Best Hikes Near
Missoula

HELP US KEEP THIS GUIDE UP TO DATE

Every effort has been made by the author and editors to make this guide as accurate and useful as possible. However, many things can change after a guide is published—trails are rerouted, regulations change, techniques evolve, facilities come under new management, and so on.

We would appreciate hearing from you concerning your experiences with this guide and how you feel it could be improved and kept up to date. While we may not be able to respond to all comments and suggestions, we'll take them to heart, and we'll also make certain to share them with the author. Please send your comments and suggestions to the following address:

GPP
Reader Response/Editorial Department
P.O. Box 480
Guilford, CT 06437

Or you may e-mail us at: editorial@globepequot.com

Thanks for your input, and happy trails!

Best Hikes Near
Missoula

JOSH MAHAN

FALCONGUIDES

GUILFORD, CONNECTICUT
HELENA, MONTANA

AN IMPRINT OF GLOBE PEQUOT PRESS

FALCONGUIDES®

FalconGuides is an imprint of Globe Pequot Press.
Falcon, FalconGuides, and Outfit Your Mind are registered trademarks of Morris Book Publishing, LLC.

TOPO! Explorer software and SuperQuad source maps courtesy of National Geographic Maps. For information about TOPO! Explorer, TOPO!, and Nat Geo Maps products, go to www.topo.com or www.natgeomaps.com.

All interior photos by Josh Mahan unless otherwise indicated.

Text design: Sheryl Kober
Layout artist: Maggie Peterson
Project editor: Ellen Urban

Maps by Trailhead Graphics, Inc. © Morris Book Publishing, LLC

Library of Congress Cataloging-in-Publication Data

Mahan, Josh.
  Best hikes near Missoula / Josh Mahan.
    pages cm
  Summary: "Featuring 40 of the best hikes in the greater Missoula area, this exciting new guidebook points locals and visitors alike to trailheads within an hour's drive of the city" — Provided by publisher.
  ISBN 978-0-7627-8246-8 (paperback)
  1. Hiking—Montana—Missoula Region—Guidebooks. 2. Trails—Montana—Missoula Region—Guidebooks. 3. Missoula Region (Mont.)—Guidebooks. I. Title.
  GV199.42.M92M575 2014
  796.5109786—dc23
                                                                                    2014015192

Printed in the United States of America

10 9 8 7 6 5 4 3 2 1

For the people of Missoula. Play hard. Preserve the place.

Contents

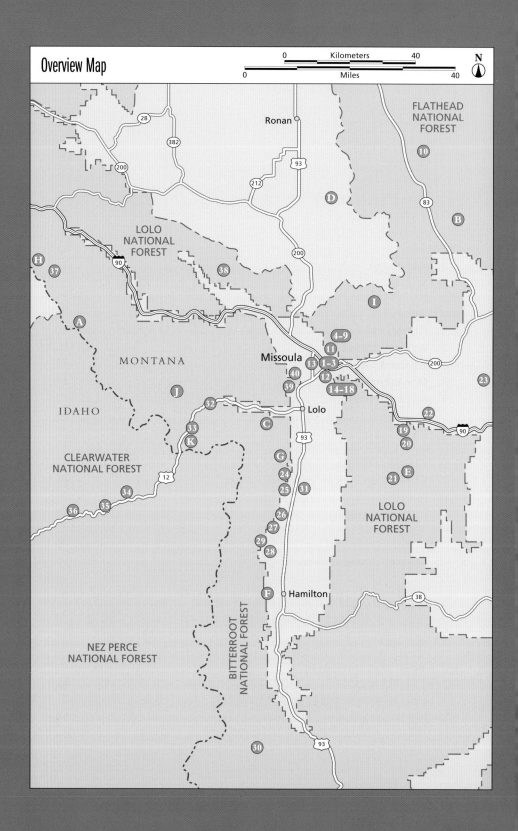

Acknowledgments

This project is the culmination of many people's efforts. Thank you to everybody who has offered trail suggestions. Special thanks to John Fothergill, Morgan Valliant, Nicole Klapper, Cory Ackerman, and Wayne Fairchild for finding secret trails and encouraging me to pursue certain hikes. Thank you to Alesha Bowman and Yuval Avneil for photos. Thank you to the Break Espresso for strong cups of coffee and for always being there.

This acknowledgment would be incomplete if I didn't thank the FalconGuides editorial team. Their professionalism and attention to detail is unsurpassed, providing hope to the future of journalism.

I also want to thank the agencies that manage the public's land: the City of Missoula, Lolo National Forest, Bitterroot National Forest, Flathead National Forest, Nez Perce-Clearwater National Forest, Missoula Bureau of Land Management, Lee Metcalf Wildlife Refuge, and Montana Fish Wildlife & Parks. All of these agencies are working in concert to maintain and preserve a resource that cannot be measured with money.

A strong thank-you is also owed to my family for introducing me to the beauty of nature and helping me to understand the value of untrammeled tracks of land. Additionally, I would like to acknowledge the many people who have invested great time and energy into creating vast sanctuaries for two-legged and four-legged creatures to breathe the pureness of the wild, wide-open spaces surrounding our fair city. Thank you.

Introduction

All too often in our lives in Missoula it is easy to get stuck by traffic circles, train delays, and endless errands in big box stores. The grind of the workweek traps us in the same industrial trail, leading to the same cubicle, classroom, job site, kitchen, or coffee shop. Sometimes it's hard to find a moment to look up at the summits and canyons that surround our city. Other times it's hard to not look away, wondering what secret a particular patch of forest on the side of Mount Sentinel might hold.

This book is intended to help unlock the mysteries of Missoula that are only a ridgetop away, to take you to those access points where you can plunge into a pristine swimming hole on a hot summer day. It's intended to get you out of town and into the mountains that originally drew us here.

There are no shortage of paths (some less than a mile from downtown) to slip away from the buzz of machines and return to a sanctuary where flowers grow at your feet, birds serenade, and deer warily gaze at you across a dewy field. Bicycle paths connect the city with the Rattlesnake, Mount Jumbo, North Hills, and Mount Sentinel Trailheads.

It's always easy to come up with a reason not to enjoy the wild trails that lay at the edge of our neighborhoods, as well as the wildernesses that are a short drive away. I've always said that if conditions had to be perfect in order for me to go for a hike, I would never get off the couch. Maybe the weather's not perfect or you don't have much time, but no matter the weather or the amount of time you spend on the trail, walking a few hundred feet next to a creek to watch a kingfisher catch a trout will change the way you feel about the day. I've never actually gotten out on the trail and been disappointed.

The next time you say there is nothing to do in Missoula, pick up this guide and see that, in fact, there are always at least forty things to do. With minimal proper provisions (a backpack, warm clothes, space blanket, water, headlamp, lighter, and trail food), you can spend a day traversing the trails above the city. This entertainment is both cheap and healthy, recharging your energy—like driving your car when its battery is low.

Most of the trails in this book have been known to locals for some time. It is my hope that this work brings new understanding to the history, flora, and fauna steeped in the trails around Missoula. I hope it encourages new generations to explore the natural gardens of our city's unique heritage.

The landscape connects us with the people of the place. Following the hikes outlined in this book, we have the opportunity to put our feet directly where Nez Perce moccasins fled on the Lolo Trail during the war in 1877. We can put our boots on the same path the Corps of Discovery took up Wendover Ridge when the going got so tough that horses starting rolling down the hill. We can stand at the Curry Cabin, where a family labored in a Montana wilderness, or eat lunch where a Civil War veteran etched a stunningly scenic picnic spot on a knoll in the Garnet Mountains a century ago. We can visit a field at Maclay Flat, where Salish Indians once gathered to dig for bitterroots and strip cambium from ponderosa pines. Doing these things helps us understand the people who stood at the same corner of space, even if it was in another time.

The landscape also connects us directly to the place. On a rock slab at Bear Creek Overlook, with the jagged peaks of the Bitterroot Mountains filling your full frame of view, the city seems trivial and far away. The same goes for when you relax into a view of the Mission Mountains across Holland Lake with a waterfall thundering at your back. Or ease into a pool at the base of a hot cataract in Weir Creek with the scent of cedars on the breeze. This sense of place can be found lying in a bloom of arrowleaf balsamroot in the North Hills. These are the treasures that nature offers us; if we are willing to visit and internalize them, we can hold on to them forever.

Hiking is part of Missoula's daily ritual. Some of our hiking trails serve not only as recreational quests but also as transportation routes. The successful open space program, bike trail system, and surrounding vast wilderness areas make Missoula a perfect trail town. Throw in the adventure of seeing a black bear and the cuteness factor of a newborn fawn and what we have here each day is post-card perfect.

It is wilderness mixed with civilization. There is no set line where the creatures of the woods stop and human development begins. Instead there is a gentle overlap until on one end you have Higgins Avenue and on the other end you have Spring Gulch, with Rattlesnake Creek and the Greenway trail system connecting the two.

So go out to hike these trails, to find meaning in the paths that are a healthy endeavor for our minds and bodies. Strive to walk someplace new each week, to see a new bend in the trail, to set foot in a new valley. Following this guide can keep you busy for years. As Thomas L. Greenough said upon donating his land to the city, we need locations for "poetic and romantic retreat." Adventure is waiting for you.

History of the Missoula Area

People have lived here for 12,000 years, arriving after crossing the ocean in boats from Asia. At that time an ice age had the river backed up so that the valley was filled with a giant puddle of water now known as Glacial Lake Missoula, larger than the Great Lakes put together. When the ice dam holding the river finally burst, the lake drained in 48 hours, sending a river unlike any other on Earth screaming toward the ocean and carving out the Columbia River Gorge. The Clark Fork is a fork of the Columbia.

Evidence suggests that native peoples established settlements here in roughly 3500 BC. The Salish people lived in the Missoula and Bitterroot Valleys. The Nez Perce traveled through the area from the west to hunt buffalo. The Blackfeet, who lived to the north, often waited on the slopes of a narrow canyon east of town, stealing, killing, and littering the ground with bodies. The first French fur trappers called this passage La Porte d'Enfer, or "Gate of Hell."

European civilization came through the valley with the Lewis and Clark expedition in 1806. Others quickly followed, with David Thompson coming through for the British in 1808. A treaty was signed with the natives on the banks of the Clark Fork River at Council Grove State Park in 1855. John Mullan punched a wagon road through the valley in 1859 (although much of it was immediately destroyed by a flood and then rebuilt). The next year 20,000 people traveled through the valley.

Missoula was founded as Hellgate Trading Post in 1860; Fort Missoula added to the security of the region in 1877. The state legislature set the University of Montana here in 1893, and the USDA Forest Service moved to town in 1908.

Bob Marshall came to the forest service's Northern Rocky Mountain Experiment Station in Missoula in 1925. This young man from New York had a passion

for hiking. At that time the concept of preserving land was foreign because the forests were so vast. Marshall was famous for climbing multiple peaks in one day. Aside from exploring the upper Flathead drainages, now a wilderness named in his honor, Marshall was the first to explore and map major sections of the Brooks Range in Alaska. He founded the Wilderness Society in 1934 to preserve land that is "sound-proof as well as sight-proof from our increasingly mechanized life."

The next one hundred years were times of growth in the Missoula Valley, but a healthy environment remained a core concept for the city, along with opportunities for recreation and access to city lands. The valley has changed from the time when the present-day city was a series of braided river channels and massive cottonwood groves. But remnants of this epoch remain at Tower Street, Greenough Park, and east of town in Beavertail Hill State Park. The ancient ponderosa groves of Pattee Canyon and Rattlesnake Creek still stand. Why does this matter to us? I'm not completely sure, but it does. We love to visit big trees.

Weather

Generally the weather that moves into Missoula comes out of the west, from the Pacific Ocean. In winter, Arctic air comes from the north. The farther west you are from Missoula, the greater the chances are that the climate will be wetter. Missoula itself is very dry, receiving only 14 inches of rain per year. April is the wettest month. In the high mountains that precipitation is captured as snow. June can be wet too.

Hiking access is limited in spring because the high mountain roads and trails are snowed in. Once the snow starts melting, the rivers and creeks around western Montana surge and become dangerous to cross. High water has traditionally been around Memorial Day, but in recent years waters have peaked weeks earlier.

The Bitterroot Range creates a classic rain shadow. The western slopes of the mountains confront Pacific moisture, and much of it dumps on those slopes. The crest of the range receives 80 inches of rain, while the valley floor below captures only 12 inches. The result is two different worlds: the high country and the low country. Nothing compares with hiking the western Montana high country during the dog days of summer, which can be hot in the low country.

Fire season becomes a concern in July and August. Thunderheads are common in summer and can lay fury on the peaks and high basins of local mountain ranges. Use caution. Hike early in the morning. Make sure you are protected— not on peaks or ridgetops or in open basins—in the afternoon, when thunderstorms can move in quickly.

Fall is a nice time to get out in the forest. The temperatures are cooler for hiking. Snow can start coming down as soon as late September, but generally it holds off until late October. Your hiking season can extend into November with a pair of good boots, warm clothing, and a determined attitude.

In the valley bottoms and foothills surrounding Missoula, hiking occurs year-round. If you do venture out into the cold, be prepared to walk on ice. Metal tracks on boots can be helpful.

Flora and Fauna

A variety of forests surround Missoula: the massive western red cedar and grand fir of the Lochsa Country, the stout ponderosas of the Bitterroot, and the stately cottonwoods of the Clark Fork bottoms. Higher up in the mountains, aspen, larch, and whitebark pine grow slowly each year. Junipers like drier sites like Rock Creek and the Garnet Range. Douglas fir and lodgepole pine are common and are often found growing together.

A variety of shrubs fill in the understory. Huckleberry grows thick in places and is utilized as a food source for both humans and animals. Thimbleberry is a broad-leafed plant that dominates the landscape in moist areas. Serviceberry was used by natives as food and to make weapons. Wild rosehips are a good source of vitamin C, and the blossoms smell delicious. Snowberry, currant, chokecherry, sumac, and many more shrubs round out the lot.

Wildflowers in Montana bloom just after the snows melt, which means, the higher the country, the later the wildflowers bloom. Glacier lilies are the first flower to emerge on the mountainsides. Creek bottoms produce trilliums in the spring. Paintbrush, lupine, bear grass, and balsamroot are common in the region. Strawberry, bearberry, Oregon grape, wild raspberry, and of course bitterroot were all sought after by area tribes.

The mountains surrounding Missoula have some of the most interesting and charismatic animals in the continental United States. Grizzly bears roam close to Missoula, where people work hard to keep their trash from interesting the big bruins. Grizzlies are more prevalent in the Rattlesnake Mountains, Swan Mountains, Garnet Range, Great Burn, and the Welcome Creek Wilderness than in the Lochsa or the canyons of the Bitterroot. But bears can pop up anywhere these days. As noted elsewhere in this book, a bear encounter is not to be dreaded. If you hike Montana trails long enough, you might be lucky enough to see one of these powerful, intelligent animals. Be sure to have your bear spray ready for that rare occasion you may need it.

Other top predators roam the region too. Wolves have appeared on the great winter stage that is Mount Jumbo. Mountain lions make the Rattlesnake their home. Black bears swing from the maple trees of Greenough Park. Deer prance about the yards of the city. Elk winter on the hillside. Bighorn sheep take refuge in the cliff bands of Rock Creek. Moose can be found in the Lolo/Lochsa. Otters swim in mountain lakes and rivers. Mink scamper down creek beds at the most unlikely times. Coyotes, bobcats, foxes, and mountain goats are frequently seen. More rarely spotted are the wilderness-specific wolverine, fisher, and lynx. Smaller mammals include badger, hare, marten, weasel, skunk, pika, and porcupine. A moment with any of these animals can make your entire hike.

Birdlife is robust in Montana. Over 400 species of winged warblers inhabit the state. Geese are a common sight, as is the merganser. On the Lochsa in spring you might spot a harlequin duck. Holland Lake is a good place to see a loon. Bald eagles are frequently found in any of the river bottoms. The Lee Metcalf Wildlife Refuge, Tower Street, and Beavertail Hill State Park are prime bald eagle habitat. But they've also been spotted in trees on Mount Jumbo, which is typically more golden eagle habitat. Great blue herons are found in rivers and creeks, standing motionless for minutes stalking trout. Grouse ramble the hillsides, springing up out of the trees and brush with loud wing movements.

The northern goshawk is a Bitterroot canyon wilderness bird. Kingfishers always put on a good show, their small figures snatching large trout. Peregrine falcons, several species of hawks, and the tiny kestrel all swoop through the skies. Owls live here too: great gray, flammulated, and great horned. Steller's jays, Clark's nutcrackers, and ravens clean up any mess humans or animals leave behind. Woodpeckers work over snags. Larks, swallows, thrushes, nuthatches,

and warblers create songs as they snatch insects from the mountain shrubs. It's a bird's world.

One animal cannot be left off this list, which is by no means comprehensive: the trout. There are several species in the Missoula area. The most revered trout in the area is the endangered bull trout. Cutthroat trout are native to the region. Rainbow trout and brown trout cruise the currents, and brook trout are stocked in lakes and streams. Steelhead trout and salmon run from the ocean into the Lochsa drainages. Other fish include Arctic grayling and mountain whitefish, which ply the rivers.

Wilderness Restrictions and Regulations

Three officially designated wilderness areas are covered in this guide: Rattlesnake, Selway-Bitterroot, and Welcome Creek. Other hikes are along the edge of the Bob Marshall Wilderness or near the proposed Great Burn Wilderness.

Overnight campers face more regulations than day hikers when in the wilderness. Always clean up your trash—no matter what. Carry a Ziploc bag or a little trash bag. Clean up other people's trash too. Nothing puts the skids on a fun

day like a half hour of campsite reclamation, but ultimately you will feel better for doing it, and your actions may encourage future visitors to follow suit. Stay organized while you are hiking.

Tools and wheeled vehicles are prohibited in theses wilderness areas, as is any type of engine. This includes mountain bikes, game carts, and chain saws.

Practicing Leave No Trace ethics ensures safety for you and wildlife. It also creates a pristine experience that will withstand generations of use. Here are some Leave No Trace guidelines to consider.

Plan ahead and prepare. Learn local regulations. Prepare for emergencies, hazards, and weather. Repackage your food to eliminate waste. Bring a map, and don't build cairns or other trail markers.

Travel on durable surfaces. Walk single file on established trails, and protect delicate riparian areas by walking around wetlands.

Dispose of waste properly. Pack it in, pack it out. Deposit human waste in cat holes at least 6 inches deep, and 200 feet from water sources. Be sure to cover the hole when you are finished, and pack out the toilet paper. Use all soap, even biodegradable, away from the water's edge, and never do your dishes in any type of water source.

Leave what you find. Do not remove historical or cultural artifacts. Leave rocks, plants, and other natural objects the way you found them. Do not dig trenches, build dams, or build lasting structures.

Minimize fire impacts. Use established fire rings. Keep your fire small, using small-diameter sticks you find on the ground. Try to burn the big chunks down when you are ready to extinguish the fire. Put out your campfire completely. When it is cool enough to touch, scatter the ashes.

Respect wildlife. Give wildlife distance. If an animal changes its behavior because of your presence, you are too close. For instance, if an animal stops eating and stares at you, you are too close. If an animal that has been sitting down stands up, you are too close. At least 100 yards is a good standard. Never feed wildlife, and protect your food against animal raids. Control your dog, and respect closures for wildlife during sensitive times of year, such as mating, nesting, rearing, or wintering season.

Be considerate of other visitors. Respect other visitors you encounter on the trail. You are both sharing your public land—play nice! Yield the trail to other users. Downhill is the textbook side of the trail to go to when encountering stock. Don't take rest breaks directly on the trail. Finally, in the age of the iPod and the traveling speakers, let the delicate sounds of nature prevail. You can listen to your jam anywhere, but you can only hear a wolf's howl in the wilderness.

Getting Around

Several of the hikes in this book can be accessed by either bicycle or foot. The city's Mountain Line bus system can get people within walking distance of trailheads for the North Hills, Mount Jumbo, the Rattlesnake, Greenough Park, Mount Sentinel, and the Clark Fork trails. The out-of-town hikes are in rural areas and require a vehicle. In most cases, getting to the trailhead does not require a special stunt vehicle with winches and 12-foot tires. However, some of the dirt roads are primitive, where a durable and tested mountain rig will come in handy. Don't negotiate these roads when they are icy or snow covered.

How to Use This Guide

This guide is designed to be simple and easy to use. The overview map at the beginning of the book shows the location of each hike by number, keyed to the table of contents. Each hike is accompanied by a route map that shows access roads, the highlighted featured route, and directional arrows to point you in the right direction. This map indicates the general outline of the hike. Due to scale restrictions, it is not as detailed as a park map might be or even as our Miles and Directions are. Use these route maps in conjunction with other resources.

Each hike begins with summary information that delivers the trail's vital statistics, including distance, difficulty, fees and permits, park hours, canine compatibility, and trail contacts. Directions and GPS coordinates to the trailheads are also provided, followed by a general description of what you'll see along the trail. Finally, a detailed route finder (Miles and Directions) sets forth mileages for significant landmarks along the trail.

Difficulty Ratings

This guide has a trail for every hiker, ranging in difficulty from a few easy miles on a flat trail to all-day adventures with long distances and intense climbs. To help you select a hike that suits particular needs and abilities, each is rated easy, moderate, or strenuous. Bear in mind that even the most challenging routes can be made easier by hiking within your limits, taking rests when you need them, and simply turning around when you feel you've had enough.

Easy hikes are generally short and flat, and take 1 to 2 hours to complete.

Moderate hikes involve increased distance and relatively mild changes in elevation, and will take more than 2 hours to complete.

Strenuous hikes feature some difficult terrain, greater distances, steep ups and downs, and generally take longer to complete.

These are mostly subjective ratings—what you think is easy is entirely dependent on your level of fitness and the adequacy of your gear (primarily shoes). If you are hiking with a group, you should select a hike with a rating that's appropriate for the least-fit and least-prepared person in your party.

Trail Finder

Hike No.	Hike Name	Best Hikes for Backpackers	Best Hikes for Waterfalls	Best Hikes for Geology Lovers	Best Hikes for Children	Best Hikes for Dogs	Best Hikes for Peak Baggers	Best Hikes for Hot Springs	Best Hikes for Great Views	Best Hikes for Lake Lovers	Best Hikes for Canyons
1	Cherry Gulch Loop				●	●					
2	Mountain View Loop				●	●					
3	Mount Jumbo Loop			●							
4	Backbone Trail										
5	North Loop					●					
6	Woods Gulch Loop	●									●
7	Rattlesnake Creek to Spring Gulch Loop			●							●
8	Sawmill Gulch to Curry Gulch Loop				●						
9	Ravine Creek Trail	●					●				
10	Holland Falls National Recreation Trail		●	●	●				●	●	
11	Greenough Park Loop, Bolle Birdwatching Trail				●	●					
12	Clark Fork Riverbank Loop				●						
13	Tower Street Conservation Area Loop				●	●					

Trail Finder

Hike No.	Hike Name	Best Hikes for Backpackers	Best Hikes for Waterfalls	Best Hikes for Geology Lovers	Best Hikes for Children	Best Hikes for Dogs	Best Hikes for Peak Baggers	Best Hikes for Hot Springs	Best Hikes for Great Views	Best Hikes for Lake Lovers	Best Hikes for Canyons
14	Mount Sentinel Loop / The "M"			●							
15	Kim Williams Trail			●	●						●
16	University Mountain from Crazy Canyon										●
17	Meadow Loop Trail				●	●					
18	Sam Braxton National Recreation Trail										
19	Valley of the Moon Nature Trail				●						
20	Babcock Creek Trail to Mormon Spring			●							●
21	Welcome Creek Trail	●									●
22	Beavertail Hill State Park Trail			●	●	●					
23	Warren Park Trail			●	●				●		
24	Bass Creek Trail	●		●							●
25	Kootenai Creek Trail	●	●	●	●						●
26	Big Creek Trail	●		●	●						●

Trail Finder

Hike No.	Hike Name	Best Hikes for Backpackers	Best Hikes for Waterfalls	Best Hikes for Geology Lovers	Best Hikes for Children	Best Hikes for Dogs	Best Hikes for Peak Baggers	Best Hikes for Hot Springs	Best Hikes for Great Views	Best Hikes for Lake Lovers	Best Hikes for Canyons
27	Glen Lake Trail	●		●					●	●	
28	Bear Creek Trail	●	●	●	●				●		●
29	Bear Creek Overlook Trail			●			●		●		●
30	Boulder Creek Falls Trail	●	●	●					●		●
31	Kenai Nature Trail				●					●	
32	Lolo Trail at Howard Creek			●							
33	Lee Creek Interpretive Trail			●	●						
34	Wendover Ridge								●		
35	Warm Springs Creek Trail				●			●			
36	Weir Creek Trail							●			
37	Lost Lake Trail	●	●	●					●	●	●
38	Sleeping Woman Trail to Cha-paa-qn Peak			●			●				
39	Vista Point Loop								●		
40	Maclay Flat Nature Trail				●	●					

Map Legend

Transportation

═══〔90〕═══	Freeway/Interstate Highway
═〔12〕═	U.S. Highway
═〔200〕═	State Highway
═〔1136〕═	Forest/Paved/Improved Road
═ ═ ═ ═	Unpaved Road
┼──┼──┼	Railroad

Trails

▬▬▬▬▬▬	Selected Route
------	Trail/Fire Road
——————	Paved Trail
→	Direction of Route

Water Features

◯	Body of Water
≃ ≃ ≃	Swamp/Wetland
〜	River or Creek
·⁄·	Intermittent Creek
⚲	Spring
≋	Waterfall

Symbols

20	Trailhead
■	Building/Point of Interest
P	Parking
🚻	Restroom
◈	Scenic View/Overlook
?	Park Headquarters
⛩	Picnic Area
▲	Campground
•―•	Gate
‿	Bridge
⛴	Boat Launch
○	Towns and Cities
×	Spot Elevation
▲	Mountain/Peak
🏠	Ranger Station/Headquarters
▭	Bench

Land Management

▢	National Park
▢	State/Local Park
▢	Wilderness/Recreation Area

North of Missoula

The North Hills of Missoula.

Hikers have it easy in Missoula, especially when it comes to hiking north of the city in the Rattlesnake Valley and Mountains. The city limit–sign to trailhead-sign distances are staggeringly short. As a general rule, the farther you go up the valley, the wilder it becomes. That's not to say you can't have wolves on Mount Jumbo. The legacy of the Rattlesnake National Recreation Area and Wilderness is a gift to the people of Missoula. Equally visionary land-use planning by the city protected Mount Jumbo (on the east side of the Rattlesnake) and the North Hills (on the west side of the Rattlesnake) from development. Now combine these wide open spaces with walking and biking trails that allow you to access trailheads without ever having to get in a car. Only in Missoula can you lazily pedal next to a creek after hiking several miles of backcountry trail!

The Holland Falls National Recreation Trail is a lone outlier far away in the Seeley Valley. This beautiful hike on the edge of the Bob Marshall Wilderness has it all: scenic lake, symmetrical peak, and classic mountain waterfall. Combine the hike with canoeing or fishing on Holland Lake.

Mount Jumbo peeks up above the North Hills.

The Cherry Gulch Loop combines the Cherry Gulch Trail with the North Hills Ridge Trail. The Cherry Gulch section of the hike is incredibly scenic and serene. It's often hard to imagine that a thin ridgeline separates you from Missoula. At the head of Cherry Gulch, the trail climbs up to the ridgeline at the site of the old peace sign. The final 1.0 mile will take you down the North Hills Ridge Trail with a bird's-eye view of Missoula. A spur trail leads to the current peace sign that is visible over Missoula 0.1 mile before reaching the trailhead. The beginning of this trail may be rerouted in the near future.

Start: North Hills Trailhead

Distance: 2.2-mile loop

Hiking time: About 1 hour

Difficulty: Moderate; small climb

Trail surface: Dirt path

Best season: Year-round

Other trail users: None

Canine compatibility: Leashed dogs permitted

Land status: City of Missoula open space, private conservation easement

Fees and permits: None required

Schedule: Open 6 a.m. to 11 p.m.

Maps: USGS Northeast Missoula; City of Missoula Parks, Open Space & Trails

Trail contacts: Missoula Parks and Recreation, 600 Cregg Lane, Missoula, MT 59801; (406) 721-7275; ci.missoula.mt.us

Special considerations: In spring the native wildflower blooms are brilliant. Don't pick these flowers; leave them to reseed for next year. When identifying a flower, always bring your eye to the flower, not the flower to your eye. Bitterroot, the state flower, is common in the North Hills. The largest population of the rare Missoula phlox also occurs in the North Hills. This incredibly rare flower is easily trampled, and disturbing these plants brings a hefty fine. Stay on the trails to prevent erosion and to avoid trampling the native vegetation.

Finding the trailhead: From the Van Buren Street exit off I-90, go north on Van Buren Street for 0.1 mile. Turn left; go to the end of the block and turn left onto Jackson Street, which turns right and becomes Vine Street. Go 0.1 mile and turn right on Greenough Drive. Go 240 feet and veer left onto Minckler Loop, a short unassuming dirt road that leads to the top of a hill and the trailhead. **GPS:** N46 52.55' / W113 58.94'

THE HIKE

Cherry Gulch on Waterworks Hill is the closest patch of native wildness to Missoula that a hiker can experience. It is one of the crown jewels of the city's open space system, and one of the many reasons Missoula could be dubbed Hiking Town USA. When in the folds of Cherry Gulch, visitors are completely ensconced within a native grassland canyon, tranquility, and birdsong. Car horns, train tracks, and the buzz of tote bags on bicycle commuters are on just the other side of the North Hills ridge (to the south). Upon summiting the ridge, the bird's-eye view of downtown is uniquely juxtaposed against nature. You are literally straddling the line between wilderness and civilization.

View of Mount Sentinel from the North Hills Ridge. ALESHA BOWMAN

In spring, the thick blooms of elegant pink bitterroot flowers cannot be missed. The state flower of Montana, bitterroot was an essential food source for the native Salish tribe that frequented these hills until the 1890s. Views of Mount Sentinel and Mount Jumbo dominate parts of the hike, as does Hellgate Canyon to the east. Hellgate Canyon is famous for its furious and frigid winds during late fall and winter. It is named for the numerous raids by Blackfoot Indians against other regional tribes traveling through the narrow notch with pack strings of meat after successful buffalo hunts.

Your journey up Cherry Gulch begins with an intimate encounter within the shallow and narrow gulch. It is mostly open, but peppered with young pine trees. All trees fade away as the canyon gently gains elevation. This is private conservation easement land that Missoula's Peschel family has graciously allowed the city to use instead of developing it into condos. You'll pass through a gate and onto city land. Shortly after, follow a set of switchbacks over the North Hills ridge, on your left. Upon summiting the ridge you will arrive at four round pillars about 2 feet high, with a collection of stones forming a peace sign in the middle of the pillars. This is all that remains of Missoula's famous peace sign that adorned Waterworks Hill for decades. Take a moment here to rest and enjoy the view of the city that unfolds in front of you.

The peace sign is a piece of Missoula's underground history. County commissioners never planned for the symbol to be emblazoned on the television repeater above town. It simply appeared one morning in May 1983. Nobody knew at the time that the prank, labeled by some as art and others as vandalism, would come to define the city.

The peace sign remained on the North Hills for close to twenty years. Sometimes it was painted over by the company that owned the repeater, but always, in the dead of night, the peace symbol returned. Legends grew about the genesis and background of the group behind the peace sign, but nothing was ever confirmed or denied. Missoula came to embrace the peace sign; it served as a daily reminder of conduct. Then, one day in 2001, the television repeater was removed. A row ensued, and the Peace Park was eventually developed. Not the original, it is a small white symbol that is hard to see.

The old peace sign lives on, though. It lies in nine separate pieces in backyards around Missoula, held by a group known as the Peacekeepers who are looking for a location to reassemble the sign. The old peace sign lives on artistically too. It has become a frequently painted icon, referred to as the Mona Lisa of Missoula.

From the skeleton of the old peace sign, turn left and head downhill. You are now on the North Ridge Trail. A mile's walk down this ridge, which can be a little steep in sections, will return you to the trailhead. The City View Trail connects at 1.8 miles; the Peace Park Trail intersects at 2.2 miles.

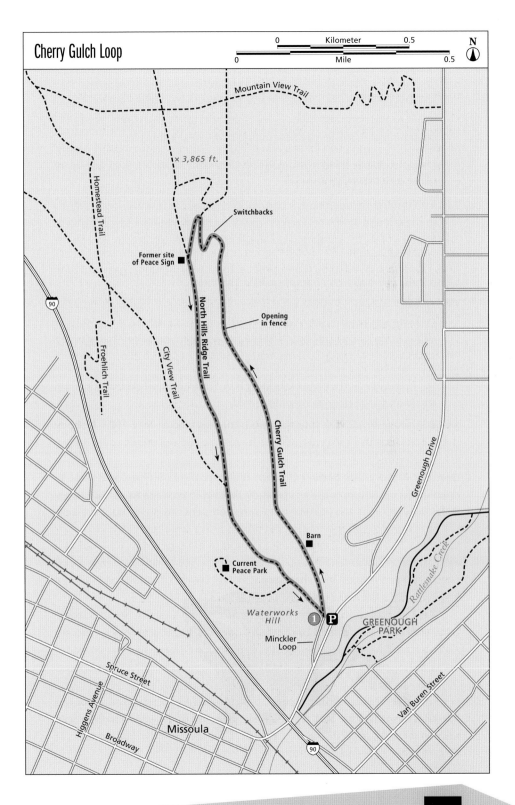

Cherry Gulch Loop

0 Kilometer 0.5

0 Mile 0.5

N

Mountain View Trail

× 3,865 ft.

Switchbacks

Former site
of Peace Sign

North Hills Ridge Trail

Opening
in fence

Homestead Trail

90

Froehlich Trail

City View Trail

Cherry Gulch Trail

Barn

Current
Peace Park

Greenough Drive

Rattlesnake Creek

Waterworks
Hill

GREENOUGH
PARK

Minckler
Loop

Spruce Street

Higgens Avenue

Missoula

Broadway

Van Buren Street

90

0.0 Start at the trailhead and go right at a brown wooden sign with arrows. One arrow points straight and says Ridge Trail. The other points at a 45-degree angle to the right and says Cherry Gulch. Go up Cherry Gulch. (Note: The beginning of this hike may be rerouted in the near future.)

0.2 Enter the gulch just beyond an abandoned barn. Enjoy the gentle gradient of the hike through the gulch.

0.7 Pass through an opening in a barbed-wire fence. The trail veers very slightly to the left and continues straight past a sign and map that says WELCOME TO MISSOULA'S TRAILS. From here you can see the switchbacks coming up on the North Hills ridge.

0.9 A short series of switchbacks begins up the ridge.

1.1 Summit the ridge at the pillars of the old peace sign and enjoy views of Mount Jumbo (with the "L"), Mount Sentinel (with the "M"), Hellgate Canyon, and the city of Missoula with the Bitterroot Mountains in the background. Turn left here onto the North Hills Ridge Trail and head downhill.

1.8 Come to a junction with the City View Trail. The trail intersects from the right and leads to the Orange Street trailhead.

2.1 A spur trail to the right leads to the current peace sign.

2.2 Arrive back at the trailhead.

Options: At the pillars of the old peace sign, turn right and hike up the North Hills Ridge Trail. Return to the trailhead by walking east on the North Hills Ridge Trail.

Mountain View Loop

Wildflower enthusiasts must take advantage of this hike in spring. The variety of species and colors are the crown jewels of scenery surrounding the city. This hike is located midway up the Rattlesnake Valley and a short distance from town. Begin by climbing up to the North Hills Ridge via the Mountain View Trail. Loop around, with an option to hoof out to the historic and working Moon-Randolph Homestead. Descend via the Sunlight Trail and finish the hike walking a nice doubletrack on the banks of Rattlesnake Creek next to the organic farm.

Start: Turnout on right, just beyond Mountain View Drive

Distance: 3.7-mile loop

Hiking time: About 1.5 hours

Difficulty: Moderate

Trail surface: Dirt; single- and doubletrack

Best season: Year-round; spring for flowers

Other trail users: None

Canine compatibility: Leashed dogs permitted

Land status: City of Missoula

Fees and permits: None required

Schedule: Open 6 a.m. to 11 p.m.

Maps: USGS Northeast Missoula; City of Missoula Parks, Open Space & Trails

Trail contacts: Missoula Parks and Recreation, 600 Cregg Lane, Missoula, MT 59801; (406) 721-7275; ci.missoula.mt.us

Special considerations: In spring the native wildflower blooms are brilliant. Don't pick these flowers; leave them to reseed for next year. When identifying a flower, always bring your eye to the flower, not the flower to your eye. Bitterroot, the state flower, is common in the North Hills. The largest population of the rare Missoula phlox also occurs in the North Hills. This incredibly rare flower is easily trampled, and disturbing these plants brings a hefty fine. Stay on the trails to prevent erosion and to avoid trampling the native vegetation.

Finding the trailhead: From the Van Buren Street exit off I-90, go north on Van Buren Street, which becomes Rattlesnake Drive. Turn left onto Lolo Street at 1.8 miles. Go 0.5 mile and turn right onto Duncan Drive. Go another 0.5 mile to reach Mountain View Drive. The parking area is on the right next to the soccer fields, immediately after Mountain View Drive. Access the trail across the street from the turnout; it cuts between two house lots. **GPS:** N46 53.55' / W113 58.58'

THE HIKE

This classic suburban Missoula hike begins in the heart of the middle Rattlesnake neighborhood and takes hikers into the North Hills. Ornate blooms of lupine, balsamroot, and bitterroot mark this section of trail in spring. But even if the flowers are not in bloom, hikers can find solace on the ridges any time of year. Don't be fooled by this path's proximity to the city. It whisks you to another world. Unique views of Mount Jumbo loom above. An option to visit the working Moon-Randolph Homestead offers a cultural aspect to this journey.

Bitterroot, the state flower, offers a glimpse into the region's past as well. The roots beneath the graceful pink flowers were a highly valued food source for Native Americans. The roots carried tribes through tough winters, and a sack of them could be traded for a horse. Patties made from ground bitterroot, deer suet, and lichen were used as fast food while traveling. Bitterroot was so important to tribal survival that spring migrations were coordinated with the blooms. While most harvest grounds around Missoula have been obliterated by development, the flowers and their carrot-like roots still have a foothold in the North Hills. It is illegal to disturb these plants.

An arrowleaf balsamroot marks the beginning of spring.

The Moon-Randolph Homestead offers another glimpse into history. This 13-acre working farm is open to the public on Saturday from 11 a.m. to 5 p.m., May through October. Hosts offer tours of the historic compound, and the apple orchard is an opportune place to picnic, take a nap, or glimpse some wildlife. Chickens, sheep, and goats mill about the property. Caretakers live on the property in a converted chicken coop and revel in the dichotomy between twenty-first-century Missoula, just over the hill, and nineteenth-century living on the homestead. Visitors can share this same sense of time travel, including enjoying the journey through pre-development on the hike. Private tours during off-hours can be arranged upon request.

The hike begins near the PEAS Farm, midway up the Rattlesnake Valley. The organic farm marks a large quiet section of land on the west side of the creek. Its fields are prominent at the end of the hike as the trail skirts the property.

An unmarked turnout just beyond Mountain View Drive marks the trailhead. Begin the hike by crossing the street and following the Mountain View Trail between two houses and up the hill. The trail is marked by a sign and a garbage can. The path switchbacks up into the North Hills, traversing through scattered ponderosa pine and thick blooms of wildflowers when the hills are green in spring.

The North Hills trail junction is at 0.7 mile; keep going straight, climbing the ridge. At 0.9 mile turn right onto the North Hills Ridge Trail; turn right again at 1.4 miles at the intersection of the trail leading to the Moon-Randolph Homestead. The next junction is at 1.6 miles. A right turn takes hikers back to the Mountain View Trail and shortens the hike. Turn left and follow the fence line for the full hike.

Mountain bluebird nest boxes are spaced throughout the field. Clutches of young are raised here. Bright flashes of blue prevail as the birds dart to feed on insects. Their songs carry on the breeze.

At 2.1 miles turn right and go downhill. The trail crosses Duncan Drive at 2.7 miles and then winds down to Rattlesnake Creek. Turn right again at 2.9 miles. This section of trail is between the PEAS Farm and Rattlesnake Creek. It's a peaceful spot and a good wind down after the hike through the hills. Turn right at 3.6 miles onto Mountain View Drive to complete the loop.

Most studies of mountain bluebirds are of birds that live in nest boxes. Knowledge of their natural nesting habits is limited. Local bird enthusiasts and Sentinel High School students manage the North Hills bluebird boxes and have noticed large population increases on-site.

MILES AND DIRECTIONS

0.0 Start at the trailhead and cross the street. Proceed up the trail that goes between two houses. A garbage can and signs mark the trail.

0.6 Reach a crest rise after a series of switchbacks up the trail.

0.8 Intersect the North Hills Trail; go straight.

0.9 Intersect the North Hills Ridge Trail; turn right.

1.4 Arrive at trail junction to the Moon-Randolph Homestead. Go right to complete the loop. (**Option:** Turn left to visit the homestead.)

1.6 Reach a fence line and the North Hills Trail. Turn left, following the fence.

2.1 The Sunlight Trail turns right just below the power line; go downhill.

2.6 Intersect a doubletrack path. Turn right for the last bit to the Sunlight Trailhead. Dogs must be leashed here.

2.7 Cross a paved road (Duncan Drive). On the far side descend to Rattlesnake Creek on the Papoose Walkway, part of the Rattlesnake Greenway.

2.9 Turn right onto a gravel doubletrack near the creek.

3.0 Veer left on a spur doubletrack and drop down to creek level.

3.3 Return to the doubletrack; turn left.

3.5 Pass a green gate. Cars are allowed on the road for next 2 blocks.

3.6 Turn right at the intersection with Mountain View Drive.

3.7 Arrive back at the trailhead.

Options: At 1.6 miles turn right onto the North Hills Trail to return to the Mountain View Trail. Turn left onto the Mountain View Trail to complete a 2.9-mile hike.

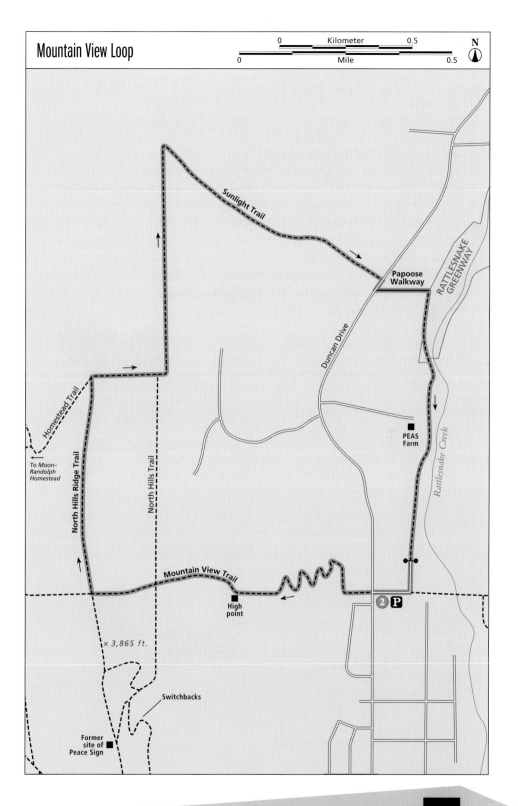

Mountain View Loop

0 — Kilometer — 0.5
0 — Mile — 0.5

N

Sunlight Trail

Papoose Walkway

RATTLESNAKE GREENWAY

Duncan Drive

Homestead Trail

To Moon–Randolph Homestead

North Hills Ridge Trail

North Hills Trail

PEAS Farm

Rattlesnake Creek

Mountain View Trail

High point

× 3,865 ft.

2 P

Switchbacks

Former site of Peace Sign

MOUNT JUMBO
Mount Jumbo Loop

This hike starts in the Lower Rattlesnake neighborhood of Missoula. Though you park in the grid of the city, changes in altitude quickly alter the dynamics of your surroundings. Turn-of-the-twentieth-century homes with lawns and invasive Norwegian maples are soon replaced by native grasslands of fescue and bunchgrass, creating prime deer and elk habitat. The summit of the mountain is forested in areas and offers shelter for mountain lion and black bear. There have even been reports of a band of gypsy wolves that occasionally make an appearance. Views from the top include the Rattlesnake Wilderness to the north and the Bitterroot Mountains to the south, as well as a bird's-eye gander of the Missoula Valley. This hike is strenuous, but with a little grit and determination, the top is quite attainable after negotiating switchbacks with a medium grade. For a shorter option, consider just tackling the "L," which is encountered on the downhill part of the loop.

Start: Mount Jumbo trailhead, at the corner of Polk and Poplar Streets

Distance: 4.5-mile loop

Hiking time: About 2.5 hours

Difficulty: Strenuous

Trail surface: Dirt; single- and doubletrack

Best season: Spring through fall

Other trail users: None

Canine compatibility: Leashed dogs permitted

Land status: City of Missoula

Fees and permits: None required

Schedule: Winter closure, Dec 1 to Mar 15

Maps: USGS Northeast Missoula; City of Missoula Parks, Open Space & Trails

Trail contacts: Missoula Parks and Recreation, 600 Cregg Lane, Missoula, MT 59801; (406) 721-7275; ci.missoula.mt.us

Special considerations: Closed in winter to protect the elk herd. Use caution during dry weather so as to not create any fires. No water available; bring adequate amounts.

Finding the trailhead: From the Van Buren exit off I-90, drive north on Van Buren Street 0.1 mile to Poplar Street. Turn right and go 0.3 mile to the intersection with Polk Street. Parking is allowed anywhere on both sides of the street. **GPS:** N46 52.12' / W113 58.55'

On the northeast side of Missoula, a grassy slope rises above the city. This is the locally famous Mount Jumbo, home to the "L." Early settlers thought this mountain looked like an elephant with its haunches in the Clark Fork River. Its head and trunk are to the north and face the Rattlesnake Wilderness. It was called Elephant Hill until a copper mine located close by hit a mother lode, which they named the Jumbo Lode. The name stuck, and Mount Jumbo was born.

Some historians say the legendary explorer David Thompson was the first European to climb the summit of Mount Jumbo, in February 1812. Other scholars have argued that the hill Thompson climbed on that winter day was actually a small knoll west of Missoula. Thompson was accompanied by one other man, and it appears they may have been the only two in the valley. Things have changed a bit since then.

Today dozens of people climb Jumbo everyday, largely thanks to the 1995 voter-approved Open Space Bond. Most of Jumbo became city land, designated never to be developed. This was at a time when the south side of the city was expanding by leaps and bounds. The open space legacy has since become one

A mule deer buck rambles after the does.

of Missoula's greatest achievements and a model in urban planning. Its passage protected Missoula's viewshed, recreation opportunities, and critical wildlife habitat.

The south end of Mount Jumbo is closed to public recreation from December 1 to March 15. During this time the Mount Jumbo elk herd frequents the area exclusively. Since the closure was initiated, the size of the elk herd has doubled. The elk, in turn, attract a roving wolf pack from the Rattlesnake Wilderness that appears very occasionally. This life-and-death wintertime drama plays out on the stage above the city.

Wildlife is abundant on the mountain. During the summer months a domestic sheep herd feeds on noxious weeds like leafy spurge and Dalmatian toadflax. This opens up space for native plants to grow, which is critical for a healthy ecosystem.

Your dog must be well behaved and under voice control or on a leash. Well behaved or not, a leash is mandatory on the first 200 yards of the hike. After that, good dogs can stretch their legs a little.

While there are a number of options for your journey on Mount Jumbo, the hike outlined here is a loop that efficiently explores most of what the south side of the mountain has to offer. When the hike begins, you will be navigating a series of trails. Don't get overwhelmed. Just follow the detailed instructions below.

Once you are on the South Face Trail, your goal is the ridgeline in front of you. Soon the trail starts to switchback and leaves the noise of I-90 behind. The trail winds around onto the back side of Jumbo with views of East Missoula and the upper Clark Fork River valley. At 2.3 miles you will hit a fence line on the ridgetop. Here the trail becomes doubletrack again. Follow the trail over two more knolls. The second knoll, at mile 2.5, is the top of Jumbo (4,768 feet).

Go back through the fence line and look for a subtle trail turning to the right and downhill at mile 2.8. It's marked by low-lying circle of rocks. You will now be heading toward the city instead of the canyon. At mile 3.6 you will encounter the "L." Follow the switchbacks down the mountain until you loop back into the original trail.

MILES AND DIRECTIONS

0.0 Start at the trailhead at the corner of Polk and Poplar Streets. Walk up the steep singletrack for 250 feet between some rocky outcrops. Turn right onto the doubletrack US West Trail (which starts at an alternative access point at the end of Cherry Street).

0.1 Pass a no-name singletrack.

Mount Jumbo Loop

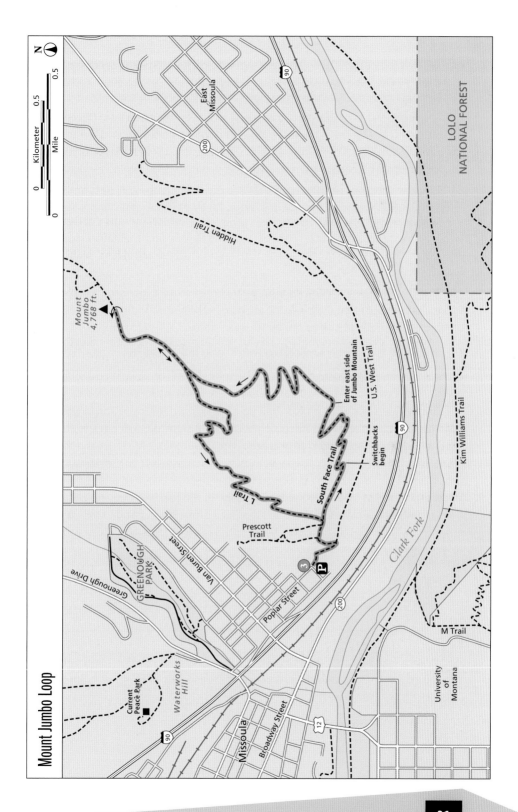

0.2 Turn left onto the Prescott Trail. Walk 200 feet and turn right on a singletrack. You are now heading up the southern flank of Mount Jumbo on the South Face Trail. Your destination is the ridge in front of you. Game trails abound.

0.4 Switchbacks begin climbing the ridgeline.

1.0 The trail reaches the back side of Mount Jumbo, with views of East Missoula. Continue up the trail.

2.3 The fence line on the ridgetop marks the point where the trail becomes a doubletrack. Continue through the fence. Go over a knoll and climb a second knoll.

2.5 The top of the second knoll is the top of Mount Jumbo. Turn around here and go back through the fence.

2.8 The "L" trail spurs off here. It's a subtle trail marked by a low-lying circle of rocks. Turn right and downhill. You are now heading toward the city instead of Hellgate Canyon. Follow the switchbacks down.

3.6 Reach the "L." From here follow the switchbacks down the hill.

4.3 Intersect the Prescott Trail; turn left.

4.35 Intersect the US West Trail; turn right.

4.4 Turn left back down the steep singletrack for a short descent back to the intersection of Polk and Poplar Streets.

4.5 Arrive back at the trailhead.

Options: For a shorter hike, consider just tackling the "L." Up and down is 1.6-miles round-trip.

Backbone Trail

The Backbone Trail is the steepest route up Mount Jumbo. It leads from the saddle to the summit on the forested north ridge. As you make your way up this route, you are following the hoofprints of the elk migration. Though steep, this is shorter than other Jumbo summit routes. Before you know it, you are standing on the summit perched for a 360-degree view. The views of the Clark Fork flowing through Missoula are especially good. The Backbone Trail ties together the Mount Jumbo Loop and North Loop hikes.

Start: Trailhead on Lincoln Hills Drive

Distance: 3.7 miles out and back

Hiking time: About 2 hours

Difficulty: Strenuous

Trail surface: Dirt; single- and doubletrack

Best season: Spring through fall

Other trail users: None

Canine compatibility: Dogs permitted

Land status: City of Missoula

Fees and permits: None required

Schedule: Closed Dec 1 to Mar 15

Maps: USGS Northeast Missoula; City of Missoula Parks, Open Space & Trails

Trail contacts: Missoula Parks and Recreation, 600 Cregg Lane, Missoula, MT 59801; (406) 721-7275; ci.missoula.mt.us

Special considerations: This is the steepest route up Mount Jumbo.

Finding the trailhead: From the Van Buren Street exit off I-90, go north on Van Buren Street . (Van Buren Street becomes Rattlesnake Drive.) Turn right onto Lincoln Hills Drive at 2.0 miles. Wind up the hillside through a neighborhood for 1.4 miles. The trailhead is a turnout on the left, right after the paved road becomes dirt. The trail is a singletrack across the road from the parking area. There are two trails at the trailhead, which merge almost immediately. **GPS:** N46 53.88' / W113 56.95'

THE HIKE

The Backbone Trail is the fastest way to Mount Jumbo's summit . It's also the steepest route, though not unbearable. The trail stretches from the historic saddle to the scenic summit, giving you the option of a switchbacking singletrack or a doubletrack that goes straight up the mountain. The journey up into the clouds is a swift one from the saddle. Before you know it, you emerge from the trees onto the summit, victorious and feeling like Rocky Balboa.

Jumbo hasn't always had forest to emerge from. Native Americans frequently managed the landscape with fire, and Jumbo was no different. It was burned regularly, contributing to its open faces. During the last century, fire suppression has facilitated thick tree growth on Jumbo's north-facing slopes. Although in this era of climate change, the trees are starting to die off from both drought and bark beetle infestation.

Even though drought has affected the trees of Jumbo's slopes, its famous seeps and springs are still flowing, resulting in the hawthorn thickets you see in its nooks and crannies. Chokecherry, serviceberry, and wild rose grow along with the hawthorn in a microenvironment that creates critical habitat for songbirds and perfect shelter for deer, bear, and coyote.

The Missoula Valley weathers a fall snow storm.

The roots of Jumbo run deep in this community. Mount Jumbo has been patiently forming since Precambrian times. The processes that have shaped the modern mountain began a billion years ago. During that time Montana had a tropical climate. A great mountain range was washed away by an inland sea, and large amounts of sediment piled up. The sediment was filled with iron, giving it a redness, and chlorite, giving it a greenish color as well. As this mud hardened into rock, it was carved by the forces around it. Looking closely at a hardened chunk of this mud, you can see ripple marks from ancient waters, impressions from raindrops that slammed into the soft soils, and cracks from when it was baked by the sun. Three types of rock were eventually formed: Miller Creek argillite (a purple shale), Hellgate quartzite, and Newland limestone.

More recently Jumbo was shaped by the power of ice. The last ice age began two million years ago; ice sheets covered the land and blocked the flow of the Clark Fork River, forming Glacial Lake Missoula. Windswept waves slammed into the shores of Jumbo, which was an island sticking out of the water. This lake formed and reformed over the years as the ice dam succumbed to the pressure of water. The last Glacial Lake Missoula existed only 15,000 years ago. Early migrants from Asia most likely stood on its shores or perhaps plied the waters with oars. Rumor has it that these wanderers from Asia read *A River Runs through It* and arrived at the glacial lake to try their hand at shadow casting, though they didn't have much luck landing a lunker—fossil evidence suggests that the lake supported no life.

To explore these wonders of Jumbo, the trail takes off from the parking area on Lincoln Hills Drive. Climb the singletrack trail as it weaves through young ponderosa forests, eventually running back into the doubletrack trail in the historic Jumbo Saddle. That trail climbs straight for the ridgeline, climbing above the saddle and providing a good view of the immediate area. At 0.9 mile you enter a shaded north-slope forest. The trail gets steeper here.

A lookout point at 1.2 miles is a good place to turn around if you are feeling winded, cold, or unmotivated. The lower knoll has good views of the Missoula Valley and the Bitterroot Mountains. Take the singletrack trail at the knoll. It winds around the west face of the knoll. (The doubletrack trail takes a straight line over the top. You will rejoin the doubletrack trail at 1.3 miles.)

From here you are in the heat of the hike. Singletrack trails weave off of the doubletrack, scurrying up the hill in a series of switchbacks. Take these trails as you climb for the summit. You emerge onto the 360-degree perch at 1.85 miles, with views of all the area's landmarks. Retrace your steps to the trailhead. Consider taking the doubletrack down for a steep, yet direct, descent.

4

0.0 Start at the pullout and cross the dirt road. There are two trails that meet up almost immediately.

0.1 The trail veers right and follows a power line.

0.3 The trail forks; take the right fork into a grove of young ponderosa pines.

0.4 The singletrack returns to doubletrack.

0.6 Climb a hill above the saddle.

0.9 The doubletrack becomes a singletrack path as the grade steepens. The trail enters the forest and climbs the ridge. The singletrack weaves in and out. It is always the least-steep choice.

1.2 Take the right fork to enjoy the views from this knoll.

1.3 Rejoin the doubletrack.

1.85 Reach the summit of Mount Jumbo and a 360-degree perch. Return the way you came.

3.7 Arrive back at the trailhead.

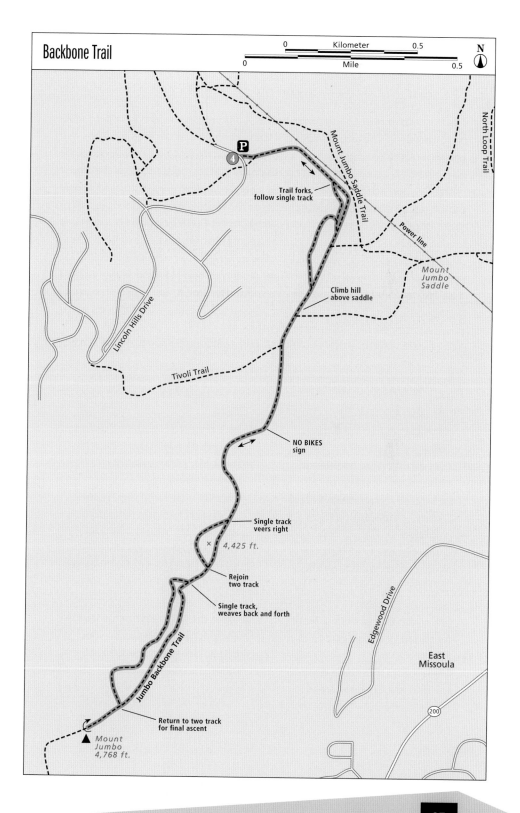

Backbone Trail

0 — Kilometer — 0.5

0 — Mile — 0.5

N

Mount Jumbo Saddle Trail

North Loop Trail

P

④

Trail forks,
follow single track

Power line

Mount
Jumbo
Saddle

Climb hill
above saddle

Lincoln Hills Drive

Tivoli Trail

NO BIKES
sign

Single track
veers right

✕ 4,425 ft.

Rejoin
two track

Single track,
weaves back and forth

Jumbo Backbone Trail

Edgewood Drive

East
Missoula

200

Return to two track
for final ascent

▲ Mount
Jumbo
4,768 ft.

5

North Loop

The North Loop starts on the west side of Jumbo and runs over an upper saddle on the ridgeline. The grassy slopes of Mount Jumbo are interrupted by draws and patches of forest. Unique views of the North Hills and the Rattlesnake Valley mark the hike. The trail is a road that the city occasionally uses for maintenance of the area. It makes for good side by side walking with a gentle gradient. A variety of wildlife calls the forested portions of this hike home. Be on the look out for elk and deer, as well as the more rare black bear (which uses Danny O'Brien Gulch as a travel corridor) and mountain lion. It intersects the Ridge Trail leading up to Woods Gulch and then drops slightly into Marshall Canyon before circling down into the main Jumbo saddle. The saddle is a historic travel route for Native Americans and Montana settlers alike as a way to avoid Hellgate Canyon. Follow the Saddle Trail to complete the loop and finish out the hike. This trail is closed from December 1 to May 1 to protect elk winter range. A large deer herd takes refuge here too.

Start: Parking area on Lincoln Hills Drive

Distance: 4.6-mile loop

Hiking time: About 2 hours

Difficulty: Moderate

Trail surface: Dirt; doubletrack

Best season: Year-round

Other trail users: Hunters in fall

Canine compatibility: Dogs permitted

Land status: City of Missoula; Montana Fish, Wildlife & Parks; Lolo National Forest

Fees and permits: None required

Schedule: Closed during winter for elk range, roughly Dec 1 to May 1

Maps: USGS Northeast Missoula; USDAFS Lolo National Forest, available at Fort Missoula; City of Missoula Parks, Open Space & Trails

Trail contacts: Missoula Parks and Recreation, 600 Cregg Lane, Missoula, MT 59801; (406) 721-7275; ci.missoula.mt.us

Lolo National Forest Supervisor's Office, Fort Missoula Building 24A, Missoula, MT 59804; (406) 329-3750; www.fs.usda.gov/lolo/

Special considerations: There are a couple sections of state land on this hike where hunting is permitted in the fall. Wear hunter orange and put hunter orange on your dog as well when hiking here during hunting season.

THE HIKE

This loop is another option to explore the massive flanks of Mount Jumbo's native grassland and thick forest. The trail begins in the saddle of Mount Jumbo. To the north, the mountain ridge extends up toward Woods Gulch and Sheep Mountain. Salish Indians used the saddle as a travel route over the mountain they referred to as Sin Min Koos, meaning "obstacle" or "thing in the way." Not the most romantic designation for the mountain that Missoulians have come to love for its open space and winter elk herds, but it's certainly a practical treatment for the broad mass.

Missoula's famous open space.

The mountain meant more to the Salish than just a thing in the way, though. The Salish used the mountain to harvest bitterroots and ponderosa pine cambium, which were religiously harvested together.

Sin Min Koos also held spiritual value. A lone pine on the southwest slope of the mountain that served as a medicine tree was cut down by vandals in the 1930s. Jumbo also provided safety. The threat of ambush by the Blackfeet in Hellgate Canyon encouraged use of the Saddle Trail to bypass the canyon. Rock piles can still be found marking this trail's path, which extended across the valley into the North Hills.

Later, after the Mullan Road was punched through Hellgate Canyon, stagecoaches used the saddle when the Hellgate road was too muddy, as it often was during periods of rain. In 1866 Civil War veteran Robert Marshall established the first settlement near Mount Jumbo, on the east side of the mountain in Marshall Creek.

Today recreationists use the Mount Jumbo saddle during the summer months and turn it over to the elk herds in winter. The elk use the saddle as an essential travel corridor to move from higher ground in the north to travel to the grasslands of southern Mount Jumbo, where the snows are thinner and grasses more accessible. The herd is often seen feeding in the morning and evening. The elk tend to move into the trees during the middle of the day. It is important not to stress these animals during the winter months. It's hard to survive out there. Even the slightest extra use of calories can send a struggling elk over the edge. Enough energy is expended avoiding predators like mountain lions, coyotes, and the occasional wolf.

To begin hiking in this historically rich natural region, enter the North Loop Trail behind the locked gate from the parking area. The path is going to take you to the north, crossing Danny O'Brien Gulch, an active black bear corridor.

At 1.0 mile the Elk Ridge Trail veers to the left. Stay right. The North Loop Trail leads you into a switchback that turns the trail back to the southeast. The trail maintains a gentle gradient uphill and moves across the forested hillside until it merges with the Three Trees Trail near the ridgeline at 2.3 miles. Continue straight for another 0.1 mile until you hit the Ridge Trail (326) at the left, leading toward Woods Gulch. To the right is another, unnamed option. Continue straight to stay on the North Loop, which descends slightly before turning to the south and onto the east side of Mount Jumbo overlooking Marshall Canyon.

A trail intersects the North Loop at 3.3 miles just after the trail bends to the west. It leads downhill to the left and into Marshall Creek. Continue straight on the North Loop past a spur trail that leads to Mount Jumbo's Backbone Trail. Staying on the North Loop, you pass an ephemeral pond (dry in summer), all that

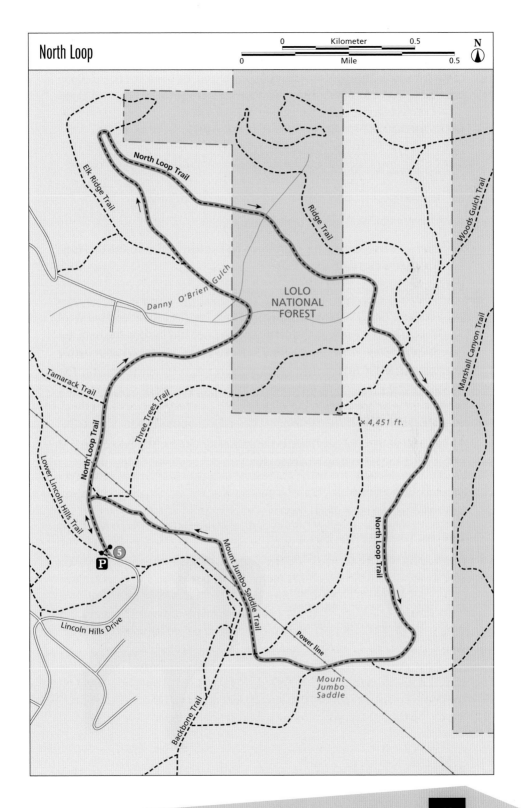

remains of a former Dutch colony. The main Backbone Trail takes off from here to the left and up the mountain. Go right, staying on the doubletrack trail. Complete the loop and turn left to return through the locked gate to the parking area.

MILES AND DIRECTIONS

0.0 Start on the doubletrack trail (a road) behind a locked gate. The trail heads north from the Mount Jumbo saddle.

0.9 The trail crosses Danny O'Brien Gulch and heads northwest.

1.0 The Elk Ridge Trail extends to the left; stay right.

1.4 The trail bends tightly in a switchback and heads southeast. The Elk Ridge Trail rejoins the North Loop Trail.

2.3 The Three Trees Trail turns to the right; go left.

2.4 The Ridge Trail (326) turns to the left and leads into the national forest toward Woods Gulch, 0.7 mile to the north. An unnamed trail leads to the right. Go straight to stay on the North Loop. The trail descends a short distance before swinging to the south.

3.3 A trail to the left leads to FR 2122 and down into Marshall Canyon.

3.4 A spur trail leads to the Backbone Trail.

3.6 Pass an ephemeral pond left behind by early settlers. The Backbone Trail leads to the left and up Mount Jumbo. Veer right onto the Saddle Trail.

4.2 Complete the loop; turn left to return to the parking area.

4.6 Arrive back at the parking area.

Options: Take the Ridge Trail at mile 2.4 to climb up the ridge toward Woods Gulch, only 0.7 mile away. It connects with the Sheep Mountain Trail. This same area offers access to the Backbone Trail, the northern route up Mount Jumbo.

Woods Gulch Loop

The southernmost trail in the Rattlesnake, this loop up and above Woods Gulch is partly on the Sheep Mountain Trail (513). The route leads up the bottom of this rocky, shrubby gulch, surrounded by parklike ponderosa forest. The trail eventually tops out on a ridge overlooking Marshall Creek with views up toward Blue Point and Wisherd Ridge. Continue climbing and take a left on a logging road. This winds around an old clear-cut and provides big views of the Missoula Valley and the Bitterroots. The road merges with Trail 513.1, taking hikers back toward Woods Gulch. At 5.6 miles connect back with the gulch-bottom trail to return to the trailhead.

Start: Woods Gulch Trailhead
Distance: 6.9-mile loop
Hiking time: About 2.5 hours
Difficulty: Moderate
Trail surface: Dirt
Best season: Spring through fall
Other trail users: Bikers, equestrians; hunters in fall
Canine compatibility: Unleashed dogs permitted year-round
Land Status: USDA Forest Service
Fees and permits: None required
Schedule: Closed 10 p.m. to 6 a.m.
Maps: USGS Northeast Missoula; USDAFS Lolo National Forest Map, available at the district office

Trail contacts: Lolo National Forest Supervisor's Office, Fort Missoula Building 24A, Missoula, MT 59804; (406) 329-3814; www.fs.usda.gov/lolo
Special considerations: Watch for out-of-control mountain bikers. During hunting season, wear hunter orange; put hunter orange on your dog too. Yield the trail to equestrians. This is mountain lion country. Grizzlies can wander through too. Watch kids, carry bear spray, and remain alert.

Finding the trailhead: From the Van Buren Street exit off I-90, go north on Van Buren Street, which becomes Rattlesnake Drive. At 1.6 miles turn right to stay on Rattlesnake Drive. After a small jog, the road continues up the valley. Go 2.5 miles and turn right onto Woods Gulch Road. After 0.3 mile arrive at the intersection with Madera Drive; bear right at the fork. The trailhead is on a bend in the road after another 0.1 mile. Parking is available in the small turnouts on the left, with a sign marking the otherwise minimally developed trailhead. **GPS:** N46 55.213' / W113 56.887'

THE HIKE

Woods Gulch receives less attention than other trails in the Rattlesnake, due to its location a short distance to the east of the main trailhead. This route immediately ensconces hikers in the tight confines of Woods Gulch. Cliff outcrops and dense shrubs define the beginning of the trail as it criss-crosses the creek, first by bridge, then by a foot crossing at 0.8 mile. Hikers doing the full loop will return to Trail 513 at this location from up the hill to the north. First, though, climb out of the drainage and use the trail to climb the sidehill on the south side of the gulch.

At mile 1.3 you encounter a three-way trail junction. Trail 513.1 is one of the trails at the junction. You may return to this junction if you follow the full loop outlined in this hike. For now, go right and stay on Trail 513, marked by a diamond-shaped sign on a tree. You will reach the ridgetop separating Woods Gulch and Marshall Creek. Feast your eyes on the first big vistas of the hike at mile 1.5. You are looking at the former Marshall Mountain Ski Area and upward into the country above the Blackfoot River: Sheep Mountain and Wisherd Ridge. This is a good place to turn around for an out-and-back hike.

The Bitterroot Mountains rise above the Missoula Valley.

A variety of wildlife can be encountered through here. It's a critical travel corridor between the habitat of the Rattlesnake and Blackfoot country to the north and the sanctuary of the Sapphire Mountains to the south. Black bear, elk, moose, deer, and mountain lion regularly wander through this area, though a larger variety of wildlife is also afoot. Big stands of open ponderosa span the area.

Turn left when you hit the trail junction on top of the ridge. Continue to climb and work through a series of switchbacks. Eventually, at mile 2.0, the trail intersects a logging road. An option to continue up toward Sheep Mountain is possible here, though the round-trip will give hikers a 16-mile day.

Turn left onto the logging road to complete the Woods Gulch Loop. This road proceeds at a gentle gradient as it winds around the side of the mountain through a recovering clear-cut. The road offers some views down into the Missoula Valley and the massive Bitterroot Mountain range beyond. Trail 513.2 intersects the road at mile 2.3, just before a hairpin turn on the road. After leaving the clear-cut and reentering the forest, you encounter a fork in the road. Go left and come to Trail 513.1 at mile 3.3. Turn left and descend through a beautiful ponderosa grove, eventually winding around and down on the bench above the north side of Woods Gulch.

At mile 5.1 an unnumbered connector trail, marked with a No Bikes sign, drops steeply down to the bottom of Woods Gulch. This is not an official forest service trail. Continue straight and rejoin the Woods Gulch Trail at mile 5.6. Turn right and retrace your steps back to the trailhead.

MILES AND DIRECTIONS

0.0 Start at the brown sign marking the Sheep Mountain Trail (513). Follow this trail up the gulch along the right (south) side of the creek.

0.2 The trail crosses the creek via a bridge and then switchbacks briefly up the left (north) side of the gulch.

0.8 The trail crosses back to the right (south) side of the creek (no bridge). An unmarked trail descends and connects from the left (north) side. Hikers doing the full loop have an option to connect back with Trail 513 here; though the short connector trail is unofficial, it is certainly there. For the time being, cross the creek to the south side and follow the trail as it begins to climb up the side of the gulch.

1.3 Reach a three-way intersection. Take the right fork, staying on Trail 513. The trail switchbacks to the ridgetop from here. The trails are marked by gray diamond-shaped signs on trees. Trail 513.2 goes straight; Trail 513.1 goes left and downhill. You will complete the loop and return to this spot on Trail 513.1.

1.5 Arrive on the ridgetop and the site of a trail junction and views of Marshall Creek. Turn left (north) to stay on the Sheep Mountain Trail as it enters a series of switchbacks. (Turning right takes hikers down toward Mount Jumbo.)

2.0 Intersect a doubletrack road. The Sheep Mountain Trail continues up the ridge on the far side of the road. (**Option:** Turn around here to retrace your steps to the trailhead.) To complete the loop, turn left on the road. The road winds around through a recovering logging site with good views of Missoula Valley.

2.3 Trail 513.2 enters from the left. Continue straight on the doubletrack. The road makes a hairpin turn over small creek.

2.8 The road reenters the tree line, leaving the recovering cut.

3.0 Reach an intersection on the road; go left.

3.3 Turn left off the doubletrack at Trail 513.1, marked by a metal sign on a tree in a large larch grove. The trail descends through a beautiful grove of large and well-spaced ponderosas.

5.1 Intersect an unnumbered trail that is marked with a No Bikes sign. This is not an official trail.

5.6 Intersect Sheep Mountain trail. Turn right and retrace your steps to the trailhead.

6.9 Arrive back at the trailhead.

Options: Hikers who want to go for the gusto can tackle Blue Point (10 miles total round-trip) or Sheep Mountain (16 miles round-trip) by continuing on Trail 513 at the intersection with the doubletrack road at mile 2.0. There is a more moderate loop in Woods Gulch bottom. From the three-way intersection at mile 1.3, take Trail 513.1. Then turn left onto the unnamed connecter trail to get back down to Trail 513.

> 🌿 **Green Tip:**
> *Maintain control of your pet even when it is unleashed.*
> *Never let your dog chase wildlife.*

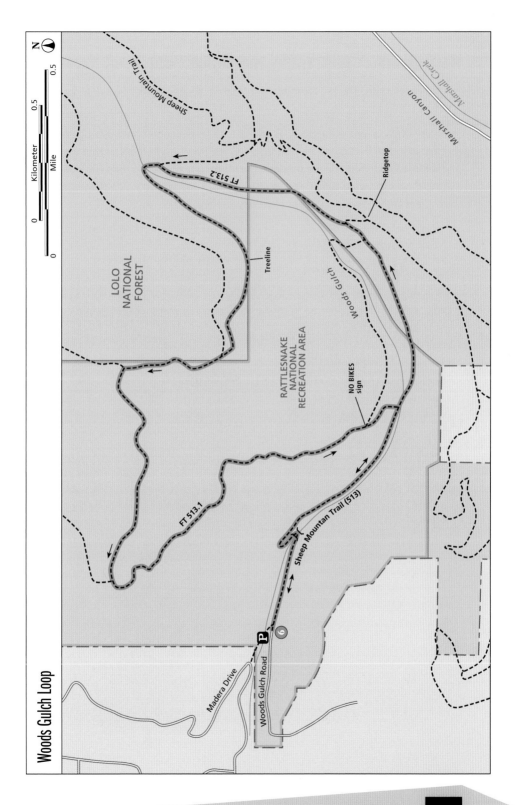

Woods Gulch Loop

Rattlesnake Creek to Spring Gulch Loop

Enjoy a leisurely walk up the Rattlesnake on a network of trails tracing the course of the creek. Traverse past secret beaches and quiet swimming holes. Then climb out of the drainage onto the Wallman Trail and crest over Strawberry Ridge. Scents of pines and wildflowers drift on the breeze. From the high point of this hike, descend down into neighboring Spring Gulch. Follow the trail until it reconnects with the Rattlesnake Creek Trail, creating a pleasant half-day journey.

Start: Main Rattlesnake Trailhead
Distance: 8.5-mile loop
Hiking time: About 4 hours
Difficulty: Strenuous
Trail surface: Dirt; single- and doubletrack
Best season: Year-round
Other trail users: Bikers, equestrians; hunters in fall; skiers in winter
Canine compatibility: Dogs permitted, leashed partway; seasonal restrictions
Land status: USDA Forest Service
Fees and permits: None required
Schedule: Closed 10 p.m. to 6 a.m.
Maps: USGS Northeast Missoula; USDAFS Lolo National Forest, available at the district office
Trail contacts: Lolo National Forest Supervisor's Office, Fort Missoula Building 24A, Missoula, MT 59804; (406) 329-3814; www.fs.usda.gov/lolo
Special considerations: Watch for out-of-control mountain bikers. During hunting season wear hunter orange and put hunter orange on your dog as well. Yield the trail to equestrians. This is cougar country. Grizzlies can wander through too. Watch kids, carry bear spray, and remain alert.

Finding the trailhead: From the Van Buren Street exit off I-90, go north on Van Buren Street, which becomes Rattlesnake Drive. At 1.6 miles turn right to stay on Rattlesnake Drive. After a small jog, the road continues up the valley. After 2.5 miles turn left onto Sawmill Gulch Road. Drive over the bridge and turn right into the main Rattlesnake trailhead after 0.2 miles.
GPS: N46 55.522' / W113 57.611'

THE HIKE

The main Rattlesnake Trail is one of the most popular trails near Missoula. This loop combines the classic singletrack creekside hike with a journey up Strawberry Ridge to find solitude and take in elevated views. The return to the trailhead takes you down Spring Gulch. The route encounters several trail junctions, and numbered spur trails abound on this section of the trail. Though they may seem confusing, they are actually straightforward. The trails get you off the beaten path, and the effort is worth it.

An elegant beach awaits next to Rattlesnake Creek.

The journey up Rattlesnake Creek begins immediately from the parking area. Access the doubletrack trail, actually a small road, from the main Rattlesnake Trailhead, just beyond the toilets. Trailhead signs and brochure maps are available. Dogs are allowed on this route (except December 1 to February 28), but they must be leashed part of the way—up to1.7 miles along Rattlesnake Creek and up to 1.3 miles from the trailhead in Spring Gulch.

There are warning signs about mountain lions at the trailhead. The area certainly is home to these fanged creatures, and encounters have been reported over the years. Dealing with predators is one aspect of mountain travel that all Montana hikers should feel comfortable with. First, remember the old adage: Lions and bears are more scared of you than you are of them. Mountain lions, especially, are incredibly secretive and capable of moving quickly and quietly. You will be lucky to see one in your hiking career. If you do run into the business end of a mountain lion, never turn your back on it. Make yourself appear big (open your jacket) and take charge of the situation; think Tarzan. Don't act scared. Do not appear weak. Pick up your children; draw your dog close; wave your arms. Make sharp noises, but no squeaks. Make sure you are not cornering the animal or threatening its young. In a worst-case scenario, fight back. Use bear spray, jackets, hiking sticks, backpacks, sticks, rocks, even your own two fists, in the battle to determine who is king of the pines. You could well be fighting for your life.

Cross Spring Gulch on a small concrete bridge, located just beyond the big bridge across Rattlesnake Creek. Just beyond Spring Gulch, the network of singletrack trails will cut off to the right at 0.6 mile. Explore this network and enjoy the myriad respites offered along the waterway. Small beaches and swimming holes are scattered about. A perfect picnic site is located at 1.2 miles.

Emerge from the network of singletrack paths and turn right onto Trail 515 at 2.0 miles. Shortly after, turn left and follow the cutoff trail through the forest to the Wallman Trail, leading over Strawberry Ridge, which lies ahead. The trail switchbacks as it climbs the ridge. Glacier lilies emerge in the spring on this hillside. The big double leaves of this delicate yellow flower provide a tasty and zingy snack for hikers. Bearberry, a low-lying dwarf shrub, is scattered across the ground too. The bearberry—known as bear's grape in Europe—produces a mealy red berry that can be ingested, but it's no huckleberry. Native Americans used this plant recreationally and spiritually. The leaves were collected, dried, and mixed with red-willow bark or tobacco and smoked. Called kinnikinnick, the name of this mixture has been passed on to the bearberry as a common reference.

As you crest the ridge at 4.4 miles, small use trails lead to the left, offering views of the valley below. Continue over the spine of the ridge and drop down a series of switchbacks into Spring Gulch. Turn left when you meet Trail 517 in the

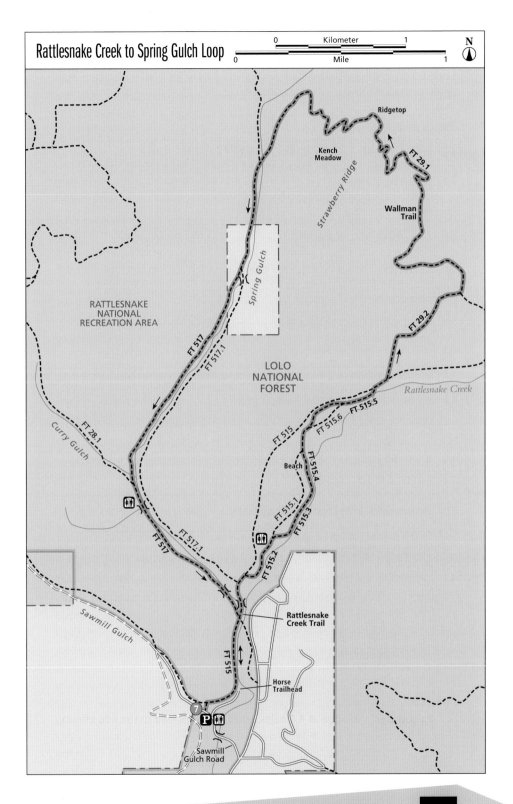

0 Kilometer **1**
0 Mile **1**

N

Ridgetop

Kench
Meadow

Strawberry Ridge

FT 29.1

Wallman
Trail

FT 29.2

RATTLESNAKE
NATIONAL
RECREATION AREA

Spring Gulch

LOLO
NATIONAL
FOREST

Rattlesnake Creek

FT 517

FT 517.1

FT 515

FT 515.6

FT 515.5

Curry Gulch

FT 28.1

Beach

FT 515.4

FT 517

FT 512.1

FT 515.1

FT 515.3

FT 515.2

Rattlesnake
Creek Trail

Sawmill Gulch

FT 515

Horse
Trailhead

7

P

Sawmill
Gulch Road

bottom of the gulch. Stay on the right side of the creek all the way down, past Curry Gulch, to the junction with the main Rattlesnake Trail. From there turn right and finish out the final 0.4 mile.

MILES AND DIRECTIONS

0.0 Start at the main Rattlesnake Trailhead.

0.4 A bridge spans the creek, leading to a neighborhood and the horse trailhead. A trail breaks off the left, leading up Spring Gulch. Go straight on Trail 515.

0.5 A small concrete bridge spans the creek flowing in Spring Gulch.

0.6 To the left is another trail leading up Spring Gulch. Immediately past this junction, Trail 515.2 turns off the right. Follow this singletrack directly next to the creek.

0.8 Merge with Trail 515.1 (restroom).

0.9 Turn right onto Trail 515.3.

1.1 Merge back with Trail 515.1 for a few steps; then turn right onto Trail 515.4.

1.2 Arrive at a nice beach and swimming hole. At the end of the beach, the trail veers left and climbs a small bench. Turn right at the junction. Several trails run through here; all lead to the same place.

1.5 Trails come together to form Trail 515.6. The trail becomes a doubletrack.

1.7 Turn right onto Trail 515.5.

2.0 Merge with Trail 515; go right (upstream).

2.1 Turn left onto the cutoff to the Wallman Trail. Technically this is Trail 29.2, but the old wooden sign says Trail 29.

2.7 Merge with Trail 29.1; turn left (uphill). Follow the old wooden sign that points to Spring Gulch. The trail immediately begins the climb up Strawberry Ridge.

4.4 Reach the top of Strawberry Ridge. Little spur trails lead to views. Descend the far side into Spring Gulch via a series of switchbacks.

5.5 Intersect Trail 517 in a meadow down in Spring Gulch.

6.0 A bridge leads to the far side of the creek and Trail 517.1. Go straight, staying on Trail 517.

7.2 Reach junction with Trail 28.1, leading up Curry Gulch; go left.

7.3 Reach another junction with a trail leading to a bridge and restroom. Go straight to stay on Trail 517.

8.1 Return to the main Rattlesnake Trail 515; turn right.

8.5 Arrive back at the trailhead.

Options: Return on Trail 515 when the singletrack network intersects it at 2.0 miles for a loop strictly along Rattlesnake Creek.

Missoula's network of bike lanes makes it easy to cycle to the Rattlesnake Trailhead, reducing vehicle emissions and adding a multi-sport workout to your day.

Sawmill Gulch to Curry Gulch Loop

This hike ties four key Rattlesnake National Recreation Area drainages into a tidy loop close to town. A large meadow, ridgetop, historic site, and creek bottom mark the diverse landscape on this walk. The trails are single and double dirt tracks. Hike up to the big meadow in Sawmill Gulch, starting from the main trailhead. From there, crest the ridge and descend into Curry Gulch, home to a historic homestead. The trail then descends and merges with the Stuart Peak Trail in Spring Gulch. Keep following that creek down to the junction with the Rattlesnake Creek Trail. Be prepared to share the trail with mountain bikers. No dogs are permitted in either Sawmill or Curry Gulch.

Start: Main Rattlesnake Trailhead
Distance: 5.9-mile loop
Hiking time: About 3 hours
Difficulty: Moderate
Trail surface: Forested dirt path; single- and doubletrack
Best season: Summer and fall
Other trail users: Bikers, equestrians; hunters in fall; skiers in winter
Canine compatibility: No dogs permitted
Land status: USDA Forest Service
Fees and permits: None required
Schedule: Closed 10 p.m. to 6 a.m.
Maps: USGS Northeast Missoula; USDAFS Lolo National Forest, available at the district office
Trail contacts: Lolo National Forest Supervisor's Office, Fort Missoula Building 24A, Missoula, MT 59804; (406) 329-3814; www.fs.usda.gov/lolo
Special considerations: Watch for out-of-control mountain bikers. During hunting season, wear hunter orange and put hunter orange on your dog as well. Yield the trail to equestrians. This is cougar country. Grizzlies can wander through too. Watch kids, carry bear spray, and remain alert.

Finding the trailhead: From the Van Buren Street exit off I-90, go north on Van Buren Street, which becomes Rattlesnake Drive. At 1.6 miles turn right to stay on Rattlesnake Drive. After a small jog, the road continues up the valley. After 2.5 miles turn left onto Sawmill Gulch Road. Drive over the bridge, and turn right into the large parking area after 0.2 mile. The main Rattlesnake Creek Trailhead is past a roundabout and the toilets. *This is not the trailhead for this hike!* As you face the roundabout, the Sawmill Gulch Trail (24.2) is on your left, closer to the intersection of the parking lot and Sawmill Gulch Road. **GPS:** N46 55.522' / W113 57.611'

THE HIKE

The Rattlesnake National Recreation Area and wilderness is as iconic to the identity of Missoula as fly fishing, the farmers' market, and the peace sign. The Rattlesnake offers wildness directly out of Missoula's backdoor. True megafauna roam the forested hills and meadows: deer, elk, moose, wolf, bear, and mountain lion.

The Rattlesnake is also a restoration success story. Long before it became a national recreation area and wilderness in 1980, the land was inhabited by humans and light industry. Reminders of settlers abound in the region, mainly in the form of aging foundations and chimneys. At its peak more than one hundred people lived in the Upper Rattlesnake. There was even a schoolhouse where Spring Gulch joins the Rattlesnake.

During the early 1880s crews working for Missoula businessman Thomas Greenough pulled 20,000 railroad ties out of unsettled land in the Rattlesnake drainage, floating them down the creek to the Missoula Valley.

Natives used the Rattlesnake for hundreds of years before Greenough's crews roamed the land. The name of the creek is derived from the Salish word for rattlesnake, perhaps because the creek sounded like a rattling rattlesnake during high-water months.

A row of healthy ponderosa pines stands tall above Rattlesnake Creek.

Today the Rattlesnake Trailhead is a bustling station for recreationists. The Sawmill Gulch to Curry Gulch Loop begins at one end of the parking lot and ends at the other. The route takes hikers through varied terrain and makes the most of a journey through four different drainages: Sawmill Gulch, Curry Gulch, Spring Creek, and Rattlesnake Creek. To begin your journey, start at the less-emphasized Sawmill Gulch Trail (24.2), which begins on the west side of the parking lot. It is marked by a brown sign bearing a NO DOGS symbol. The trail begins to climb uphill immediately and parallels the road.

Note: If you get turned around and take the Rattlesnake Creek Trail to the north, you will be following Rattlesnake Creek. This is not the trail to Sawmill Gulch!

At mile 1.2 the trail and road are cut off by a closed gate, a trailhead sign, and a parking area. This is the official Sawmill Gulch Trail (24.0). Continue past the gate on the doubletrack dirt path that leads through the large meadow. Various trails spur off from the main trail. At mile 1.8 a large tree with a sign marks Trail 24.0. The path joins from the right and leads up a side drainage.

Within 0.5 mile the trail switchbacks and goes up the ridge separating Sawmill Gulch from Curry Gulch. Go left when you reach the trail junction on top of the ridge at mile 2.8. Twenty paces later you will see a sign directing you to turn right onto Trail 28.2. It descends into Curry Gulch, home of the Curry Cabin. Take a small detour, with a left turn at the intersection of Trails 28.2 and 28.1, to reach the cabin.

This historic homestead is intact and littered with tools and other bits that mark a life lived in the mountains at the turn of the twentieth century. From the cabin, walk downhill (southeast) along the wooded Curry Gulch until it runs into Spring Gulch. Follow Trail 517 down Spring Gulch until it merges with the Rattlesnake Creek Trail. During the early 1900s a school house stood at this location. A bridge leads across the creek to a nearby neighborhood and equestrian trailhead. Follow the trail, more of a small road, down the creek. The path leads past striking cliffs among cottonwood trees.

MILES AND DIRECTIONS

0.0 Start on the trail marked by a brown sign showing a dog with a red slash through it. The trail parallels the road as it climbs Sawmill Gulch.

1.2 Reach the official Sawmill Gulch Trail (24.0). The car road up the gulch ends here at a metal gate with additional parking. The doubletrack trail enters a large meadow surrounded by ponderosa pine forest. Various spur trails cut off to the right and left. Continue straight, staying in the meadow.

1.8 Veer right to stay on Trail 24.0, marked by a sign on a tree. Follow the trail up a side drainage out of the main meadow.

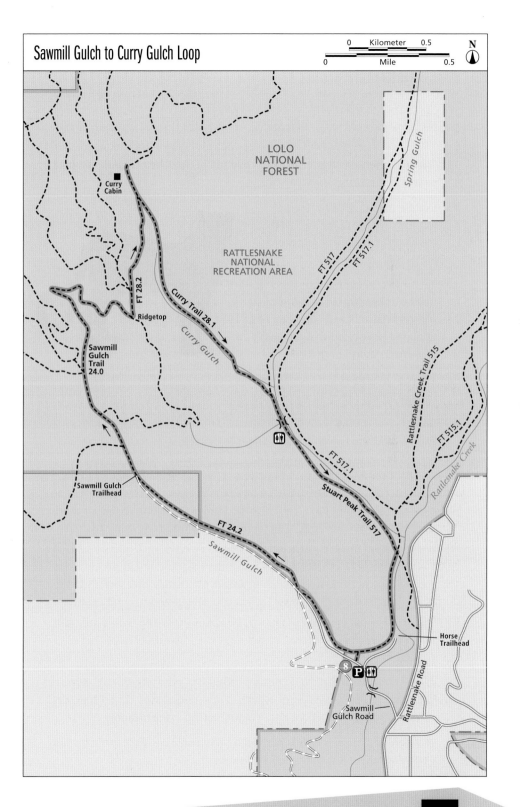

Sawmill Gulch to Curry Gulch Loop

Kilometer 0 · 0.5

Mile 0 · 0.5

N

Curry Cabin

LOLO NATIONAL FOREST

Spring Gulch

FT 28.2

Ridgetop

Curry Trail 28.1

Curry Gulch

RATTLESNAKE NATIONAL RECREATION AREA

FT 517

FT 517.1

Rattlesnake Creek Trail 515

Sawmill Gulch Trail 24.0

FT 517.1

FT 515.1

Stuart Peak Trail 517

Rattlesnake Creek

Sawmill Gulch Trailhead

FT 24.2

Sawmill Gulch

Horse Trailhead

8 P

Sawmill Gulch Road

Rattlesnake Road

2.2 Encounter a big switchback and continue climbing up the ridge dividing Sawmill and Curry Gulches.

2.8 Arrive on a ridgetop. Turn left and follow sign with arrows to Curry Gulch. Walk 20 paces and turn right onto Trail 28.2. This trail descends into Curry Gulch and to the Curry Cabin.

3.3 The trail intersects the main Curry Trail (28.1). Turn left to take the small detour to the Curry Cabin.

3.5 Explore the Curry Cabin; then return down the Curry Trail. (**Note:** It is illegal to disturb or remove artifacts.)

3.7 Pass an intersection on the right that leads back up to the ridge between Sawmill and Curry Gulches. Continue straight down Curry Gulch on a forested path.

4.6 The trail intersects the Stuart Peak Trail (517) in Spring Gulch. Turn right and follow the trail down the creek.

4.7 A quick spur leads left, across a bridge, to Trail 517.1. An outhouse is located here. Go straight to stay on the more primitive Trail 517.

5.5 Spring Gulch opens up into the Rattlesnake Valley and the Rattlesnake Creek Trail (515). Turn right on the trail and walk down the creek to complete the loop.

5.9 Arrive back at the main Rattlesnake Trailhead.

Options: There are several variations of this loop. You can simply explore Sawmill Gulch via the network of trails in and above the meadow. If you decide to do this, you can park at the Sawmill Gulch Trailhead. Alternately, hike directly to the Curry Cabin via the main Rattlesnake Trailhead for an out-and-back hike with less elevation gain.

Ravine Creek Trail

Ravine Creek is Grant Creek's little-known backdoor access point to the Rattlesnake Wilderness and Recreation Area. This trail instantly places hikers into thick Douglas fir forest as it winds up the mountainside from the bottom of Ravine Creek. Views stretch into upper Grant Creek. The trail ends on a ridgetop at the intersection of Trail 24.1. Turn left and a brief walk will lead you to a rocky outcrop with a view of upper Grant Creek at a trail junction. Continue up the trail and eventually you will top out on Stuart Peak. This trail is the most direct route to that peak.

Start: Ravine Creek Trailhead
Distance: 6.2 miles out and back
Hiking time: About 3 hours
Difficulty: Moderate
Trail surface: Dirt; singletrack
Best season: Spring through fall
Other trail users: Bikers, equestrians; hunters in fall
Canine compatibility: Dogs permitted; leashed for first 0.25 mile
Land status: Lolo National Forest
Fees and permits: None required
Schedule: Closed 10 p.m. to 6 a.m.
Maps: USGS Northeast Missoula; USDAFS Lolo National Forest, available at the district office
Trail contacts: Lolo National Forest Supervisor's Office, Fort Missoula Building 24A, Missoula, MT 59804; (406) 329-3814; www.fs.usda.gov/lolo
Special considerations: A special elk hunting season opens on Sept 15. Make sure you are wearing hunter orange; put some on your dog too. Watch out for kamikaze mountain bikers.

Finding the trailhead: From the Reserve Street exit off I-90, drive north on Grant Creek Road for 4.6 miles. A RAVINE ROAD sign marks the pullout, 0.8 mile past Snowbowl Road. The pullout (not actually a road) holds about five cars. **GPS:** N46 58.41' / W113 59.79'

THE HIKE

This tiny, quiet access point to the Rattlesnake National Recreation Area and Wilderness is often overlooked. When most people think of Rattlesnake access, they naturally think of Rattlesnake Creek, with its four trailheads and numerous drainages. This sort of thinking keeps the tiny parking lot at Ravine Road empty. Cars do come and go, but they're mainly locals taking the dog for a 0.5-mile trot. In many ways, the Ravine Creek Trail (34) serves as a Grant Creek neighborhood access to the meadows of Sawmill Gulch, the Curry Cabin, and the most direct route up Stuart Peak.

Sure there is some uphill involved from this trailhead—maybe one reason it is so small. The trail isn't steep, but it climbs steadily uphill on a series of switchbacks starting at 0.3 mile. It climbs to a ridgetop at 2.8 miles, where it joins the rest of the Rattlesnake trail system. Rattlesnake aficionados who usually use the main trailhead may find that the Ravine Creek Trail offers a fresh perspective on well-known places.

This is also the route you want to take for the most direct access to one of Missoula's sentinel peaks: 7,960-foot Stuart Peak. Once you arrive at the

A fall snow storm blankets the trail, but not enough to keep hikers from playing in the hills.

Ravine Creek Trail

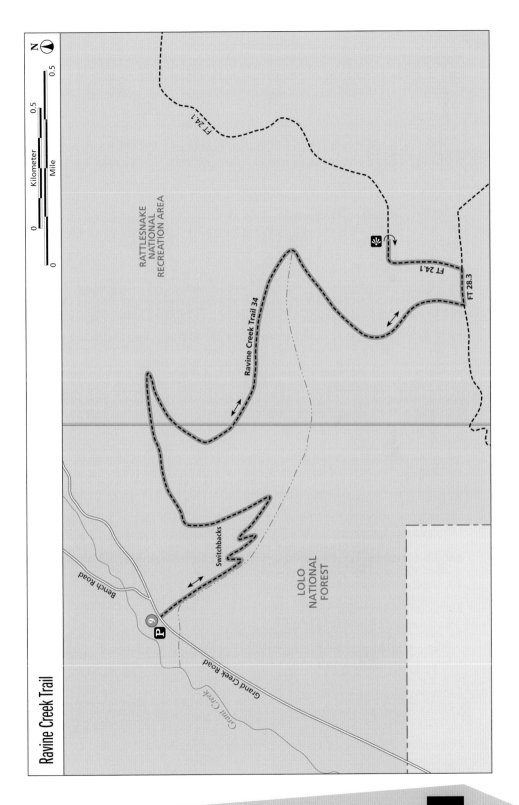

ridgetop at 2.8 miles, turn left and walk 0.1 mile to an intersection between Trail 24.1 and Trail 28.3. Go left at this junction and walk another 0.2 mile until you arrive at a rocky promontory that overlooks the upper Grant Creek Valley. From this promontory, continue to follow the trail system uphill to reach the Stuart Peak Trail (517).

The elk that live in this section of the Rattlesnake are culled in an early hunt each year. Since the Rattlesnake became a federal wilderness in 1980, the elk herd has grown from 40 to 300 head. The hunters who stalk this section of forest for elk number in the forties. Those hunters tend to take fewer than ten elk per year from the southern Rattlesnake.

To get onto the trail from the trailhead, pick up the singletrack on the north side of the small parking area.

The Ravine Creek Trail is well marked. The only place that isn't marked is an intersection with a narrow trail at 0.7 mile that follows the path of the creek. This trail has been closed to allow the area to recover. The main trail continues to climb up the hill with a series of switchbacks. Shortly after the Ravine Creek Trail ends, watch out for the junction between Trails 24.1 and 28.3. Take the left fork to make the final 0.2 mile out to the rock promontory.

MILES AND DIRECTIONS

0.0 Start at the trailhead at the north side of the parking area. The trail starts between two houses and leads up Ravine Creek (34).

0.3 The trail makes a hairpin turn and begins to switchback up the side of the ridge.

0.7 Reach an unmarked trail junction. A smaller, singletrack path continues straight, following the path of the creek. Follow the larger trail that continues to switchback up the hill.

1.6 The trail bends from facing into Grant Creek to facing back into Ravine Creek.

2.8 Reach a junction with Trail 24.1; turn left.

2.9 Go left at the junction of Trails 24.1 and 28.3.

3.1 Arrive at a small rocky promontory that overlooks upper Grant Creek. Retrace your steps to the trailhead. (Trails continue up toward Stuart Peak from here; see "Options.")

6.2 Arrive back at the trailhead.

Options: The Ravine Creek Trail can be used to climb Stuart Peak. Turn left onto Trail 24.1 at 2.8 miles and follow it until it merges with the Stuart Peak Trail. This is an 18-mile round-trip, with more than 4,000 feet of vertical gain followed by an equal descent. The Curry Cabin and Sawmill Gulch can be reached by turning right at the intersection with Trail 24.1. Upper Spring Gulch can be reached by following Trail 28.3.

HIKE INFORMATION

Organizations: Rocky Mountain Elk Foundation, 5705 Grant Creek Rd., Missoula, MT 59808; (800) 225-5355; www.rmef.org. The foundation's national headquarters is in Missoula at the base of Grant Creek, where the Elk Country Visitor Center is located. The center has a museum and a small nature trail.

SWAN VALLEY
Holland Falls National Recreation Trail

The Swan Mountains north of Missoula are a quintessential Montana mountain range. Holland Falls, thundering just above Holland Lake, is one of the natural features that define the state. This hike traces a route on the lakeshore and then winds up to the impressive falls. Pyramid-shaped Carmine Peak is a commanding presence above. The view of the Mission Mountains, Holland Lake, and Holland Falls—all from a natural boulder field platform—is unique. In fall, larch and birch trees add brilliant color to the scene. The waterfall is particularly powerful in spring.

Start: Holland Falls Trailhead

Distance: 3.0 miles out and back

Hiking time: About 1.5 hours

Difficulty: Easy

Trail surface: Dirt; singletrack

Best season: Spring through fall

Other trail users: None

Canine compatibility: Dogs permitted

Land status: USDA Forest Service

Fees and permits: None required

Schedule: None

Maps: USGS Holland Lake; USDAFS Flathead National Forest

Trail contacts: Swan Lake Ranger District, 200 Ranger Station Rd., Big Fork, MT 59911; (406) 837-7500; www.fs.usda.gov/main/flathead/home

Special considerations: This is grizzly country; carry bear spray.

Finding the trailhead: From Van Buren Street go east on I-90 for 4.1 miles to exit 109. This is MT 200 East. Continue through Bonner and up the Blackfoot River. Go 32.9 miles and turn left onto MT 83 at Clearwater Junction. Go through the town of Seeley Lake. After 35.5 miles turn right onto Holland Lake Road. Veer left onto Holland Lake Lodge Road after 2.5 miles; pass a campground and Holland Lake Lodge. The trailhead is at road's end after another 1.4 miles. **GPS:** N47 27.18' / W113 36.20'

THE HIKE

The Holland Falls National Recreation Trail is on the edge of the Bob Marshall Wilderness. While a walk into the "the Bob" is an expedition-worthy endeavor, hikers can get a taste of this massive wilderness where Holland Falls rushes into Holland Lake.

It takes only a moment along the shores of Holland Lake to realize the unique importance of the area. The classic beauty of Carmine Peak rises above the lake. Views of Holland Falls—a mere ribbon at this distance—with the lake in the foreground add to the surrounding grandeur.

Carmine Peak in Montana's Swan Range rises above Holland Lake. The falls is but a tiny ribbon in the trees.

The area loses its snowpack well after Missoula, so hiking begins here in late spring. Car camping is available near the trailhead, as well as the opportunity to stay in the historic Holland Lake Lodge. Canoeing is popular on the lake and can be combined with a hike to the falls.

Native Americans have used this path for thousands of years to enter the South Fork of the Flathead via Gordon Pass. In 1908 a tragic conflict that shaped relations between natives and settlers played out near the shores of Holland Lake. Eight Pend d'Oreille Indians were attacked by a Montana game warden in what is now known as the Swan Valley Massacre. The Indians were on an excursion off reservation land, making rounds through their aboriginal hunting grounds to provision up on as much meat as possible to get the tribe through winter. Although the 1855 Hellgate Treaty allowed them to hunt without permits, they purchased licenses.

The party had hunted in the South Fork of the Flathead and was camped at a place known as "It Has Skunk Cabbage." They planned to return to the Flathead Reservation over the nearby Mission Mountains, which form the reservation boundary.

While the hunting rights of the natives were well known, the motives of state game warden Charles Peyton remain unclear. He encountered the party and proceeded to harass the women, who had stayed behind in camp while the men hunted. When Peyton returned to again examine permits, the hunting party was together in a tepee and a small skirmish broke out. Peyton left but returned the next day. He is rumored to have been drunk and in the company of another gunman. Whatever happened next happened fast. When the smoke cleared, the three men in the party, who were unarmed, and a 13-year-old boy who scrambled for a rifle once the shooting started were dead. The women in the party responded by grabbing rifles and killing Peyton. One of the women, six months pregnant, rode for help; she escaped Peyton's accomplice and located another tribal hunting party for help.

These troubling events are etched in the stones along the lake's shore, as sure as its elegant shape. You can contemplate this story as you overlook the upper Swan Valley at Holland Falls. It's not that hard to imagine a world where Native Americans on horseback still roam in the rhythm of an ancient hunter-gatherer ritual.

From the parking area, walk south toward the lake. The trail forks almost immediately, at 0.1 mile. The left fork, East Holland Trail (415) goes left. This trail climbs the steep mountain flank on the left side of the lake. Take the right fork, Holland Lake Trail (416), which stays along the lakeshore. At this same junction, a primitive picnic area opens up on the lakeshore.

Weave through nooks of larch, fir, and birch along Holland Lake and cross a small footbridge over a side creek at 1.1 miles. Shortly after, the trail climbs fairly gently up to the base of the falls. A boulder field creates a natural platform for viewing the cascade, which roars in spring. The area's autumn colors are renowned.

Fishing in the lake can be productive, and motors are allowed.

Be Bear Aware

This is grizzly country, and bears are active in the area, especially in spring and fall. Make sure to carry your bear spray where it's easily accessible. It's a good idea to replace any spray you have had for a number of years; it can expire.

The spray forms a cloud that envelops the bear. The range of the spray is about 30 feet, which is about 10 paces for most people. That's about 2 seconds before a charging grizzly makes contact. Don't spray too early. There are only 8 seconds of spray in the full-size canisters. Aim low, and spray in short bursts.

Although bear spray is extremely effective, it's best to avoid a bear encounter altogether. Remain aware of fresh bear sign: tracks, scat, flipped-over rocks, and ripped-up logs on the ground.

If you see this sort of sign, be aware of the wind direction. If the wind is blowing in your face or across the trail, chances are a bear can't use its most powerful sense—scent—to detect your approach.

Bears attack humans when they are surprised at close range. So if visibility is limited on the trail, make noise by clapping your hands or talking loudly in a low-pitched voice (for instance, saying "Hey, bear") to let bears know you are in the area. This way they can clear out—and take their cubs with them!

Never crowd a bear, and never run from a bear. If you encounter a bear at close range, slowly back away. If you are in a group, stand together. If the bear charges, stand your ground. If it makes contact with you, play dead. This actually works, so ride it out.

Chances are, you will never see one of these wily and powerful bruins in the wild. If you do, it will most likely run from you. But if it doesn't, have that bear spray handy—and know how to use it. A grizzly encounter can be a defining moment in your life.

MILES AND DIRECTIONS

0.0 Start on the East Holland Trail (415).The trailhead is on the south (lake) side of the parking area.

0.1 Bear right at the trail junction to follow the Holland Falls National Recreation Trail (416) along the lakeshore. (The East Holland Trail heads off to the left, eventually climbing to high elevations.) Spur trail leads off to the right to the lake's edge.

0.7 Reach a view of the waterfall and Carmine Peak across the lake.

1.1 Cross a footbridge over a small creek. From here the trail begins to climb to the base of Holland Falls.

1.5 Reach a jumble of boulders at Holland Falls. Enjoy the thundering cascade above before returning the way you came.

3.0 Arrive back at the trailhead.

Options: The adventurous and surefooted can rock-hop and bushwhack up the creek above the falls (to the east) to intersect Trail 415. Trail 415 crosses the creek and merges with the Holland-Gordan Trail (35). Turn left. There is an upper falls at 0.5 mile and Upper Holland Lake at 2.0 miles. Return to the trailhead via Trail 415. If you don't want to bushwhack, Trail 415 starts near the trailhead.

HIKE INFORMATION

Camping: Holland Falls Campground (seasonal) has 39 sites in two loops on the lakeshore before you reach the trailhead. For more information visit www.forest camping.com/dow/northern/flatcmp.htm; for reservations call (877) 444-6777.

The best times of year to catch kokanee salmon and rainbow trout in Holland Lake are early spring and late fall.

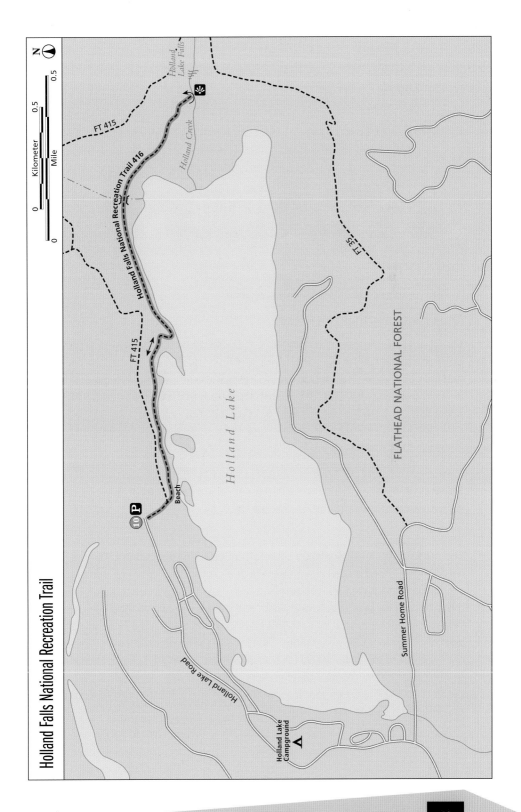

Holland Falls National Recreation Trail

In Missoula

Views of downtown Missoula from the Clark Fork River Trail.

The urban walks in Missoula are some of the nicest in the country. Thomas L. Greenough echoed a similar sentiment over a century ago when he donated a section of Rattlesnake Creek bottomland to the city to preserve it in natural harmony forever. He said he had traveled far and what is free here in Missoula, other cities try to re-create at great cost. This is why he wanted to gift a "romantic and poetic" retreat to future generations. Today there is still a place where you can sit on a bench and feel a damp leaf fall from a tree and graze your cheek. The smell of the forest will intertwine with your own, clinging to your sweatshirt after you get back to the shelter of your living room. Birdsong will make you remember that your boss should get out here more too.

It's hard to tell if the Clark Fork River walk is an urban hike with natural highlights or a nature hike with urban influences. The trail attracts people from all walks of life. On a spring weekend afternoon, the path transforms into a vibrant scene of Missoula culture, with each person using his or her preferred mode of travel. Laughter, dogs barking, and the shout of a surfer fill the air. Scents of cinnamon and lamb drift on the wind from the farmers' market. An off-course Frisbee floats by. It's caught by a stranger and returned with a flick of the wrist. Meanwhile, down in the Clark Fork Natural Area, mallards tend to their nests, nosing their eggs into protective nooks among shrubs at the water's edge. An osprey circles overhead, eyeballing you suspiciously as it grapples with a small trout before settling into a nest atop a big cottonwood tree.

Of all the urban walks, Tower Street has the most intact forest, and therefore the most bird and mammal life. The river seems different as it flows through Tower Street. It's not confined and simply floating in a big, lazy straight line like it is through downtown. It has islands in it, layers of big trees on its banks, imperceptible curves in its channels, and a community of animals living in and around it.

The question isn't which of these urban walks you will do. It's which one you will do today.

Fall colors in Greenough Park.

11

Greenough Park Loop, Bolle Birdwatching Trail

Greenough Park is the gem of the Missoula Park system. Acres of cottonwood line Rattlesnake Creek, making it an oasis during summer, when Missoulians flock to the shaded waters. Birders thrive in the park as well and have spotted over 120 species of feathered friends in Greenough. The park is a living example of the legacy that conservation provides for generations. The land was donated to the city by Thomas L. and Tennessee Greenough as a place for "romantic and poetic retreat." The Greenoughs also demanded that the park be kept in pristine natural order.

Start: Greenough Park, corner of Locust and Monroe Streets
Distance: 1.6-mile loop
Hiking time: About 45 minutes
Difficulty: Easy
Trail surface: Paved doubletrack; dirt singletrack
Best season: Year-round
Other trail users: Bikers on paved sections
Canine compatibility: Leashed dogs permitted
Land status: City of Missoula

Fees and permits: None required
Schedule: Open 6 a.m. to 11 p.m.
Maps: USGS Northeast Missoula; City of Missoula Parks, Open Space & Trails
Trail contacts: Missoula Parks and Recreation, 600 Cregg Lane, Missoula, MT 59801; (406) 721-7275; ci.missoula.mt.us
Special considerations: Black bears are known to frequent the park in the fall.

Finding the trailhead: From the Van Buren Street exit off I-90, go north on Van Buren Street for 0.2 mile. Turn left onto Locust Street. Go 0.1 mile and turn right onto Monroe Street. Turn immediately left into the Greenough Park parking area. **GPS:** N46 52.47' / W113 58.79'

G reenough Park was the city's first park. This oasis within the city is located mere blocks from downtown, but you'll never know once you're ensconced beneath the shady cottonwoods at the edge of Rattlesnake Creek. Within the 42-acre park, a winding network of trails places you squarely in epic birding habitat. More than 120 bird species make Greenough Park their home. What's most interesting about Greenough Park, however, is how it came to be.

The park was donated by Thomas L. and Tennessee Greenough in 1902. The couple lived in an A. J. Gibson–designed Victorian mansion near modern-day I-90 on the banks of Rattlesnake Creek. The two had long encouraged the city to purchase the wild land just north of their home to protect it from encroaching development and preserve it as a park for generations to come. But the city wasn't interested.

The Greenoughs, who had earned millions in the timber and mining trade, decided to take the buffalo by the horns and bought the property themselves over time. Upon gifting the land to the city, Thomas Greenough told the city council to create a park "to which the people of Missoula may during the heated days of summer, the beautiful days of autumn, and the balmy days of spring find

The sun sets on Rattlesnake Creek and Mount Jumbo.

a comfortable, romantic, and poetic retreat." The only stipulation was that the city had to protect the park as "a forest and natural growth" and prevent "desecration and destruction." If the park was mistreated in any way, the land would revert to the Greenough heirs.

Greenough had to stick to his guns to keep the park preserved in its natural state. Park managers (deemed uneducated by Greenough) immediately wanted to clear away the snowberry, elderberry, and mountain ash that make up the understory of the park. Greenough intervened; he threatened to take back the land, noting that elsewhere in the country cities were spending vast sums of money trying to re-create natural parks. "Money can hardly buy what we have here for free," he said.

A patient great blue heron ekes out a living on the banks of Rattlesnake Creek.
ALESHA BOWMAN

Greenough Park Loop, Bolle Birdwatching Trail

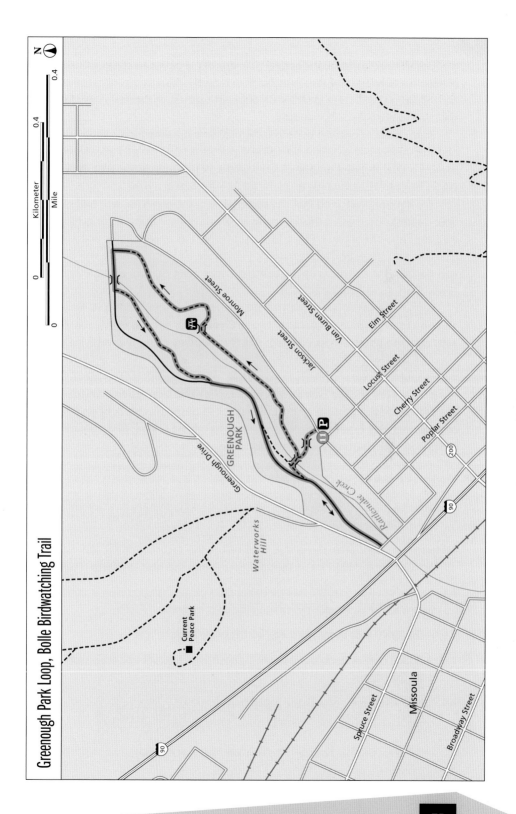

Other impediments to the natural character of the park were the installation of a cement bunker (still visible in the park) to cage two black bears and fencing a herd of captive deer. This too ruffled Greenough's feathers, and the two unsightly spectacles were eventually removed.

Today the city ensures that no unnatural developments occur within the park's boundaries. Missoulians from all walks of life flock to the park year-round, seeking a brief respite from the civilized world that surrounds the open space. Black bears have been known to do the same, especially in the fall.

The Bolle Birdwatching Trail, the centerpiece of the park's modern trail system, creates a loop with a small stem. To access the trail, walk from the parking area and cross one of two bridges. Turn right before the second bridge and walk across a small grassy field to the tree line. Pick up the trail here, next to a sign that says NO BIKES. The trail leads up the east side of the main channel of Rattlesnake Creek. Cross a small bridge at 0.4 mile, just before meandering into a picnic area.

Left of the picnic area, the trail returns to the cottonwoods and winds around, crossing a bridge over Rattlesnake Creek at 0.6 mile. Turn left immediately after the bridge to get on a foot trail that wanders down the west side of the creek. This is one of the most natural sections of the park. The trail rejoins the paved doubletrack at 0.9 mile. Turn left and arrive at the big bridge over the creek at 1.1 miles. Walk straight past the bridge to explore one last section of the park. The path leads you past the enclosure that once housed two black bears. Turn around when you reach the street, and return to the big bridge. Turn right over the bridge, which returns you to the parking area.

MILES AND DIRECTIONS

0.0 Start on the trail leading into the park over a bridge that spans a side channel of Rattlesnake Creek.

400 feet Turn right after the bridge (and before the second bridge) and walk across a grassy field. Pick up the trail near the tree line, next to a NO BIKES sign.

0.4 Cross a small bridge. The trail winds next to a picnic shelter and an alternate access to the park before reentering the cottonwoods.

0.6 A spur trail leads to the northeast corner of the park.

0.65 A bridge crosses Rattlesnake Creek. Turn left onto the foot trail immediately after the bridge.

0.9 The foot trail merges with the paved trail; turn left.

1.1 Arrive at a big bridge over the main creek. Keep going straight to explore the stem of the loop.

1.3 Turn around at the sidewalk. Follow the small footpath next to the creek to return to the big bridge.

1.5 Arrive at the big bridge. Turn right and cross the bridge.

1.6 Arrive back at the parking area.

HIKE INFORMATION

Organizations: Five Valleys Audubon Society, PO Box 8425, Missoula, MT 59807; fvaudubon.org. This local chapter periodically hosts bird walks in Greenough Park.

Becoming a birder is as easy as getting your hands on a pair of binoculars and a field guide and taking a walk around bird habitat. Find birds; observe without disrupting the flock. Note birds' unique characteristics. Cross-check these with listings in your field guide, and start a life list. You are on your way to becoming a birder!

Clark Fork Riverbank Loop

This classic loop is the heart and soul of Missoula, with sections of the route on Missoula's boardwalk. The slogan "Keep Missoula weird" is taken to heart down here. Artists of all sorts (poets, musicians, painters, chess players) flock to the parks adjacent to this urban hiking path. Kayakers, surfers, skateboarders, in-line skaters, cyclists, volleyball players, runners, and a host of other impromptu sports enthusiasts frequent this greenway trail system on both sides of the mighty Clark Fork River. Interpretative signs and art, commissioned by the city, mark the path as well. Other sections of the pathway, such as the Clark Fork Natural Area near the Orange Street Bridge, are less urban and get hikers in touch with cottonwood trees and songbirds along the riverfront.

Start: Parking lot at Boone and Crockett Club

Distance: 1.9-mile loop

Hiking time: About 1 hour

Difficulty: Easy

Trail surface: Dirt; paved double-track

Best season: Year-round

Other trail users: Several; see above

Canine compatibility: Leashed dogs permitted

Land status: City of Missoula

Fees and permits: None required

Schedule: None

Maps: USGS Southeast Missoula; City of Missoula Parks, Open Space & Trails

Trail contacts: Missoula Parks and Recreation, 600 Cregg Lane, Missoula, MT 59801; (406) 721-7275; ci.missoula.mt.us

Finding the trailhead: From the Van Buren Street exit off I-90, go south 0.1 mile to Broadway Street; turn right. After 0.6 mile turn left onto Higgins Avenue; go over the Higgins Avenue Bridge. Turn right on 3rd Street after another 0.6 mile, then immediately turn right again onto a small street, Station Drive, that descends down to the river level. There is a parking lot next to the former Railroad Depot building. **GPS:** N46 52.09' / W113 59.95'

THE HIKE

This is the most urban hike in the book, though the downtown Missoula riverfront offers more opportunity to enjoy the rhythms of nature than most suburban locations. The Ron MacDonald Riverfront Trail Loop links several parks together on a journey through the heart of Missoula on the north and south banks of the Clark Fork River. In warm weather these boardwalks rival any of the great people-watching places in America. Enjoy shameless, fun-time recreation at each step, and before you finish your hike, you may find yourself in a game of ultimate Frisbee, high-stakes volleyball, or a casual game of hacky sack.

Caras Park is one of the many parks that are linked together by the Clark Fork Riverbank Loop.

The large orange building at the trailhead now houses the Boone and Crockett Club (with a collection of wildlife mounts open to visitors), but for years it was a depot for the Milwaukee Railroad. When the company went belly up in 1980, the tracks were removed and the Riverfront Trail was born.

From the parking area, walk east on the Riverfront Trail and pass under the Higgins Street Bridge. At 0.3 mile pass the Clark Fork Native Prairie in the John H. Toole Park. The prairie comprises native plants that don't require excessive water. You can find yarrow, larkspur, and bitterroot blooming among the native grasses and shrubs. The prairie is the size of a postage stamp—a token few intriguing acres, a little window into the native prairie that once covered the Missoula Valley.

A famous Missoula-area historical photo shows six tepees encamped in 1890 at what is today the running track. The flat was a productive bitterroot patch, and Native Americans camped here well into the early 1900s. Times have changed. Today the Riverfront Trail is frequented by joggers, hikers, and power walkers. At peak times—for instance, weekends and rush hour—this trail can be incredibly busy.

After you hike past the track, turn left over the footbridge below the Madison Street Bridge at 0.6 mile. Cross the bridge, admiring the river's current. (Don't jump off the bridge; it is dangerous.) Turn left once across the bridge and continue west on the Riverfront Trail North. Before long, at 0.8 mile, the paved trail veers to the right and descends a short distance through Kiwanis Park near the volleyball courts.

After passing through Kiwanis Park, the trail weaves through a neighborhood for a couple blocks on an alley and a street. Follow the trail signs. The trail leaves the street and enters Bess Reed Park at the corner of Clay Street. A winding sidewalk takes you through nicely manicured grass and a stand of shade trees before continuing down the river. At 1.0 mile the trail passes the statue of the three fish; at 1.1 miles is the pier where you can watch surfing on Brennan's Wave.

At this same spot a trail turns to the right and drops down into Caras Park, famous for concerts and food events. Caras used to be called Island Park because it was an island until 1961, when the north braid of the river was filled in with soil from the rebuilding of the Higgins Avenue Bridge. Until that time, the river ran against the historic Wilma building.

Continue downriver. At the end of Caras Park you pass the famous Carousel for Missoula—a high-speed, hand-carved attraction for kids and adults alike. Orange Street Bridge is at 1.4 miles. Turn right before you go under the bridge and go up the stairs. At the top of the stairs, turn left and cross over the river.

At 1.5 miles a paved blacktop path veers to the left and down to the Riverfront Trail as it comes out of the tunnel that passes under Orange Street. Turn left, cross a small gray bridge with wooden arches, and enter the Clark Fork Natural Area at 1.6 miles. A short loop takes hikers through some excellent birding area

Clark Fork Riverbank Loop

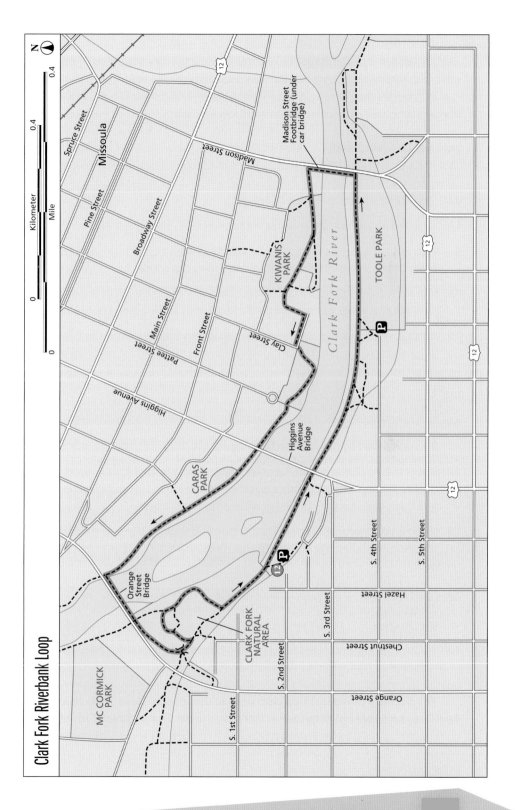

and a small but meaningful grove of cottonwoods. The city intentionally pre-serves this land with the idea of education and habitat conservation.

At 1.8 miles the short loop rejoins the Riverfront Trail. Turn left and return to the parking area next to the Boone and Crockett Club to finish out the loop.

MILES AND DIRECTIONS

0.0 Start at the parking lot and go right (east) on the Riverfront Trail.

0.1 Go under the Higgins Avenue Bridge.

0.4 A spur trail leads to a parking area at the end of 4th Street; go straight.

0.6 Turn left over the footbridge under the Madison Street Bridge. Turn left again on the Riverfront Trail North after crossing the bridge.

0.8 Veer right on a cement path that leads down from the levee above the river. (The trail that continues straight on the levee ends at the tennis courts.)

0.9 Reach a small roundabout marked by a boulder; turn left. Go a short dis-tance and through two wooden posts with reflectors. The trail becomes an alley, then a street for 2 blocks.

0.95 Turn right onto Lavasseur Street.

1.0 Turn left at the corner of Clay Street. A paved trail enters Bess Reed Park.

1.1 Pass under the Higgins Avenue Bridge again.

1.2 Reach the viewing deck for Brennan's Wave, a surf feature for kayaks and boards. A roundabout around a commemorative kayak statue leads down into Caras Park. Go straight to stay on Riverfront Trail North.

1.4 The trail intersects the Orange Street Bridge. Turn right before you go under the bridge and climb the stairs. At the top of the stairs, turn left and cross the bridge.

1.5 Veer left onto a blacktop path and descend back down to the Riverfront Trail after it comes out of a tunnel under Orange Street. Turn left when you merge with the trail.

1.6 Turn left over a small gray bridge with wooden arches into the Clark Fork Natural Area. This is a short but worthwhile loop that rejoins the main trail.

1.8 The Clark Fork Natural Area loop rejoins the Riverfront Trail; turn left.

1.9 Arrive back at the parking area.

Options: Extend your walk into McCormick, Ogren, and Silver Parks, downstream (west) of the Orange Street Bridge. The best trail to use is off the Clark Fork Natural Area Loop. Use the unnamed trail that goes under the bridge on the riverbank, which leads down to the picturesque California Street Pedestrian Bridge, 0.7 mile away. The walk leads past the skate park, Osprey baseball field, and a river access. On the return trip, turn right onto the Bitterroot Branch Trail, then left on the Milwaukee Trail until you go through the tunnel under Orange Street. At that point you are back on the loop described in this guide.

Another option to extend your hike is to stay on the south side of the river to intersect the Kim Williams Trail at 1.7 miles.

HIKE INFORMATION

Local events/attractions: YMCA Riverbank Run, 3000 South Russell St., Missoula; (406) 721-9622; ymcamissoula.org/index.php. This event, which occurs annually during the second weekend in May, has blossomed into one of the country's biggest footraces.

13

Tower Street Conservation Area Loop

This thick Clark Fork River floodplain is a birder's dream. Fat cottonwoods dominate the foliage here and make a tempting home for beaver. These trees also shelter young morel mushrooms in springtime, available for harvest just before the high-water floods in May. Serenity is abundant here. The small trailhead parking area is often jammed full, but you can park on nearby Tower Street. Do not park on the private Kerwald Drive. Many locals take advantage of this little-known spot to walk their dogs, shake off the day's stress at the river's edge, or throw a fishing line into the water. This is a perfect walk for families, as there are two loops. Walk one loop for a shorter excursion, or take in both to extend your city's-edge getaway.

Start: Tower Street Trailhead

Distance: 1.5-mile double loop

Hiking time: About 45 minutes

Difficulty: Easy

Trail surface: Dirt and rock; single- and doubletrack

Best season: Summer through winter

Other trail users: Archery hunters late Oct through Jan

Canine compatibility: Leashed dogs permitted

Land status: City of Missoula

Fees and permits: None required

Schedule: None

Maps: USGS Southeast Missoula; USDAFS Lolo National Forest, available at the district office; City of Missoula Parks, Open Space & Trails

Trail contacts: Missoula Parks and Recreation, 600 Cregg Lane, Missoula. MT 59801; (406) 721-7275; ci.missoula.mt.us

Special considerations: During the annual spring flood, this area can be swallowed by the river and impossible to hike. Parking on the private Kerwald Drive can get you ticketed. Late spring produces impressive mosquito hatches; use repellent. The active floodplain also can change the trail system slightly from year to year.

Finding the trailhead: From the Reserve Street exit off I-90, go south on Reserve Street 2.3 miles to 3rd Street West. Turn right and drive 1.1 miles to Tower Street. Turn right and go 0.2 mile to the end of Tower Street. Turn right into the dirt parking lot at the edge of a mass of cottonwood trees. **GPS:** N46 52.247' / W114 03.795'

Until the Tower Street cottonwoods were purchased by the city, this flood-plain received little attention as a hiking destination. In the past it was defined by rambling trails, mostly haunts for vagabonds. Now it is cele-brated as a cornerstone of Missoula's open-space vision. The area is clean and safe and has marked trails that attract scores of hiking enthusiasts looking for a quick jaunt into nature. This trail system is a local favorite and a guarded secret among locals because of the relatively pristine forest and river experience so close to town. Hikers can encounter bald eagles, ospreys, red-winged blackbirds, beavers, river otters, and white-tailed deer—all of this just a few minutes from Reserve Street, Missoula's western demarcation line.

The small trailhead parking area may be full. If it is, park on nearby Tower Street. Enter the trail system by walking past a length of chain between two posts. There is a red loop and a blue loop, and there are several ways to approach this hike.

A good way to go is straight to the river on the doubletrack behind the chain gate. This is an overlap of the blue and red trails and is marked by blue and red

A beaver made short work of this cottonwood along the Clark Fork River at Tower Street.

blazes on trees. The red loop kicks out to the right 100 feet after you begin your walk. The blue loop turns left at 0.1 mile. Continue straight along the doubletrack. The blue loop comes back in from the left shortly before you reach the Clark Fork River at 0.2 mile. Continue to the right. You are now on the red loop. Follow the river upstream past a small riffle and enjoy overlooking the islands in the Clark Fork. There's good fishing here.

At 0.4 mile the red loop veers away from the river and begins to wind its way back around toward the parking area. Snowberry, juniper, and aspen intersperse beneath the cottonwood canopy. Vireos, flycatchers, catbirds, waxwings, Lewis's woodpeckers, and a variety of owls and warblers are among the many species that birding enthusiasts can discover here. You will complete the red loop at 0.7 mile. Call it a day, or continue on to explore the blue loop.

To reach the blue loop, turn right and go down the doubletrack trail you started on until you reach 0.8 mile. Go left at the intersection of the blue loop trail. This loop is a little more primitive and a nice singletrack trail winding through the cottonwoods. At mile 1.0 the trail takes a sharp turn and starts heading toward the river. A spur trail continues straight toward some houses. Turn right here and head toward the river. You will reach the river at 1.3 miles. Complete the loop and return to the parking area at 1.5 miles.

MILES AND DIRECTIONS

0.0 Start at the Tower Street Trailhead; 100 feet into the hike, a trail comes in from the right. This is the completion of the red loop. Continue straight down the doubletrack.

0.1 The trail turns left. This is the beginning of the blue loop. (The red and blue loops overlap here.) Continue straight.

0.2 The blue loop comes in from the left. Go right on the red loop. Shortly reach the Clark Fork River; continue walking upstream.

0.4 The trail turns away from the river and back toward the parking lot.

0.7 Complete the red loop. Turn right to hike the blue loop.

0.8 Turn left onto the blue loop.

1.0 The blue loop turns toward the river. A spur trail heads off toward houses. Turn right.

1.3 The blue loop reaches the riverbank. Continue following the loop.

1.5 Arrive back at the parking area.

Tower Street Conservation Area Loop

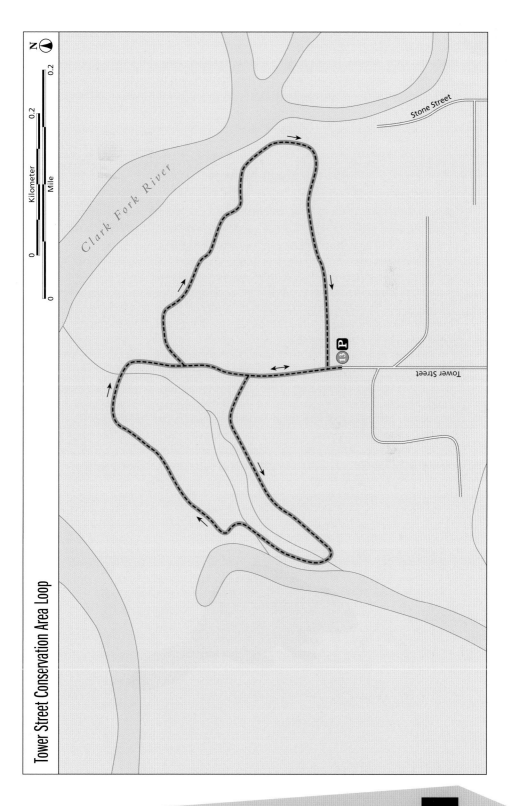

Options: Turn left off the doubletrack onto the blue loop at 0.1 mile. Continue onto the red loop when you reach the river. Then return to the parking area for a 1.0-mile hike with no backtracking. Or simply enjoy just the blue or red loop.

About Beavers

Beaver sign is abundant at Tower Street. Beavers don't always build a dam. They can carve a burrow in a riverbank and live quite happily, eating aquatic vegetation and bark from willow, aspen, and cottonwood trees. When beavers do fell trees to construct dams (a fully grown beaver can chew through a 10-inch tree in as many minutes), they back up streams and create excellent habitat for trout. This attracts animals like otters and ospreys that feed on fish. Beaver dams are also an important part of forest succession, creating meadows and then shrub lands, which shade tree seedlings and allow the next generation of forest to flourish.

Beavers give birth in May and June. During that time of year you may see the kits riding on their mother's back as they learn to hold their breath and dive. While beavers still flourish in the area, their numbers are greatly reduced from the 1800s, when they dominated the landscape. Trapping eradicated the beaver from much of its habitat and weeded out larger members of the species. Historically beavers could weigh as much as 100 pounds. Though beavers are generally regarded as docile, they are ferocious fighters when cornered. If you spook one, it will most likely dive beneath the water after slapping the surface with its tail to warn other beavers of danger.

A monster ram takes a quick drink in Rock Creek before retreating back to the security of the cliffs during hunting season.

Missoula lies in Mount Sentinel's shadow when the sun comes up in the morning. The mountain is due east of town. On Sentinel is the "M," Montana's most famous letter. This giant chunk of concrete draws the crowds. And why shouldn't it? The view is beautiful. Above the "M," nooks lead various ways to the summit. Beyond the summit is Hellgate Ridge. Extending beyond the ridge is University Mountain, an unassuming mass but one of the highest points surrounding the valley. Below University Mountain, Crazy Canyon leads down into Pattee Canyon and the site of more good hiking, with two easy loops in the valley bottom.

World-famous Rock Creek is only 20 miles east of Missoula. Renowned for its big game wildlife habitat and blue-ribbon trout fishing, the modest-size valley is always worth a journey out of town. Just remember your binoculars. You can get lost in the side drainages of Rock Creek for days. Herds of bighorn sheep and deer frequent the lower stretches of the creek, and grizzly bears have taken hold in the Welcome Creek Wilderness, farther up Rock Creek, deep in the Sapphire Mountains. This rugged section of land was one of the last bastions of outlaw country in the early 1900s, rife with horse thieves until the USDA Forest Service tamed the trails. It was also the site of wild mining history for both gold and sapphires.

Garnet Ghost Town, nestled in the arid high country of the Garnet Range, contains a forgotten gem called Warren Park Trail that leads to a homemade turn-of-the-twentieth-century picnic site with Big Sky Country–approved views of the Swan Mountains.

The journey up Mount Sentinel is a great way to get to know Missoula, train for wilderness hikes, and take in views of the city and surrounding mountains. Its proximity to town makes it a popular destination for crowds looking to squeeze in some essential recreation any time of the day. The switchbacks will get your attention, and many people turn back at the "M." But those looking to find more solitude close to town can keep climbing and stand at the summit alone. Deer frequent the slopes; spring brings wildflowers. There's even an old mining shaft for adventurous souls to peer into.

Start: Mount Sentinel Trailhead
Distance: 3.6-mile loop
Hiking time: About 2.5 hours
Difficulty: Strenuous
Trail surface: Dirt; singletrack
Best season: Spring through fall
Other trail users: None
Canine compatibility: Leashed dogs permitted
Land status: City of Missoula, University of Montana
Fees and permits: None required
Schedule: None
Maps: USGS Southeast Missoula; City of Missoula Parks, Open Space & Trails
Trail contacts: Missoula Parks and Recreation, 600 Cregg Lane, Missoula, MT 59801; (406) 721-7275; ci.missoula.mt.us
Special considerations: There are a limited number of free parking spaces for hikers. Otherwise parking in Lot L requires a paid University of Montana parking permit Monday through Friday, 9:30 a.m. to 4 p.m. You can park your bike for free here anytime.

Finding the trailhead: Take the Van Buren exit off I-90 and go south 0.1 mile to Broadway. Turn right and drive 0.2 mile to Madison Street. Turn left. Go over the bridge and continue 0.4 mile to 6th Street; turn left. In 0.2 mile the one-way street turns left. Follow the turn to the stop sign at the end of the block. Turn right onto Campus Drive and follow it as it veers right along the base of Mount Sentinel. After 0.3 miles turn left into Parking Lot L across the street from Washington-Grizzly Stadium; park anywhere. There are restrooms here. Walk up the flight of stairs and through the gate. **GPS:** N46 51.739' / W113 58.832'

Mount Sentinel has been attracting hikers since the trail to the "M" was first etched onto the mountain in 1908. The thirteen switchbacks that lead to the concrete letter that defines not only the University of Montana but also Missoula itself offer a glimpse into the past of the garden city below.

On Mount Sentinel it's easy to let the mind wander to Missoula's history, posing the question, "How did all this begin?" Only 12,000 years ago an ice age gripped the land and conditions were cold and wet. The large, flat valley tucked in among surrounding mountains was formed by a body of water plugged up behind an ice sheet on the Clark Fork River. The depth reached 2,000 feet in places. Called Glacial Lake Missoula, this lake splashed 400 feet above where the present-day "M" is located on the side of the hill. This ice reservoir carved unique ripple marks on Mount Sentinel that can still be seen today. Regardless of the large ice jams, the power of the river always won. On average it would take the river fifty-five days to build up enough energy to break through the barrier. A volume of water larger than several Great Lakes with the power of sixty Amazon Rivers would then drain in 48 hours and rush to the sea. This event occurred dozens of times, eventually forming the Columbia River Gorge.

Once the high water retreated, it wasn't the end of turbulent times in the now-tranquil valley. The flat swath of land left behind by the great flood was at

The bustle of the city is visible, but far away, up on the grassy slopes of Mount Sentinel.

a crossroads of five valleys. Each housed various Native American communities. The narrow confines of Hellgate Canyon directly adjacent to Mount Sentinel were known as one of the best places to ambush a tribe hauling heavy loads of buffalo robes and steaks. The Blackfeet were the most notorious for this tactic. The result was a veritable killing field with human remains littering the landscape, prompting French trappers to name the place for the gates of hell.

These days the only combat of this magnitude can be witnessed from a hike up Mount Sentinel on Saturdays in fall. This is when the Montana Grizzly football team takes to the gridiron in the stadium below. Fans have been known to take in sold-out games and concerts from a lawn chair with a pair of binoculars.

Continuing up the trail, you will reach the base of the massive "M" at 0.8 mile. From here a series of trails are available. This guide recommends taking the switchback left above the "M" on the main trail. Cross over the fire road at 1.0 mile, continuing up on a singletrack trail. This will lead you up through yet more switchbacks, traversing some rocky points.

As you move beyond the "M," the crowd thins and the largeness of the valley floor seems small. It becomes easier to focus on nature's craftsmanship: the beauty of the native bunchgrasses, the warble of songbirds from shrubs, and the grace of deer herds as they shy away from hikers. An abandoned mine shaft lies just off the trail at mile 1.3, where the adventurous can peek into the murky blackness. Shortly after, hikers enter a forested area.

At mile 1.6 you come to a trail junction with the Hellgate Ridgeline Trail. Follow this for 300 feet and then turn right. You are now on the Sentinel Summit Trail, which winds around the face of the mountain. Continue through the forest and the trail opens up again, following the sidehill above a gulch. Chokecherry and serviceberry house meadowlarks and sparrows. The landscape is enchanting through here. The trail winds up around a knoll and intersects the Crazy Canyon Road on the back side of the mountain. Old-growth ponderosa pines mark this intersection on a ridge at mile 2.4. Turn left for the final few feet of vertical climb to the top of Mount Sentinel at mile 2.5.

The view from the top affords a panorama of the entire region. Continue the loop down the steep descent of the Hellgate Ridgeline Trail, which widens into three tracks. This section offers a bird's-eye view of the historic canyon below. It's a 1.1-mile beeline to the bottom.

MILES AND DIRECTIONS

0.0 Start at the parking lot and go up the flight of stairs and through the gate. Turn right and proceed up the thirteen switchbacks to the "M" on the "M" Trail.

0.8 Reach the legendary "M." As you face the "M," continue on the trail directly below it that goes to the left and uphill. You are now on the Sentinel Summit

Trail, though no sign distinctly marks it. Two hundred feet later you reach the Hellgate Ridgeline Trail. At this junction turn hard right.

1.0 The Sentinel Summit Trail intersects the Sentinel Fire Road, a doubletrack heading level across the mountain. At this fork continue up and to the left on a singletrack. Continue up more switchbacks, traversing through some rocky points.

1.3 Pass a mine shaft in the rocks on the right.

1.4 Enter a forested area.

1.6 The Sentinel Summit Trail intersects the Hellgate Ridgeline Trail again. The trails merge for 300 feet. Turn right as the Sentinel Summit Trail breaks away. Continue through the forest. The trail opens up again and follows a sidehill above a gulch as it winds around a knoll.

2.4 The trail intersects the Crazy Canyon Road on the back side of Mount Sentinel in an old-growth ponderosa pine grove. Turn left for the final few feet of vertical gain.

2.5 Reach the summit of Mount Sentinel. To complete the loop, continue straight down the front side of the mountain. You are now on the Hellgate Ridgeline Trail.

2.7 Veer right along the drop-off's edge. Continue down the steep hill.

3.3 Pass a rock marking the 4,200-foot high-water mark of ancient Glacial Lake Missoula.

3.4 Intersect the Sentinel Summit Trail / "M" Trail. Bear right and continue descending straight down.

3.6 Arrive back at the parking lot.

Options: There are a number of options available from the summit of Mount Sentinel. It is 3.0 miles down to the Kim Williams Trail via the Hellgate Canyon Trail then another 1.0 mile back to the trailhead for a loop. A longer route from the summit involves hooking into the Crazy Canyon Road to the Pattee Canyon Crooked Trail. Follow that trail to the Sentinel Fire Road, which eventually intersects back into the Hellgate Ridgeline Trail. It is 5.8 miles one-way to the parking lot from the summit.

HIKE INFORMATION

Local events/attractions: Sentinel Hill Climb and "M" Trail Trot each fall. Contact the Runner's Edge at (406) 728-9297 for more information.

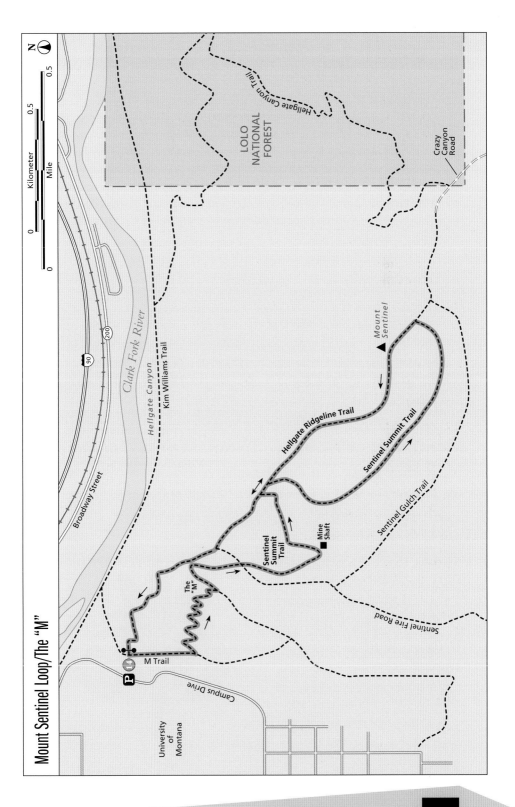

Mount Sentinel Loop/The "M"

Kim Williams Trail

The Kim Williams Trail is a corridor that cuts straight out of town among the cliffs and forests of Hellgate Canyon. The doubletrack, gravel trail is flat and follows the path of the old Milwaukee Railroad. The bottleneck canyon in the Clark Fork River is a popular recreation destination any time of the year. A variety of wildlife can be encountered here. The hike begins at the Sentinel Trailhead. There is an option to climb the Hellgate Canyon Trail to the top of Mount Sentinel and descend down the face. There are plans to extend this trail over the river and connect it with the Canyon River Loop on Bandmann Flats.

Start: Mount Sentinel Trailhead, Lot L
Distance: 5.4 miles out and back
Elevation: Minimal
Hiking time: About 2 hours
Difficulty: Easy; flat walking
Trail surface: Dirt and gravel; doubletrack
Best season: Year-round
Other trail users: Bikers, joggers, equestrians
Canine compatibility: Dogs permitted
Land status: University of Montana, City of Missoula, Lolo National Forest
Fees and permits: None required
Schedule: Open 6 a.m. to 11 p.m.
Maps: USGS Southeast Missoula; USDAFS Lolo National Forest Map, available at the district office; City of Missoula Parks, Open Space & Trails, available at McCormick Park
Trail contacts: Missoula Parks and Recreation, 600 Cregg Lane, Missoula, MT 59801 (this location is in McCormick Park); (406) 721-7275; ci.missoula.mt.us
Lolo National Forest Supervisor's Office, Fort Missoula Building 24A, Missoula, MT 59804; (406) 329-3814; www.fs.usda.gov/lolo/
Special considerations: There are a limited number of free parking spaces for hikers. Otherwise, parking in Lot L requires a paid University of Montana parking permit Monday through Friday, 9:30 a.m. to 4 p.m. You can park your bike for free here anytime.

Finding the trailhead: Take the Van Buren exit off I-90 and go south 0.1 mile to Broadway. Turn right and drive 0.2 mile to Madison Street. Turn left and go over the bridge 0.4 mile to 6th Street; turn left. In 0.2 mile the one-way street turns left. Follow the turn to the stop sign at the end of the block. Turn right onto Campus Drive and follow it as it veers right along the base of Mount Sentinel. Turn left into Parking Lot L, across the street from Washington-Grizzly Stadium after 0.3 mile; park anywhere. There are restrooms here. Walk up the flight of stairs and through the gate. **GPS:** N46 51.73' / W113 58.83'

THE HIKE

The Kim Williams Trail leads up Hellgate Canyon and traces a path along the Clark Fork River. The trail starts at the university, on the edge of town, and whisks hikers into the depths of the canyon with forest and cliff faces meeting the riverfront. Herons wade and eagles swoop in the same waters that black bears drink for breakfast.

Summer in full swing below the ridgeline of University Mountain on the banks of the Clark Fork River.

The trail is an extension of the Riverfront/Milwaukee Trail System. The Milwaukee Railroad operated a rail line here until 1980, when the tracks were torn up. The rail line was famous for using electric engines instead of steam because of Montana's inclement weather. The Hellgate winds are one example of such weather. The wind that howls out of that canyon is brutal in winter, icy and strong—the type of wind that freezes your eyes open, cripples movement out of doors, kills car batteries, and makes houses shudder with its relentless blasts of frigid Arctic air.

The Clark Fork is certainly a focal point of this hike. The Kim Williams Trail ends at the railroad bridge, though plans call for it to become a trail system bridge in the near future. Upstream of the bridge, the Clark Fork makes a big oxbow bend around Bandmann Flats, the site of a large golf course and housing development. The 2.2-mile Canyon River Loop follows the river near that development.

The river went through an extensive rehabilitation during the early 2000s. Cyanide and arsenic started showing up in the groundwater around Bonner and East Missoula, near the site of the Milltown Dam, in the early 1980s. Mining waste from the upper Clark Fork valley had been washing downstream and collecting behind the dam for more than seven decades. The waste was removed and carried by train up to Anaconda for storage on land. In 2008 the Milltown Dam was removed, historic bull trout migrations were restored, and the confluence of the Blackfoot and Clark Fork flowed free once again.

From Lot L, as you face Mount Sentinel, veer to the left on a singletrack dirt path that leads along a fence at the base of Mount Sentinel. The unmarked trail is called the Kim Williams Connection. Do not go up the stairs and through the Mount Sentinel trailhead gate. At 0.2 mile the Kim Williams Connection merges with the Kim Williams Trail. Go right on the doubletrack gravel path and pass a brown sign that says KIM WILLIAMS NATURE AREA. Kim Williams was a local author and conservationist whose passionate and witty commentaries were broadcast weekly from Missoula on National Public Radio. Williams espoused simple living and developed a large national following.

At 0.9 mile the Hellgate Canyon Trail (11) leaves the Kim Williams Trail and climbs to the ridge between Mount Sentinel and University Mountain. Reminiscent of the train track it once was, the Kim Williams Trail continues on with its even grade, straight lines, and broad width. At times the repetitive footfalls can become monotonous, but the birdlife, wildlife, rocky cliff sides, and river views provide ample stimulus for hikers.

A red, worn-down gate and a KIM WILLIAMS NATURE TRAIL sign mark the end of the trail, currently at 2.7 miles. Turn around here and retrace your steps back to the parking area.

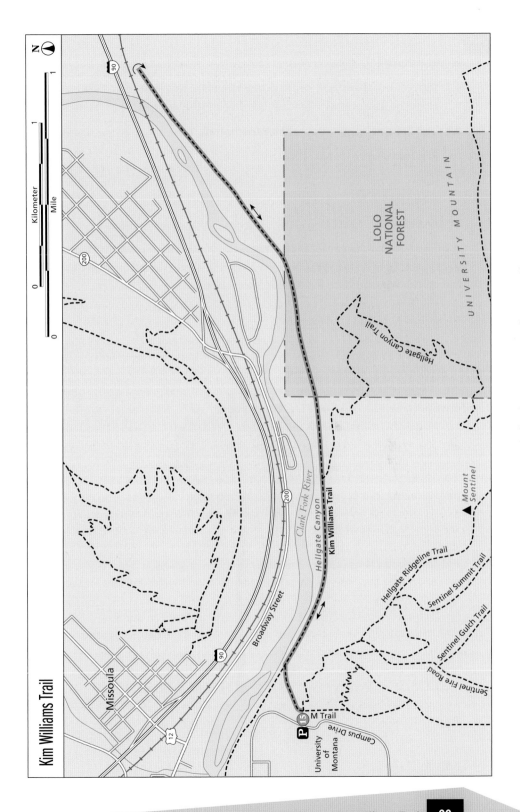

Kim Williams Trail

MILES AND DIRECTIONS

0.0 Start on the singletrack dirt path, the Kim Williams Connection, to the left along the base of Mount Sentinel. Do not climb the steps up toward Sentinel.

0.2 Veer right, merging with the Kim Williams Trail.

0.9 Pass the Hellgate Canyon Trail on the right.

2.7 Reach the end of the Kim Williams trail. Retrace your steps to the parking area.

5.4 Arrive back at the parking area.

Options: Hike the Hellgate Canyon Trail and connect into the Mount Sentinel trail system. From there climb University Mountain or head to the top of Sentinel and descend down its face for a classic loop.

Diverse terrain and a network of trails mark this dash up to one of the Missoula Valley's high points. The hike starts in the confines of Pattee Canyon. Creek bottom yields to hillside, culminating in a ridgeline approach to the mountain. It's adorned with beacons and lies 650 feet higher than, and east of, Mount Sentinel. While this developed locale may technically be the highest point along the ridge above Hellgate Canyon, the undeveloped no-name 5,709-foot knoll just west of University Mountain is also a fine place to enjoy the heights before turning around. The views offer a unique perspective of the valley and its surrounding mountains. Wildflowers dominate in the spring. A few steep pitches on this hike get your attention but are worth the extra effort.

Start: Crazy Canyon Trailhead
Distance: 7.5-mile loop
Hiking time: About 4 hours
Difficulty: Strenuous
Trail surface: Dirt; single- and doubletrack
Best season: Year-round
Other trail users: Bikers
Canine compatibility: Dogs permitted
Land status: Lolo National Forest, State of Montana
Fees and permits: None required
Schedule: Closed 9 p.m. to 6 a.m.
Maps: USGS Southeast Missoula; USDAFS Lolo National Forest Map, available at the district office; City of Missoula Parks, Open Space & Trails; Lolo National Forest brochure
Trail contacts: Lolo National Forest Supervisor's Office, Fort Missoula Building 24A, Missoula, MT 59804; (406) 329-3814; www .fs.usda.gov/lolo/
Special considerations: Black bears frequent the area. Mountain lions can be encountered too. Carry bear spray where it's quickly accessible.

Finding the trailhead: From the corner of Broadway and Higgins Street, go south (toward the river) on Higgins Street for 2.2 miles. Turn left onto Pattee Canyon Drive. After 3.4 miles there is a sign for the Crazy Creek Trailhead. Turn left into the parking area. Brown metal fence and signs separate the parking area from the trail. (**Note:** If you pass a sign for the Pattee Canyon Picnic Area, you have gone too far.) **GPS:** N46 49.55' / W113 56.30' number of trails form the route recommended here to climb and descend University Mountain, a noted Missoula high point. It makes for getting the most out of a few area trails, namely branches of the Crooked Trail, the ridgeline trail to University Mountain, and then a descent on Crazy Canyon Road. Other options are available as other trails weave in and out of the route. All trails are well marked with numbers.

The Crazy Canyon approach to the ridgeline between Mount Sentinel and the University Mountain ridgeline is a crown jewel of the 5,914-acre Pattee Canyon Recreation Area. It does require some effort, as the trail gains more altitude

A deer peers through the big trees of Pattee Canyon.

here than on either of the other Pattee Canyon hikes featured in this guide. But the reward is a stunning perspective of the Missoula Valley and a down-and-dirty ridgeline trail hike after exploring unique forest groves.

Following the Crooked Trail out of the parking lot places hikers on a well-worn footpath. Some of the largest ponderosa pines in the region used to reside up here. Massive cutting around turn of the twentieth century has toppled most of the giants that used to stand on this slope. But a second-growth forest thrives as this area recovers, and some massive pines still pepper the landscape.

Not long into the hike, the Crooked Trail begins intersecting the Crazy Canyon Road. The Crooked Trail is a bit more of an intimate experience; singletrack in many places, it weaves across a couple creek beds and forest areas, making for the best ascent. A well-formed doubletrack, the Crazy Canyon Road is great for the descent.

When the Crooked Trail descends away from the Crazy Canyon Road at 0.4 mile, it crosses Crazy Creek and then climbs up to an orange sign. Here the trail veers down a ridge and merges with the main road again. At the intersection at 1.0 mile, the Crooked Trail becomes a doubletrack again and descends into a gully. As the trail turns sharply to the left, it becomes a singletrack again. The Crooked Trail descends through a quiet, beautiful valley and you are truly in the forest, away from the hubbub of the busy area.

Keep your head up for the right turn onto Trail 302.1 at 1.8 miles, though it's well marked. You will be leaving the main Crooked Trail, which continues to the left and snakes its way down to the valley floor on Pattee Canyon's north wall. Instead continue up the massive flank of Sentinel as you climb out of the canyon and up toward the ridgeline between 5,158-foot Mount Sentinel and 5,806-foot University Mountain.

Clamber across the Crazy Canyon Road one more time at 2.4 miles. At the ridgeline at 2.6 miles, turn right onto Trail 302.2 and climb up into some steep spurts of trail. In spring this area is a thick wildflower patch, painted with paintbrush, lupine, and balsamroot against a deep spring-green background. Foliage dries as the year progresses, and the green yields to a golden hillside.

The ridgeline provides for some spectacular views down into both Hellgate and Pattee Canyons. It gains elevation and tops out on a rounded, undeveloped knoll that seems like the sort of place where a dog would like to lie belly up on a sunny day. At 5,709 feet, this is a perfectly acceptable turnaround spot. University Mountain is the next rise over, at 5,806 feet. To get there you must first descend into a saddle and then climb up to the high point, covered in beacons and radio towers. Both peer well over Mount Sentinel.

Return back down the ridgeline trail and turn left onto Trail 302.1 at 5.0 miles. Turn left again onto the Crazy Canyon Road at 5.2 miles. Follow this road all way back down to the parking area. It forms a junction with the Crooked Trail at 6.4 miles. Veer left and continue down the well-established doubletrack. At 7.1 miles turn left to return to the parking area by the most direct route.

MILES AND DIRECTIONS

0.0 Start at Crazy Canyon Road (Road 9959), which immediately leads to the right. Directly after, three trails leave the trailhead. Trail 302.3 leads to the left. The Crooked Trail (302) and Trail 302.5 split at a main junction; follow Trail 302.

0.3 Cross Crazy Canyon Road; continue straight.

0.4 Cross the road again at a three-way junction. Trail 302.3 is the right fork; Crazy Canyon Road is the middle fork. Trail 302 is the left fork, a singletrack that descends; follow it and cross Crazy Creek.

1.0 The trail veers right at an orange sign and heads down a ridge.

1.1 Intersect the Crazy Canyon Road again. Turn left and stay on doubletrack Trail 302.

1.4 The trail bends left (west) and becomes singletrack.

1.8 Turn right onto Trail 302.1; the trail gains elevation.

2.4 The trail crosses Crazy Canyon Road again. Go straight to stay on 302.1, climbing toward the ridge.

2.6 Reach the ridgeline between Pattee Creek and Hellgate Canyon. The trail begins to get steep.

3.4 Crest a 5,709-foot knoll. You can turn around here or continue on. To continue, descend the knoll, cross a saddle, and make a final approach to the destination.

3.7 Reach the top of University Mountain, marked by radio towers. Head back down the ridgeline.

5.0 Arrive back at the junction with Trail 302.1; turn left.

5.2 Intersect Crazy Canyon Road; turn left and follow the road.

6.4 Reach the junction with the Crooked Trail, which you ascended on. Turn left and stay on Crazy Canyon Road.

7.1 Turn right, back onto the singletrack Crooked Trail, for a direct return to the parking area.

7.5 Arrive back at the parking area.

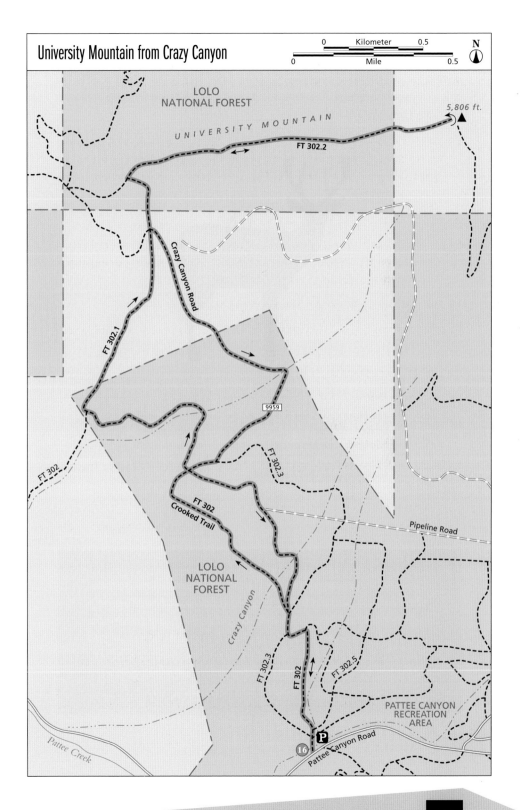

University Mountain from Crazy Canyon

Options: Hikers can take the Crooked Trail all the way to the valley floor and drive a car shuttle for a one-way downhill hike. Trail 302.3 winds a different course through the same area. Trail 302.5 connects the Meadow Loop area with the Crazy Canyon trails.

The Mountain Step is a method of walking up steep terrain. You lock your leg straight for a split second, allowing your leg muscles to relax briefly with each step. It looks a little awkward but will get you up the slope happier and healthier.

🌱 Green Tip:
Leave any unnecessary food packaging at home before your hike. If you do bring food in its original packaging, look around after you've eaten and collect any trash you may have inadvertently dropped. You might be surprised how clumsy even the most conservation-oriented hiker can be. Be especially vigilante for the smallest pieces of garbage—microtrash.

Meadow Loop Trail

Instead of hiking the traditional Meadow Loop the entire time, try the singletrack Trail 302.8 for a portion of the hike, leading out of the parking area near the Unit A picnic shelter. Cut across the meadow and then trot through the thick wildflower blooms and fat ponderosa pine stands. Huckleberries ripen here during late July, and black bears frequent the region then, although they can be found poking around the Pattee Canyon Recreation Area any time of year. Hikers will most likely encounter deer and flammulated owls, which nest near the picnic area. Frisbee disc enthusiasts share the area, as do cross-country skiers in winter.

Start: Pattee Canyon Picnic Area
Distance: 1.6-mile loop
Hiking time: About 45 minutes
Difficulty: Easy
Trail surface: Singletrack; dirt doubletrack
Best season: Spring through fall
Other trail users: Folfers (Frisbee golf enthusiasts); skiers in winter
Canine compatibility: Dogs permitted
Land status: Lolo National Forest
Fees and permits: None required
Schedule: Closed 9 p.m. to 6 a.m.; no hiking in winter
Maps: USGS Southeast Missoula; USDAFS Lolo National Forest, available at the district office; City of Missoula Parks, Open Space & Trails; Lolo National Forest brochure
Trail contacts: Lolo National Forest Supervisor's Office, Fort Missoula Building 24A, Missoula, MT 59804; (406) 329-3750; www .fs.usda.gov/lolo/
Special considerations: Black bears frequent the area. Mountain lions can be encountered here too. Carry bear spray where it's quickly accessible. During winter the trail is groomed for cross-country skiers and closed to hiking to preserve the quality of the skiing trail. The Sam Braxton Trail is open during this time.

Finding the trailhead: From the corner of Broadway and Higgins Street, go south (toward the river) on Higgins Street for 2.2 miles. Turn left onto Pattee Canyon Drive. After 3.9 miles there is a sign for Pattee Canyon Picnic Area. Turn left into the parking area. The hike starts from Unit A. **GPS:** N46 49.67' / W113 55.49'

THE HIKE

Missoula's reputation as a play-hard recreation town is well deserved given its diversity of athletic pursuits. Pattee Canyon reflects the town's desire to seek fun by creating a multi-sport recreation area at the top of the canyon at the picnic area.

The Unit A picnic shelter serves as an access point for both folfers and hikers. Watch for flying discs! Skiers slip into the snow beneath the pines in winter here on groomed trails. Immediately out of the picnic shelter, a connecter trail heads right (northeast) and moves along the edge of the meadow. There are a couple

When is the last time you sat in a field of flowers for a few minutes?

of trails you can take to cross the meadow, though none is well marked. The connecter trail eventually runs into Trail 19.3. Turning left onto this trail (which is shared by the folf course) will take you to an unmarked junction with Trail 302.8. Turn right and hike up into the ponderosa pines from the edge of the meadow.

Trail 302.8 is a quaint and quiet singletrack. The journey is peaceful. Good picnicking grounds are scattered about the shade of the forest groves. A slight uphill gradient marks this forgotten path and gets you away from the well-trodden main trail for a short spell.

The walk gets you into old, fat ponderosas and thick huckleberry bushes. This area is known for black bears but also for flammulated owls and nuthatches. Stem-to-stem balsamroot patches blanket bits of the forest not covered in huckleberry. University Mountain rises above the trail network.

Flammulated owls are tiny birds, only 6 inches long, that nest in cavities of trees and eat moths and crickets. Owls aren't usually migratory, but flammulated owls are, wintering in Central America. During the summer months these owls can be found at the Pattee Creek Picnic Area and in the surrounding forest feeding at dusk and dawn. Ponderosa forests with moderate temperatures are perfect for this little owl, which takes advantage of hollows created by flickers and other woodpeckers.

After 0.5 mile you intersect the main Meadow Loop Trail (19.2), a doubletrack trail. Turn left. The path loops around, and at 0.8 mile Trail 302.6 veers off to the right to meet up with the Crazy Canyon trail network. At 1.0 mile Trail 302.7 does the same thing. Continue following the doubletrack trail left in both cases.

To return to the trailhead, turn left in the meadow at 1.1 miles. There are a number of faint trails through this section that will deliver you back to the Unit A trailhead at 1.6 miles.

The meadow was once a US Army firing range for soldiers from Fort Missoula. Evidence of the range is still scattered about the meadow, including a backstop with earthen mounds and rotting boards.

Pattee Canyon was used by Native Americans as an alternative route to the dangerous Hellgate Canyon. The natives referred to Pattee Canyon as *Es nin paks*, which means "Crooked Trail." David Pattee left his name on the canyon after providing invaluable help to the burgeoning mill business in Missoula in 1871. He

> *For success with kids in the great outdoors, make sure that you plan a hike they can do. Be prepared to turn around early or sit passively. Make sure you have adequate supplies of warm clothes, food, and water. Carry bear spray, and keep an eye on your kids at all times. Enjoy the moment as they interact with the natural world.*

worked on a sawmill and a grain mill in the area, putting Missoula on the map as a business center. He homesteaded near the mouth of the canyon but pulled up stakes in 1878.

During winter the Meadow Loop Trail is groomed for cross-country skiers and closed to hikers.

This hike serves well as a quick loop after a day in town. It's also a great trail to get kids started on hiking. (No hiking in the winter, anyway.)

MILES AND DIRECTIONS

0.0 Start at Unit A in the Pattee Canyon Picnic Area. Proceed on the trail across the meadow.

0.1 Intersect Trail 19.3; turn left. There are many unmarked trails here.

0.2 Intersect Trail 302.8. Turn right and follow the singletrack path uphill into ponderosa pines.

0.5 Reach a junction with the doubletrack Meadow Loop Trail (19.2); turn left.

0.8 Trail 302.6 turns off to the right as the trail curves after the straightaway.

1.0 Reach a subtle intersection with Trail 302.7. Turn left onto the doubletrack and descend a steep hill.

1.1 Turn left into the meadow. A network of faint trails leads through the meadow back to the parking area.

1.6 Arrive back at the trailhead.

Options: To extend your hike beyond the Meadow Loop, take either Trail 302.6 or Trail 302.7 and tour some of the trails in the Crazy Canyon complex.

Montana's State Tree

While it is rumored that more picnics in the American West have occurred beneath ponderosa pines than any other tree, it is unknown if this is because of their sweet smell, medicinal properties, or parklike surroundings.

The ponderosa pine (*Pinus ponderosa*) has been called many common names—mainly by barrel-chested men in plaid shirts: blackjack, bull pine, brown bark pine, silver pine, pitch pine, red pine, yellow pine, even yellow belly pine.

Meadow Loop Trail

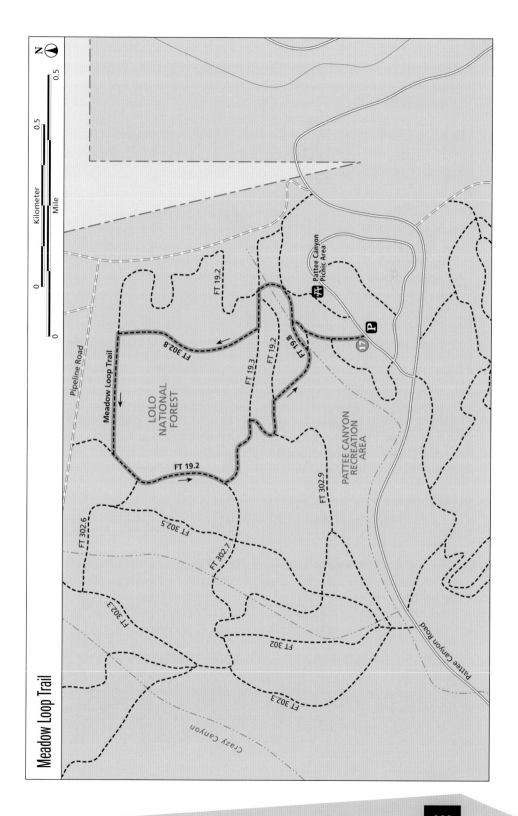

Ponderosa means ponderous, as in bulky. This is probably due to its massive stature. While its 200-foot height cannot be ignored, stubborn may be a better way to describe the ancient giants that dot Montana's hillsides up to 6,000 feet. Deep taproots nourish the frame of these beasts through times of extended drought. The tree's thick brown bark is tinted orange (though the color changes throughout its life cycle) and serves as a coat of armor against ordinary ground fires. Its towering limbs assure that its needles won't be scorched by any flames shorter than 25 feet. In this fashion, the slow-growing tree stands tall for more than 600 years, weathering even the most severe conditions. With their crooked crowns, they are royalty of trees.

Not ponderous but rather graceful and stately, its stands are elegant, clean. Thin beds of long needles lie at the foot of the tree, punctuated by rugged pinecones. Its protective bark is layered; it's smooth but comes across as rough, the individual pieces erratically abutted in round edges. Butterscotch-vanilla scent drifts from its trunk (some say coconut, maybe even cinnamon), a chemical awakened as the sap warms. Framed against a blue sky on a hot Montana summer day, the ponderosa pine symbolizes strength and freedom, shelter and abundance. Its evenly spaced stands inspire love for wide open spaces.

Long revered by Native Americans, the ponderosa was a special part of Kootenai Indians' tradition and religion. The inner bark was harvested each spring in a special ceremony that was coupled with the harvest of the bitterroot. On the first Sunday in May, the people gathered to pray to the digging sticks used in the bitterroot harvest. Medicine women would harvest the first roots in the morning to determine if they were ready. If the roots were ready, then ponderosa bark would be peeled at noon. If the bitterroots were not ready, the ceremony would be put on hold.

The inner bark beneath the scaly outer bark is moist, pliable, and sweet. Cloudy days were considered the best days to harvest because the sap flowed well. The outer bark was chipped off with a stick or bone in large chunks. Then the inner bark was removed with a goat's horn scraper. Ponderosa bark served as a sweetener in Native American communities around Missoula until well after World War I, at which time the practice became frowned upon by commercial timber interests and the cambium was replaced with sugar.

The sap of the ponderosa pine is said to have curative effects against infection. Mixed with beeswax and bear oil, Meriwether Lewis used it on his epic journey as a salve to relieve a swollen wound. Other pioneer applications involved melting a chunk of ponderosa pitch to make it pliable, rubbing it over the infected area when cool enough, and then covering it with an Oregon grape leaf.

Sam Braxton National Recreation Trail

This trail is popular with mountain bikers, and skiers glide on a groomed trail system adjacent to the Sam Braxton trail in winter. For hiking it's a good option on a hot day. The wooded area provides good shade. The route takes hikers on a loop through big pines and larches. Flowers and shrubs provide ground cover; bear grass flowers are especially prevalent every seven years during the big bloom. Elk, deer, bears, coyotes, mountain lions, birds of prey, and songbirds all make their home in this forest, which is recovering from the effects of selective logging.

Start: Pattee Canyon Trailhead
Distance: 3.6-mile loop
Hiking time: About 1.5 hours
Difficulty: Moderate due to brief elevation gain
Trail surface: Dirt; singletrack
Best season: Year-round
Other trail users: Bikers, equestrians
Canine compatibility: Dogs permitted
Land status: Lolo National Forest
Fees and permits: None required
Schedule: Closed 9 p.m. to 6 a.m.
Maps: USGS Southeast Missoula; USDAFS Lolo National Forest, available at the district office; City of Missoula Parks, Open Space & Trails; Lolo National Forest brochure
Trail contacts: Lolo National Forest Supervisor's Office, Fort Missoula Building 24A, Missoula, MT 59804; (406) 329-3814; www .fs.usda.gov/lolo/
Special considerations: Black bears frequent the area. Mountain lions can be encountered here too. Carry bear spray where it's quickly accessible.

Finding the trailhead: From the corner of Broadway and Higgins Street go south (toward the river) on Higgins Street for 2.2 miles. Turn left onto Pattee Canyon Drive. After 3.9 miles there is a turnout on the right marked by a sign that says Pattee Canyon Trailhead. **GPS:** N46 49.47' / W113 55.33'

THE HIKE

The wildlife habitat on the Sam Braxton Trail (9.0) is rich. Lush stands of shrubs line the trail and cover the forest floor. In other places, selective logging operations have visibly thinned the forest and underbrush, leaving tall pines and larches to punctuate the landscape.

Hikers have reported encounters with herds of elk, coyotes chasing deer, big black bears, and swooping owls—all in one outing. The opportunity to encounter wildlife along this loop is high and a top reason to add it to your rotation of hikes that are quick and close to town. Early morning and evening hours afford the best chance to spot these animals, though overcast days can be productive. Seasonal factors like winter snows can bring grazing animals, and thus their predators, down into Pattee Canyon. The forest along the Sam Braxton Trail provides good cover and forage.

The trailhead is obvious and well marked by a sign saying Pattee Canyon. After parking your car, follow a paved path behind a green gate until you reach a junction. Go right on Trail 9.0. Trail 9.2, a road, continues straight. At 0.1 mile you encounter an obvious sign with an arrow pointing left up a singletrack dirt path through a thick patch of shrubbery. Follow the sign and hang a left up the Sam

A trail sign marks the beginning of the loop.

Braxton Trail. The trail climbs gradually. Wild strawberries line the path, and bear grass blooms leave traces of fine white pollen on your clothes as you brush past their flowery stalks. Paintbrush and lupine add color to the groundcover.

An option to switchback presents itself at 0.4 mile. Go straight at this junction to save a little distance, or take the switchback to save some wear and tear. At 0.5 mile the trail turns right at the edge of the national forest's boundary with private timber lands that were liquidated in the 1970s and 1980s. The controversial practice of cutting beyond sustained yield is more or less frowned on now, even though there's not much left to cut on the private lands. Most of the timber companies have abandoned the Missoula area, preferring to do business in the Northeast, South, or overseas. Plum Creek's holdings in the area could one day become condos.

The trail makes a hairpin turn to the right (northeast) at 1.0 mile and a hairpin left (west) at 1.4 miles. The grounds through here are pleasant. No big views pop out as the forest keeps the scenery close. The well-fashioned trail is obvious but not intrusive.

At 2.0 miles the trail makes another major turn to the right (northwest) and rolls downhill along a ravine's edge. Trail 9.5 leads to a trail system in a rural neighborhood along Larch Camp Road (Road 9924) and intersects the Sam Braxton Trail at 2.5 miles.

In wintertime a series of groomed trails form a network of loops that create a junction at 2.6 miles. The forest service requires hikers and their dogs to stay off these trails in winter to conserve the quality of the snow for skiers.

From this point the trail crosses a small creek and heads back toward the parking area. Complete the loop at 3.4 miles and turn left, arriving back at the trailhead at 3.6 miles.

MILES AND DIRECTIONS

0.0 Start at the trailhead and walk south on a paved path. Go behind a green gate to an immediate trail junction. Go right, following a brown sign. The main route (Trail 9.2) continues straight.

0.1 Turn left onto a singletrack trail. Well marked with a sign for Sam Braxton National Recreation Trail (9.0), the trail winds uphill.

0.4 You have an option here to skip the switchback on Trail 9.2. Take either trail.

0.5 The trails come back together to continue Trail 9.0. The trail turns to the right (west).

1.0 Reach a hairpin turn in the trail; the trail heads northeast.

1.4 Come to another big bend in the trail, heading left (west).

2.0 The trail turns right (north) and goes downhill.

2.5 Stay on Trail 9.0 at the intersection with spur Trail 9.5. Go straight, but the trail veers right shortly after the junction.

2.6 Winter skiing Trail 20.4 connects with the Sam Braxton Trail. Take the left fork at the junction and cross a creek right after the junction.

2.8 Go right on Trail 9.0 at an unmarked junction. The trail meanders gently uphill. (The left fork leads back to the road and into the picnic area.)

3.4 Return to the junction of trails, completing the loop. Turn left to return to the trailhead.

3.6 Arrive back at the trailhead.

HIKE INFORMATION

Organizations: Rocky Mountaineers (rockymountaineers.com). One of the longest-standing adventure groups in the Missoula area. Membership is $10 per year, and the club is active most weekends.

Other resources: Wildflowerwalks.com is a local website that reports conditions on the Missoula area's famous spring wildflower blooms.

Bear grass blooms en masse every seven years. When the bloom is on, it can whiten hillsides, resembling snow patches. The flowery stocks can be several feet high, dusting hikers in pollen. Bear grass blooms all at once, overwhelming the elk's appetite. Otherwise, all the flowers could be eaten.

Sam Braxton National Recreation Trail

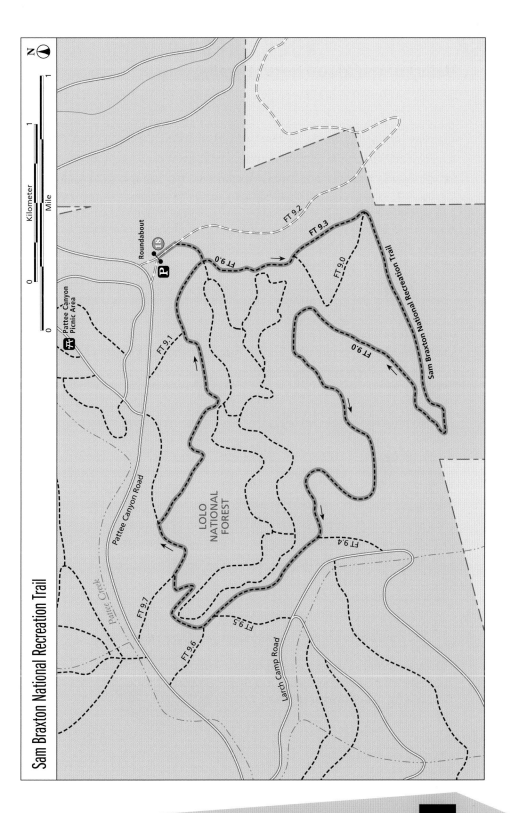

ROCK CREEK
Valley of the Moon Nature Trail

The richness of this hike, coupled with its leisure feel, make it a bang-for-your-buck stroll. This short trail wanders on the famed banks of Rock Creek. The bulk of the hike is on a small island in the creek. At the height of summer, the thick groves of cottonwood produce welcome shade. Wildlife takes shelter in here during the heat of the day. Primitive trails spur off in all directions. The signed, well-defined main path goes out and back. Investigate the spur trails with a sense of adventure. Consider carrying bear spray, even though you are right next to the road. Recurrent floods have affected the trail in the past and may do so again in the future.

Start: Valley of the Moon Trailhead
Distance: 0.8 mile out and back
Hiking time: About 30 minutes
Difficulty: Easy
Trail surface: Boardwalk; dirt singletrack
Best season: Year-round
Other trail users: Hunters in fall
Canine compatibility: Dogs permitted
Land Status: Lolo National Forest
Fees and permits: None required
Schedule: None
Maps: USGS Iris Point; USDAFS Lolo National Forest, available at the district office

Trail contacts: Missoula Lolo National Forest Supervisor's Office, Fort Missoula Building 24A, Missoula, MT 59804; (406) 329-3814; www.fs.usda.gov/lolo/
Special considerations: This area has a dense population of anglers. Do not attempt to communicate with these creatures while they are fishing. Watch for hunters in the fall. This part of Rock Creek is a wildlife corridor. Expect any type of wildlife in this small wildlife sanctuary. High water can shut down or alter the trail.

Finding the trailhead: From Van Buren Street go 20.3 miles east on I-90 to the Rock Creek Road exit. Turn right onto Rock Creek Road and go 2.1 miles. Turn right onto Rock Creek Road West. Go over the bridge and take a left into the trailhead parking after 0.2 mile. **GPS:** N46 41.89' / W113 40.24'

THE HIKE

This short path offers a lot of depth. The dense cottonwood trees on the Valley of the Moon Trail create a maze of leaves. A herd of elk could be bedded down here and you wouldn't see them until they jumped up and thundered across the creek and up the hillside in a blaze of glory. Most of the hike takes place on an island situated near the bank of the west shore. Rock Creek, a blue-ribbon trout stream, flows around the island. A bridge leads over the shallow channel that separates the island from the shore.

Rock Creek is also famous as a wildlife haven. Bighorn sheep thrive in the region. Black bears, mountain lions, mule deer, elk, moose, coyotes, and wolves live in the drainage. Grizzlies wander through, although rarely. Animals migrating from the Swan or Garnet Mountains utilize this broad valley as they travel south through the Sapphire Mountains toward the Anaconda-Pintler Wilderness.

The wide flat valley bottom of Rock Creek is a major tributary to the Clark Fork River, the confluence just 2 miles downstream. Dry, open hillsides, dotted with cliff bands, rise up above the valley floor. A quiet country road runs up the canyon.

Where's Waldo?

A pair of polarized sunglasses will help you scan the waters for fish. Native cutthroat trout live in these waters; so do rainbows, browns, brooks, and bulls, as well as mountain whitefish, suckers, and sculpin. The cutthroats face a lot of competition for food and habitat from some of these invasive species. Bull trout are an endangered species and especially sensitive to the dirt that runs into the water from roads. The silt covers the gravel the fish use for spawning beds.

High water during spring runoff can wreak havoc on this trail. At times it is impassable. After a particularly powerful high-water event, this trail can be damaged or altered.

The hike begins from the parking area and delves into the thickets of a cottonwood grove to the east. After a few curves, the trail promptly crosses a channel of Rock Creek on a bridge at 0.1 mile. Once across the bridge, you can go right or left. The right-hand option doesn't go far though; go left. The well-defined trail curves to the right before straightening out on the far side of a cottonwood thicket. Hawthorn, willow, and alder fill in the understory.

Shortly you arrive at a trail junction with a second bridge. Go left over the bridge, located at 0.2 mile. If you opt to wander around on the right side of the trail there are some spur trails and a sign, but they are erratic, unofficial, and end at the entry road.

Once over the second bridge, you arrive at the mini loop. Go right on the mini loop, eventually leaving it to reach the banks of the main channel of Rock Creek. Trails extend down the creek's bank. This is a great place to get off the trail and take in the serenity this small island in Rock Creek has to offer.

Return to the mini loop. Complete it by turning right and returning to the second bridge at 0.5 mile. Go right to return to the first bridge and retrace your steps to the parking area.

MILES AND DIRECTIONS

0.0 Start at the parking area. The trail leads east into a cottonwood grove.

0.1 A boardwalk leads to a bridge across a channel of Rock Creek. Cross the bridge and bear left at the fork; the trail curves to the right into the cottonwoods.

0.2 At the trail junction, go left over a second bridge. Go right on the mini loop trail.

0.3 The boardwalk ends. A singletrack trail leads to a high-water channel off the mini-loop toward the creek.

0.4 Turn left at the creek. Follow the creek as long as you like. Double back to the main trail.

Valley of the Moon Nature Trail

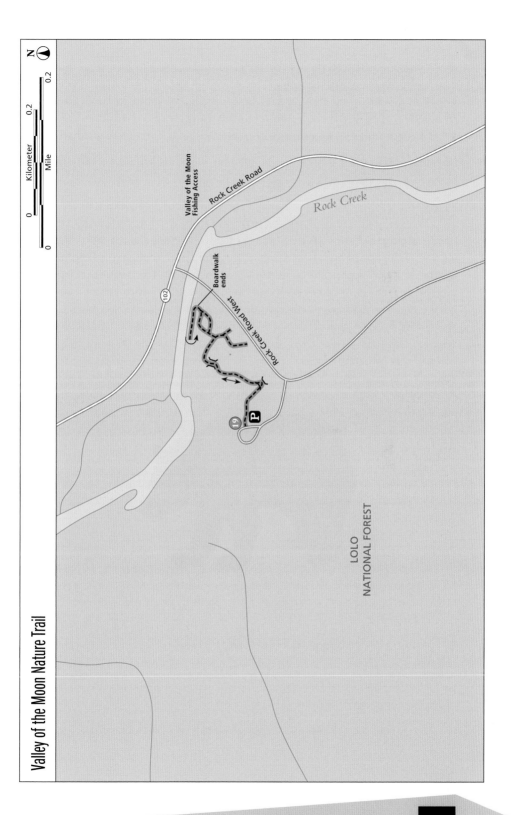

Rock Creek

Valley of the Moon Fishing Access

Rock Creek Road

102

Boardwalk ends

Rock Creek Road West

19

P

LOLO NATIONAL FOREST

N

Kilometer

0   0.2

Mile

0   0.2

0.5 Go right to complete the mini-loop. Cross back over the second bridge. Turn right to return to the first bridge.

0.6 Cross back over the first bridge and retrace your steps to the parking area.

0.7 Arrive back at the parking area.

Options: Explore the spur trails surrounding the main trail. Walk along the bank of the main channel of Rock Creek.

HIKE INFORMATION

Food/lodging: Ekstrom's Stage Station, 81 Rock Creek Rd/, Clinton, MT 59825; (406) 825-3183; ekstromstagestation.com. This outfit offers camping, cabins, and a restaurant in a historic cabin at the mouth of Rock Creek. The family that tends this uniquely Montana facility has been catering to visitors since 1883. Legend has it that the recipes haven't changed since then. Try the watermelon pickles.

Babcock Creek Trail to Mormon Spring

Babcock Creek is located in the heart of wildlife country. It is a side drainage that flows into Rock Creek in the lowers reaches of its course. The trail begins at the mouth of Spring Creek. The cliffs that tower on the hillside above are prime habitat for a local herd of bighorn sheep. Chances are high that you will encounter part of this herd on your journey. The Babcock Creek Trail (91) extends around the base of the cliffs and 1.0 mile to the north, where it turns east and climbs the steep confines of Babcock Creek.

Start: Spring Creek Trailhead
Distance: 7.0 miles out and back
Hiking time: About 3.5 hours
Difficulty: Moderate
Trail surface: Dirt; singletrack
Best season: Spring through fall
Other trail users: Equestrians; hunters in fall
Canine compatibility: Dogs permitted
Land status: Lolo National Forest
Fees and permits: None required
Schedule: None

Maps: USGS Iris Point; USDAFS Lolo National Forest Map, available at the district office
Trail contacts: Lolo National Forest Supervisor's Office, Fort Missoula Building 24A, Missoula, MT59804; (406) 329-3750; www.fs.usda.gov/lolo/
Special considerations: Hunters frequent this area in the fall. Wear hunter orange during hunting season; put it on your dog too.

Finding the trailhead: From Van Buren go east on I-90 for 20.3 miles to the Rock Creek exit. Turn right onto Rock Creek Road and go 6 miles. The small trailhead is marked by a sign on the left. **GPS:** N46 39.00' / W113 39.20'

THE HIKE

The Babcock Creek Trail (91) begins at the Spring Creek Trailhead on Rock Creek Road. This lower section of the Rock Creek drainage is major wildlife country. The steep cliffs above the trailhead are prime range for a herd of bighorn sheep that wander a region of 8,000 acres surrounding Babcock and Spring Creeks. A journey to Mormon Springs offers good opportunity to encounter the herd, which enjoys the security of the cliffs coupled with native and nutritious bunchgrasses like bluebunch wheatgrass and Idaho fescue. The sheep are especially active here in April and May, during lambing season, but fall produces sightings as well.

Babcock Creek is hemmed in by Babcock Mountain to the north and Burnt Mountain to the west. Local maps show trails above Mormon Spring and up Spring Creek, located just to the south. These trails are extremely faint and hard to follow. It is possible to create a loop by hiking above the Mormon Spring to the ridgeline between the two creeks, but this is advised only for hardy and experienced hikers who can navigate without a trail.

The hike begins by approaching the base of Spring Creek. At 0.2 mile a trail turns to the right and runs south along the base of a mountainside. Go left. Take

Babcock Creek shares a trailhead with Spring Creek in an area teeming with bighorn sheep.

another left at 0.4 mile at a trail junction marked by an aging sign. On the sign is a symbol of a hiker; a small arrow points left. This junction puts you officially on the Babcock Creek Trail. The path winds around the base of the ridge separating the two ridges. This part of the hike takes you across talus slopes and affords views of the Rock Creek drainage below. Sheep can be encountered along this section of the trail.

At 1.0 mile you encounter Babcock Creek—a narrow side drainage with fragile cliffs whose crumbled remains lie scattered across the mountainsides. A thick forest covers the bottom of the gulch. Douglas fir makes up the majority of the forest, though aspen groves are mixed in. Willows line the creek. You gain elevation steadily as you climb along the creek, but the trail is never uncomfortably steep. An unmaintained trail leads down from the north ridge at 2.0 miles.

A major side gulch joins Babcock Creek at 2.4 miles. This location is marked by big, flat rocks that are perfect for sitting. This is a good place to turn around if you are feeling hemmed in or tired, though another good 1.0 mile of trail extends before you.

Continue climbing up the creek. The trail begins to grow fainter, overgrown in places by matted-down grass. At 3.1 miles two gullies merge to form Babcock Creek proper. Both gullies are more or less dry, depending on the season. Veer right into the southerly gulch and continue following the faint trail another 0.4 mile to Mormon Spring. The gulch gets steeper during the final approach.

Mormon Spring is a rather uneventful destination, though the journey makes up for it. The spring consists of a large rectangular metal box lined with algae. A pipe drips into the box, which resembles a child's wagon. The ground begins to get moist as you approach the water source. A large human-made flat sits above the spring, marked by a sign. Turn around here and retrace your steps to the parking area.

MILES AND DIRECTIONS

0.0 Start at the Spring Creek Trailhead and walk east toward the canyon.

0.2 Reach an unmarked trail junction. One trail leads right along the base of the mountainside. Go left into Spring Creek.

0.4 An old hiker sign with an arrow pointing left marks this junction between Spring Creek and the Babcock Creek Trail. Go left. The trail traverses north along the base of the ridge between Babcock and Spring Creeks.

1.0 The trail turns east and proceeds up the narrow Babcock Creek.

2.0 Pass an unmaintained trail coming down from the ridge to the left (north).

2.4 A big side gulch merges with Babcock Creek. Flat rocks perfect for sitting mark this potential turnaround.

3.1 Two gullies merge. Main Babcock Creek is the gulch to the right. Proceed up this steep draw until you reach Mormon Spring.

3.5 Reach Mormon Spring; the spot is marked by a wooden forest service sign. Turn around here and retrace your steps to the trailhead.

7.0 Arrive back at the trailhead.

Options: Trail 91 continues on above Mormon Spring and connects into Road 2114 about 0.3 mile up the hill. The trail cuts back to the northwest and intersects the road in a saddle up on the ridge to the east of Babcock Mountain.

HIKE INFORMATION

Food/lodging: Ekstrom's Stage Station, 81 Rock Creek Rd., Clinton, MT 59825; (406) 825-3183; ekstromstagestation.com. This outfit offers camping, cabins, and a restaurant in a historic cabin at the mouth of Rock Creek. The family that tends this uniquely Montana facility has been catering to visitors since 1883. Legend has it that the recipes haven't changed since then. Try the watermelon pickles.

Bighorn Sheep

Bighorn sheep average 300 pounds; their horns (males only) alone can weigh up to 30 pounds. One of the animals' mating strategies is called tending, where a male attempts to hold the favor of a female. This requires a tremendous amount of energy for the bighorn ram. The second strategy, called coursing, involves stealing away an already spoken-for female. This results in the epic bighorn battles, where the rams rise up on their rear legs before running at each other and slamming skulls. The sound can be heard rumbling around the mountains for some distance.

Babcock Creek Trail to Mormon Spring

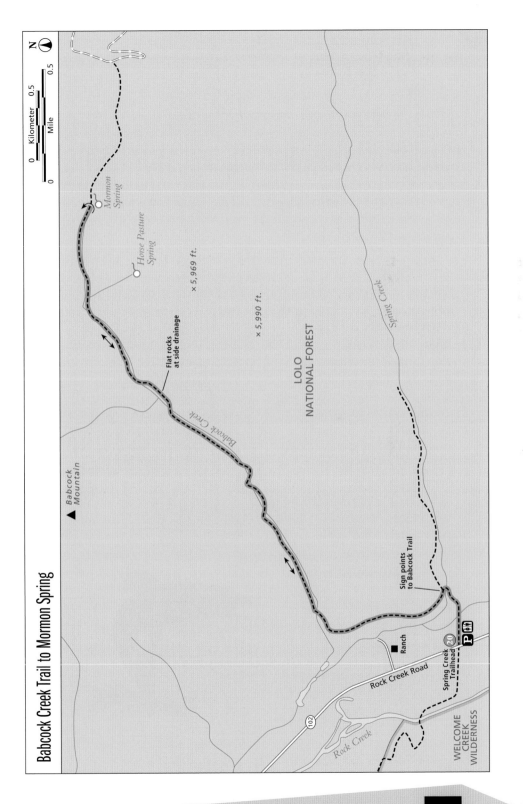

The Welcome Creek Wilderness is a little-used mountain gem located up Rock Creek. The wilderness is low elevation and heavily forested, which makes for superb wildlife habitat. The area is teeming with big game and has become home to the grizzly bear in recent years. Native American artifacts are present but hard to find. More obvious are the remnants left by the pioneers who once attempted to tame the wilds of Welcome Creek. The trail is overgrown in spots, but the untraveled feel makes up for the inconvenience. Gold mines once dotted the creek, which produced a 1.5-pound gold nugget, one of Montana's largest.

Start: Welcome Creek Trailhead
Distance: 5.4 miles out and back
Hiking time: About 2.5 hours
Difficulty: Moderate
Trail surface: Dirt; singletrack
Best season: Spring through fall
Other trail users: Hunters in fall
Canine compatibility: Dogs permitted
Land status: Lolo National Forest
Fees and permits: None required
Schedule: None
Maps: USGS Grizzly Point; USDAFS Lolo National Forest Map, available at the district office

Trail contacts: Lolo National Forest Supervisor's Office, Fort Missoula Building 24A, Missoula, MT 59804; (406) 329-3814; www.fs.usda.gov/lolo/

Special considerations: Big patches of stinging nettle line the trail; long pants are recommended. This has become grizzly territory, so carry bear spray. This is a popular locale during hunting season. Wear hunter orange during hunting season; and put it on your dog too.

Finding the trailhead: From Van Buren go 20.3 miles east on I-90. Take the Rock Creek Road exit and turn right. Continue on Rock Creek Road for 13.9 miles. The trailhead is on the right, next to a swinging pack bridge. **GPS:** N46 33.59' / W113 42.23'

THE HIKE

The rugged Welcome Creek Wilderness is infrequently visited. It has no shimmering high-country lakes, no jagged alpine peaks. There are very few vista points. Trees, streams, and rockslides mark the narrow, steep ravines that make up the majority of this area.

One of the most unique aspects of this 28,135-acre wilderness is its rugged nature—its unrelenting ability to make you tired and uncomfortable without revealing any classic visual rewards. The reward lies in the appreciation of solitude and self reliance, and in marveling at the fact that though human life tried to take permanent root here, it just couldn't thrive. Maybe this is why most photos of the Welcome Creek Wilderness are of the swinging bridge that serves as its gateway.

That being said, both adventure and beauty await you within the folds of Welcome Creek. The area is home to a host of big game, and grizzlies are now seen here more frequently than in past years. The rocky outcrops scattered on the hillsides are photogenic, as are the fields of scree at their base.

Welcome Creek Trail (225) winds along one of the largest tributaries of Rock Creek. Formed by years of erosion, this narrow canyon is larger than others in the region, but it's still confined. The trail receives more use than other parts of the

The famous footbridge that leads up into Welcome Creek.

wilderness, but this still doesn't amount to much. The trail can get faint at times and in places is overgrown with stinging nettle.

Rock Creek was inhabited extensively by Native Americans. There are many artifacts if you know where to look, although disturbing these artifacts is prohibited. The valley was also used by Western tribes, which moved east each summer to hunt buffalo. White settlers thrived here too. The amount of fish and game in the canyon was mind-boggling. In 1884 one settler who fished commercially near the confluence of the Clark Fork and Rock Creek averaged 80 pounds of fish for each half day of fishing. In 1890 four white hunters shot over 400 mule deer, poisoned the carcasses, and collected the pelts of coyotes that ate the poison meat—a "great slaughter" in the eyes of national forest rangers who took charge of the area in 1906.

Welcome Creek was the site of gold mining, most of it occurring above the hike's location near Cleveland Mountain, and produced one of Montana's largest gold nuggets, weighing in at 1.5 pounds.

From the trailhead, cross Rock Creek on the swinging bridge and then turn right (north). Cross a wooden bridge at 0.2 mile; the trail then swings to the left (west). Thick patches of trees are broken up by rockslides. Shrubs and wildflowers are thick here. The canyon tapers down at 0.8 mile.

Between the thick brush and the occasional faintness of the trail, this trail can be trying at times. But the wild and untraveled feel makes up for the discomfort. At 2.0 miles the trail peters out slightly. The trail comes up against a scree field. You can follow a cairn and off-trail it a bit through the rock before again picking up the trail in the canyon bottom. The trail crosses a small creek here, in the brush below the scree field, and continues up the valley.

At 2.5 miles you cross Welcome Creek on a log bridge. Cinnabar Creek flows into Welcome Creek at 2.7 miles. Pioneers once made a go of it here, and remnants of their life remain. This confluence is a good turnaround point. Retrace your path back to the trailhead.

MILES AND DIRECTIONS

0.0 Start at the trailhead and cross the swinging bridge across Rock Creek. Turn right (north) after the bridge.

0.2 Cross Welcome Creek on a log bridge. In 200 feet the trail turns to the left (west) and goes up Welcome Creek. A wooden sign marks the way.

0.8 The canyon tightens up. There is a large boulder field on the right side of the canyon.

1.1 Pass a backwater slough.

2.0 The trail becomes faint near a scree field on the right.

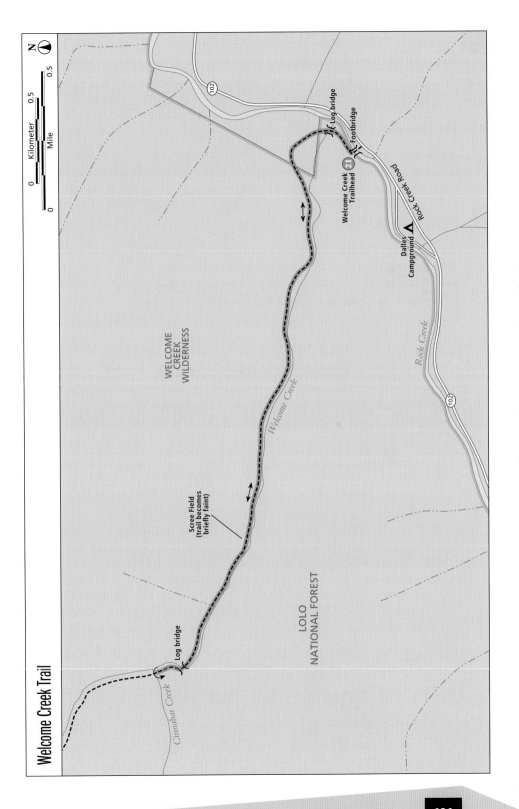

Welcome Creek Trail

2.5 Cross the creek on a log bridge.

2.7 Cinnabar Creek flows into Welcome Creek. Overgrown pioneer artifacts are scattered about. Retrace your steps to the trailhead.

5.4 Arrive back at the trailhead.

Options: To continue the adventure, continue hiking up Welcome Creek past Cinnabar Creek. The trail climbs to the divide of the Sapphire Mountains and intersects the Bitterroot Divide Trail (313) 8.0 miles from the trailhead.

HIKE INFORMATION

Food/lodging: Ekstrom's Stage Station, 81 Rock Creek Rd., Clinton, MT 59825; (406) 825-3183; ekstromstagestation.com. This outfit offers camping, cabins, and a restaurant in a historic cabin at the mouth of Rock Creek. The family that tends this uniquely Montana facility has been catering to visitors since 1883. Legend has it that the recipes haven't changed since then. Try the watermelon pickles.

Lawlessness on Welcome Creek

USDA Forest Service control marked the end of an outlaw era on Rock Creek that followed the bust of a boomtown called Quigley, located 4 miles downstream from Welcome Creek. Quigley had a population of 2,000 when it busted in 1896. The sudden economic downturn led to horse thievery. Many of the horses were held in the natural corral of upper Willow Creek, easily reached by going up Spring or Ranch Creek, before being sold on the black market in Canada.

Frank Brady, one of the rustler ringleaders, was killed at the "butte" cabin on Welcome Creek in 1904. C. K. Wyman, an undersheriff at the time, and Harry Morgan, a noted hunter, had been given the task of bringing Brady in to atone for a rash of horse thefts. Brady taunted the men, putting the word out around Bonita, an old railroad town, that the men would never make it out of the hills surrounding Rock Creek if they dared venture into the outlaw territory. The two tracked him to the cabin and called him out to make the arrest. An outlaw to the end, he answered with a hail of bullets and was killed in the gun battle that followed.

The newspaper in Philipsburg said that Brady was not without good qualities and had many friends. It also said he was reckless and daring and a bad role model for younger guys who thought he was a hero.

C. K. Wyman went on to become a forest supervisor; Harry Morgan became a district ranger.

Beavertail Hill State Park Trail

This 0.9-mile loop is located on the cottonwood floodplain of the Clark Fork River above Rock Creek. The park is only 65 acres, but the habitat is rich as the river meanders away from I-90 and into a bend laden with islands. Moose, deer, beaver, and several species of bird inhabit the park. A campground is also on-site. Beavertail Hill, the mountain to the west, is supposed to look like the silhouette of a beaver. When I-90 was constructed, it chopped off the beaver's tail, which now lies on the other side of the highway.

Start: Beavertail Hill State Park parking area
Distance: 0.9-mile loop
Hiking time: About 30 minutes
Difficulty: Easy
Trail surface: Dirt, gravel; broad path
Best season: Spring through fall
Other trail users: Archery hunters in fall
Canine compatibility: Dogs permitted
Land status: Montana Fish, Wildlife & Parks

Fees and permits: None required
Schedule: May 1 to Oct 31
Maps: USGS Ravenna
Trail contacts: Beavertail Hill State Park, FWP Region 2 Headquarters, 3201 Spurgin Rd., Missoula, MT 59804; (406) 677-6804; stateparks.mt.gov/beavertail-hill/
Special considerations: During fall the area is open to archery hunters.

Finding the trailhead: From Van Buren go east 24.7 miles on I-90 to the Beavertail Road exit. Turn right onto Bonita Station Road and drive 0.3 mile. Turn left into Beavertail Hill State Park. Parking is available just past the nature trail. **GPS:** N46 43.23' / W113 34.55'

THE HIKE

Beavertail Hill State Park lies on the banks of the Clark Fork River between the Garnet and Sapphire Mountains. It's located where the river bends away from I-90, where it is often channelized. As it moves through the natural meander around the 65-acre park, the river braids and runs through a series of islands. The result is a unique wetland that is home to beavers, herons, moose, a variety of trout species, and songbirds. The park in named for the hill to the west. The big part of the hill directly west of the park is the body of the beaver. The tail, which now stretches to the other side of I-90, was severed by the construction of that highway.

Beavertail Hill has been developed for over a century. The town of Bonita, a regional hub, was situated 1.5 miles to the west. Bonita existed to serve the railroad and dried up when that task was no longer required. Today the area near the mouth of Rock Creek, just to the west, serves as a regional hub.

The adjacent campground at Beavertail Hill has twenty-eight campsites and a couple of tepee rentals. During summer it can get busy. Early morning and dusk can be rewarding times of day to see wildlife without running into too many campers. Other times of year the campground is quiet, offering a serene experience along the shores of the Clark Fork River. The views along the waterfront are

A river runs through it.

impressive, and the fishing is good. Several gates allow access to spur trails that run outside the developed loop trail, which is wheelchair-accessible.

To begin the hike, locate where the trail heads north from the road near the entrance gate. The narrow trail is marked by a small brown sign. The parking area is just to the east of the trailhead. The trail begins on an even grade that was once part of the Milwaukee Railroad. Quickly, though, the trail circles across the campground and parallels the Clark Fork River at 0.2 mile. A green gate located in the fence here allows access to the river. From there you can wander down the riverbank on primitive trails or continue on the well-groomed trail in the state park. It leaves the riverbank and cuts across two roads that form a campground loop. A restroom is located between the road crossings. Pick up the trail again on the far side of the second road. A small brown sign marks the place.

The trail gets away from the campground at this point and heads into some larger trees and a wetlands channel of the river. Moose are said to frequent this area. White-tailed deer certainly do. This is the most natural section of the hike. Extending past the edge of the trail is a small knoll that descends down to the river.

The trail loops back to the north here at 0.7 mile. It heads pretty directly back toward the parking area and arrives there at 0.9 mile.

MILES AND DIRECTIONS

0.0 Start at the trailhead, marked by a small brown sign near the entrance gate to the state park. The trail heads north into cottonwoods and ponderosa pines.

0.1 The trail turns east and runs across a roundabout. Pick up the trail, marked by a brown sign, on the far side.

0.2 Reach the mighty Clark Fork River.

0.3 The trail leaves the river and crosses two roads that form a campground loop. Restrooms are located between the two road crossings. Pick up the trail, marked by a brown sign, on the far side of the crossings.

0.5 The path turns back toward the north near big cottonwoods and ponderosa groves.

0.7 The trail bends again near a wetland section of the trail. A side channel of the Clark Fork meanders nearby.

0.9 Arrive back at the trailhead.

Options: Get off-trail and walk down along the river's edge from one of the green gates. There is plenty of off-trail land to be explored in the region to the south of the loop. You may get your feet wet, but the adventure will be worth it.

HIKE INFORMATION

Camping: Beavertail State Park Campground, 29895 Bonita Station Rd., Clinton, MT; (406) 677-6804, stateparks.mt.gov/beavertail-hill/. The campground has 28 developed campsites and 2 rental tepees. For reservations call (855) 922-6768.

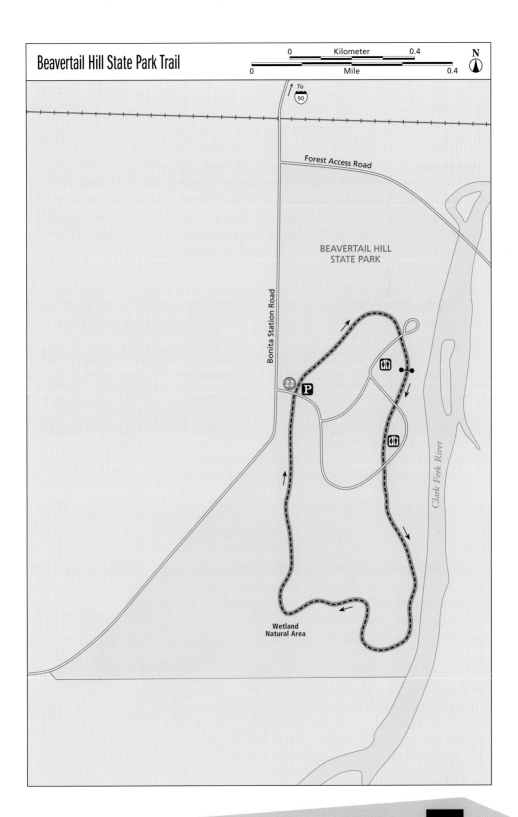

Beavertail Hill State Park Trail

BEAVERTAIL HILL STATE PARK

Forest Access Road

Bonita Station Road

Clark Fork River

Wetland Natural Area

To 90

22 P

This trail starts at the Garnet Ghost Town parking area and leads out to a picnic site that is more than a century old. Arriving at the historic site is like walking into a black-and-white photo. The place feels as inviting to a weary traveler as it did in 1900. Old benches and swings blend in among the trees. An overlook provides a sweeping view of the southern Swan Mountains, as does the hike. The trail itself meanders between lands that have been logged and sections in their natural state. The park was carved out by Edward Warren, a Civil War veteran who wanted to create a place for the community to enjoy. You pass his cabin 1.0 mile down the trail.

Start: Parking Area for Garnet Ghost Town

Distance: 2.7-mile loop

Hiking time: About 1 hour

Difficulty: Moderate

Trail surface: Dirt; singletrack

Best season: Spring through fall

Other trail users: Hunters in fall

Canine compatibility: Dogs permitted

Land Status: Bureau of Land Management, Missoula Field Office

Fees and permits: Small fee to enter Garnet Ghost Town

Schedule: Visitor center open 9:30 a.m. to 4:30 p.m., Memorial Day through Sept

Maps: USGS Elevation Mountain

Trail contacts: Bureau of Land Management, Missoula Field Office, 3255 Fort Missoula Rd., Missoula, MT 59804; (406) 329-3914; blm.gov/mt/st/en/fo/missoula_field_office.html

Special considerations: The access road gets extremely icy in late fall; no road access when snow covered.

Finding the trailhead: From Van Buren go east on I-90 for 4.1 miles. Exit onto MT 200 and continue through Bonner and up the Blackfoot Canyon for 23.2 miles. Turn right onto Garnet Range Road (between mile markers 22 and 23 on MT 200). The road, a National Back Country Byway, is marked by a sign for Garnet Ghost Town. It goes from pavement to dirt. Go 11 miles, following the signs for Garnet. Turn right into the parking area for the ghost town. **GPS:** N46 49.60' / W113 20.18'

THE HIKE

Warren Park is a tucked-away spot where a person can spend some time with a great view in the midst of a living museum. Places like this are rarely seen these days. Warren Park is a secluded picnic location overlooking the Swan Mountains and the Garnet Range. It is perched high above the valley—in the trees but with a vista point. This spot has been a picnic area since 1900.

Shortly after the Civil War, veteran Edward Brook Warren moved out to Garnet. A mile out of town he built a little cabin, which you pass on this hike. Near his claim he carved a primitive picnic area with stunning views of the surrounding countryside and encouraged the community to enjoy the grounds with him.

Coming upon the aging wooden benches, tables, and unique children's swings is like walking into a black-and-white snapshot of a picnic from bygone days. With only the wind whipping through the trees, you can almost hear forks clinking on ghostly plates. Miners aren't the only ghosts in the area. This site has also witnessed centuries of Salish use and is littered with artifacts, which should not be disturbed.

The hike begins at the Garnet Ghost Town parking area, situated just above the old mining town.

As the sun nears the horizon in the west, it illuminates the snow-capped Swan Range.

Garnet's rustic charm is worth exploring, but an afternoon in Warren Park is an altogether different experience. You get the sense that Montanans have been traveling to this secluded spot on the hill for centuries. They have come to pause and appreciate the big mountain views, to gather with friends and family beneath a shady grove of trees. They come just to be, to watch for wildlife, and to laugh. Warren Park is just the place for such things.

To reach Warren Park, leave the large parking lot and catch the trail at the large sign describing the life and times of Garnet. The trail leads west toward the ghost town. At 0.1 mile turn left at the wooden sign for Warren Park. The trail leads across the main Garnet access road, down a short path, then across two more secondary dirt roads. On the far side, the trail is marked by another wooden sign and a blue diamond trail marker. The trail leads along the edge of a timber harvest before curving into a natural drainage. At 0.5 mile the trail crosses a creek on a bridge. The trail continues uphill from there.

The next section of trail delivers a classic Montana mountain view. The broad profile of the southern Swan Range rises to the north. Pyramid Peak, Devine Peak, Marshall Mountain, and Crescent Mountain hold snow much of the year. The crests of those peaks form the Bob Marshall Wilderness Area. Timber stretches over the hills of the Garnet Range in the foreground. Toward the east is the Wales Creek Wilderness Study Area.

The Garnet Range is home to a small population of grizzlies that have wandered in from the Bob Marshall and continue to wander south to the Welcome Creek Wilderness in the Sapphire Mountains. This makes the area a critical travel corridor.

Back on the trail you will pass Warren's old cabin at 1.0 mile. The trail veers left and descends off the old road grade here. At 1.2 miles you arrive at Warren Park, marked by a sign. The benches and swings are located to the right at a three-way junction. To the left is the viewpoint. The trail continues on straight, but this is a good turnaround point. Retrace your steps back toward the trailhead. Turn left when you encounter the trail to the ghost town at 2.5 miles and enjoy the Garnet Ghost Town overlook. Return to the trailhead from here.

MILES AND DIRECTIONS

0.0 Start at the parking lot and pick up the trail at the large sign. The trail leads toward the ghost town.

0.1 Reach the junction with the Warren Park Trail, marked by a sign; turn left. After a short distance, cross the Garnet access road.

0.2 Cross an intersection of two secondary dirt roads. Pick up the trail on the far side, marked by another wooden sign and a blue diamond trail marker.

0.5 Cross a creek on a bridge in a natural section of trail. The trail climbs after the bridge.

Warren Park Trail

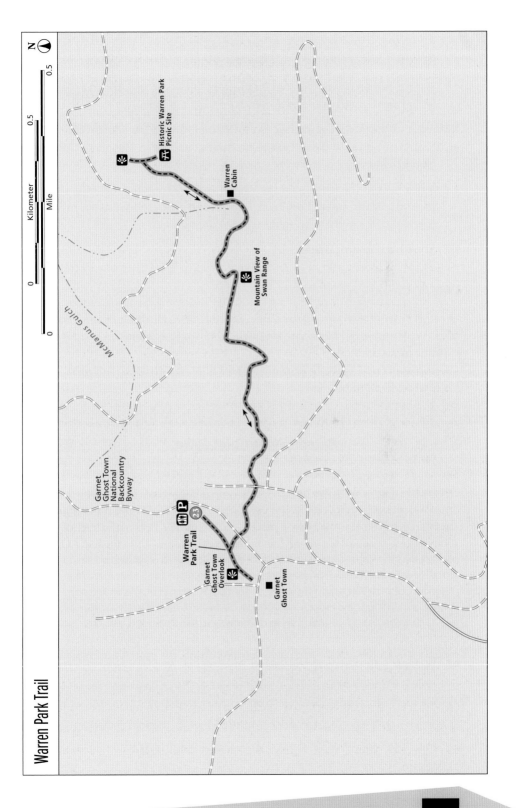

N

Kilometer

0   0.5

0   0.5
Mile

McManus Gulch

Garnet
Ghost Town
National
Backcountry
Byway

Warren
Park Trail

Garnet
Ghost Town
Overlook

Garnet
Ghost Town

Mountain View of
Swan Range

Warren
Cabin

Historic Warren Park
Picnic Site

0.8 Enjoy big views of the Swan Range to the north.

1.0 The old Warren Cabin is located on the right below the trail. The trail veers left off an old road grade and descends just past the cabin.

1.2 Arrive at the three-way intersection for Warren Park. To the right is the historic picnic area. To the left is the overlook of the Swan Mountains. Turn around here.

2.5 Arrive back at the junction of the Warren Park Trail and the trail from the parking area to Garnet Ghost Town. Turn left and walk a short distance to an overlook of the ghost town. Return to the parking area.

2.7 Arrive back at the trailhead.

HIKE INFORMATION

Local events/attractions: Garney Day Festival, BLM Missoula Field Office, 3255 Fort Missoula Rd., Missoula; (406) 329-3914. This festival, held in late June, explores Garnet's history.

Other resources: Garnetghosttown.net/index.html is a website dedicated to interpreting Garnet Ghost Town.

Boomtown to Ghost Town

Garnet was a mining town that flourished with the discovery of gold in the 1860s. By 1898, more than 1,000 people lived in the mountain boomtown. There were over a dozen rowdy saloons, a schoolhouse, four hotels, and three livery stables. The glory days were short-lived, though. By 1912 only a fraction of the population remained. The mines had played out and a fire had devastated the burgeoning settlement. Yet people stayed on and lived life in small-town tradition. Mining became profitable again in 1934 after President Franklin D. Roosevelt raised the price of gold from $16 per ounce to $32 per ounce, providing some work for townsfolk during the Great Depression.

The town finally closed up shop during World War II. Since it was an active town until the 1940s, it is one of Montana's most intact ghost towns; a stroll around town provides a convincing glimpse into the past. People report hearing pianos play or seeing the proprietor of the general store. The return route from Warren Park leads you to an overlook of the spooky town. There is a small fee if you decide to venture down to the dusty streets.

South of Missoula

Sunset over Boulder Creek.

It's impossible to ignore the jagged granite mass that rises to the south of Missoula. The Bitterroot Mountains dominate the landscape and offer a variety of creeks and ridges to walk up and a variety of high-country lakes to gaze into below alpine ridgelines. Glaciers were not gentle with these canyons, and the classic U-shape and smooth granite slabs show signs of an ice age that has only been gone for a short time. Thick groves of fat trees grow in the canyon bottoms of the Bitterroots, and all manner of wildlife lives in these mountains.

The Selway-Bitterroot Wilderness is the one of the largest national wilderness areas outside of Alaska. As a result, the Bitterroot Mountains have some of the best hiking in the country. They're picturesque; they're rugged. They look like the Tetons but are different from that range. First, they are not clogged with tour buses. The landscape teems with wildlife. And the iconic alpine range is surrounded by hundreds of square miles of forest, making it truly a place where the wolf roams.

The Lee Metcalf Wildlife Refuge is a spot that can't be missed if you like views of big mountains, even if you don't like climbing around on the mountains themselves. The acres upon acres of ponds and river channel create a playground for waterfowl and songbirds. The steep face of the Bitterroot Mountains looms in the distance.

Spruce trees in the twilight of the Bitterroot Mountains.

Bass Creek Trail

The Bass Creek Trail takes hikers among big trees and towering canyon walls. The trail leads up a cascading creek with several short spur access trails. At 2.0 miles a log dam serves as a good turnaround point. It offers good views farther up the creek to some craggy granite spires in the high Bitterroot Mountain range. The landscape has been scraped by glaciers here, and bedrock prevails in several spots. A variety of wild forest creatures live in here. Lucky hikers may even encounter a wolf or hear one howl. Mountain goats frequent the sheer cliff faces.

Start: Bass Creek Trailhead

Distance: 4.0 miles out and back

Hiking time: About 2 hours

Difficulty: Moderate; primitive trail

Trail surface: Dirt; singletrack

Best season: Spring through fall

Other trail users: Equestrians; hunters in fall

Canine compatibility: Dogs permitted

Land status: Bitterroot National Forest

Fees and permits: None required

Schedule: None

Maps: USGS Saint Mary Peak; USDAFS Bitterroot National Forest, available at the Stevensville Ranger Station.

Trail contacts: Stevensville Ranger District, 88 Main St., Stevensville, MT 59870; (406) 777-5461; www.fs.usda.gov/main/bitterroot/home

Special considerations: High water in spring turns the creeks of the Bitterroot Mountains into raging torrents; use caution. Strong currents can pin people underwater against rocks and logs. Hunting season, from late October through November, can be busy. Wear hunter orange during hiking season; put it on your dog too.

Finding the trailhead: From the intersection of Brooks and Reserve Streets, go south on Highway 93 for 20.6 miles. Turn right onto Bass Creek Road (Road 1136). After 1.7 miles the Larry Creek Loop (Road 1315) intersects from the right and Charles Waters Camp Road (Road 1136D) goes to the left. The main road becomes Larry Creek Loop; continue straight. After another 0.1 mile arrive at the trailhead, a hairpin bend in the road on the north side of Bass Creek. The road becomes Larry Creek Road and climbs up a number of switchbacks to the trailhead for the Bass Creek Overlook. **GPS:** N46 33.59' / W113 42.23'

THE HIKE

The grand firs are big in Bass Creek, but the canyon walls are much bigger. This tight canyon in the Bitterroot Mountains has been carved by glaciers and snowmelt. The resulting bedrock granite cliff faces are dramatic. In many places nothing grows, simply because there is no soil, only rock.

The creek bottom is a different world, though. Ancient grand firs and healthy cottonwood trees sprout from a dense understory of thimbleberry and snowberry. The Bass Creek Trail (4) winds its way along the creek, which is choked with large chunks of the canyon wall that have rolled down the steep confines of the canyon over the eons. Various spur trails lead to the creek from the left side of the trail. These generally take hikers to views of cascades or to small beaches and swimming holes.

All this grandeur is on the edge of the largest wilderness complex outside of Alaska, which adds an extra layer of biodiversity compared with more-urban hikes in the Missoula area.

The Bass family was a prominent part of the late 1800s in the Bitterroot Valley. They lived in nearby Stevensville and established the first fruit orchard in the

A beaver pond and the Bitterroots.

valley, growing fruit on more than 1,000 acres that they sold to mining camps. Area apples are famous, but the Bass family sold strawberries, tomatoes, plums, and livestock to round out the items available.

In 1999 a pack of wolves made history on this drainage by becoming the first wolves to den in the Bitterroot Mountains since the 1920s, when they were eradicated by poison. The two adult wolves and eight pups set up shop on a large ranch downstream from the trailhead. The pack made a go on the ranch and surrounding forestlands for a couple of months before bringing down some livestock. The pack was relocated deep in the Selway-Bitterroot Wilderness. The run-in with Fish, Wildlife & Parks agents proved too stressful for some of the wolves, though. During the relocation, three pups and the adult male died.

More wolves have filled the vacuum left by the original Bass Creek pack. They can be heard howling in these canyons on big-mooned nights. Hearing a wolf howl is mandatory to earning your Montana hiking merit badge.

The hike up Bass Creek begins at a row of boulders blocking motorized traffic from Larry Creek Road, which continues on. The trail cuts off to the left from the road and up Bass Creek. The path is broad, earthen, and stony. The overhanging rock at 0.5 miles is worth noting. The giant boulder just above the trail has a hollowed-out base, providing respite from the sun on a dusty July afternoon.

A small beach makes it home near here too, just off the main trail. A waterfall cascades into a pool with a regal grove of trees nearby. Back on the trail, the incline increases and you begin a more aggressive elevation gain. From here to the turnaround point, small spur trails cut toward the creek. At 2.0 miles the trail climbs into a relatively flat stretch of canyon. At the foot of the flat is a jumbled log dam that backs up the creek. High Bitterroot peaks form the backdrop. Keep an eye out for mountain goats, which can appear as tiny white specks on the mountainsides. Watched through a pair of binoculars, these sure-footed mountain creatures can provide acrobatic entertainment.

Turn around at the log dam and return the way you came.

MILES AND DIRECTIONS

0.0 Start at the trailhead and walk up the road 200 feet to where the trail leaves the road to the left at a boulder barrier.

0.3 Pass an old dam in the creek. There are views of cliffs on the right side of the trail.

0.4 A spur trail to the left leads to a cascade on the creek.

0.5 Reach the overhanging rock. The trail begins to gain elevation.

1.0 A small trail spurs left to the creek; go straight.

1.7 A large ponderosa pine marks a junction with a spur trail that leads left to a pool in the creek.

2.0 Reach a small pond created by logs that have dammed the creek. Spur trails lead to the water's edge. Alpine views rise from the canyon upcreek. Turn around here.

4.0 Arrive back at the trailhead.

Options: You can continue past the log dam into the Selway-Bitterroot Wilderness. Another trail departs from the Bass Creek Overlook. To get to the Bass Creek Overlook drive 5.5 miles up the switchbacks on Road 1136 from the Bass Creek trailhead. There's a great view from the parking area. Bass Creek Overlook Trail follows the ridgeline up the canyon into the wilderness.

HIKE INFORMATION

Food/lodging: Glen's Cafe, 157 Long Ave., Florence; (406) 273-2534; open 9 a.m. to 3 p.m. A rustic log cabin with a woodstove houses this cafe that makes you feel like a guest in an old-time homestead. Glen's is famous for its homemade pies and its paintings.

Wolves have very rarely acted aggressively toward humans, though the possibility always exists. This is an animal that can take down prey ten times its size. Never approach wolves or wolf kills. Be wary of any habituated wolves. If you get into an aggressive encounter, stand your ground, maintain eye contact, and don't turn your back. Never run. Large sticks and rocks can be used as weapons. Bear spray is your best bet with any creature that bothers you in the woods, though. For most, a wolf encounter is a rare and exciting moment.

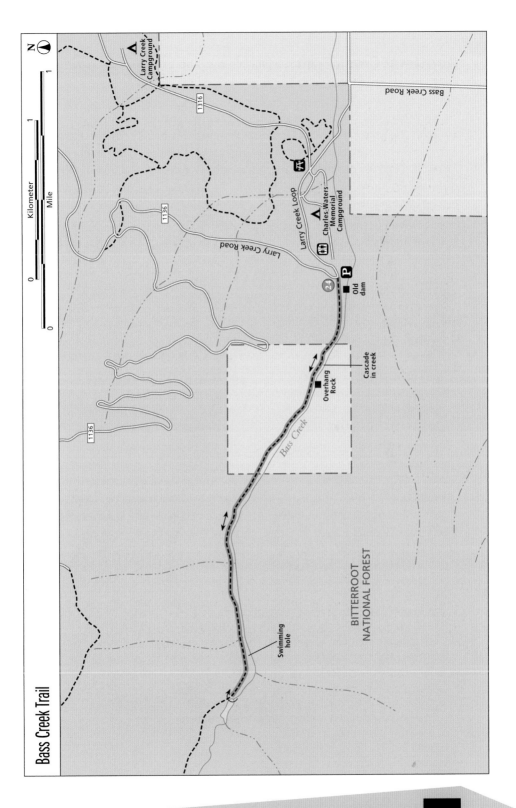

Bass Creek Trail

Kootenai Creek Trail

The Kootenai Creek Trail is a popular hike up a narrow canyon noted for its numerous pools and waterfalls—perfect for passing a Montana summer's day. Sheer granite cliffs tower above the creek bottom, which is shaded lightly by green shrubs and marked with groves of ponderosa pines and cottonwood. Otter and mink traverse the waterway. Small trout flit about the pools. The trail traces the creek on this journey, at times climbing above it for views, such as the rocky point that serves as a good turnaround spot. Hikers who want to extend the journey can proceed as far up this canyon as they wish.

Start: Kootenai Creek Trailhead
Distance: 5.6 miles out and back
Hiking time: About 3 hours
Difficulty: Moderate; some elevation gain
Trail surface: Dirt; singletrack
Best season: Spring through fall
Other trail users: Equestrians, rock climbers; hunters in fall
Canine compatibility: Dogs permitted
Land status: Bitterroot National Forest
Fees and permits: None required
Schedule: None
Maps: USGS Saint Mary Peak; USDAFS Bitterroot National Forest, available at the Stevensville Ranger Station
Trail contacts: Stevensville Ranger District, 88 Main St., Stevensville, MT 59870; (406) 777-5461; www.fs.usda.gov/main/bitterroot/home
Special considerations: High water in spring turns the creeks of the Bitterroot Mountains into raging torrents; use caution. The current can pin people underwater against rocks and logs. Hunting season, from late October through November, can be busy. Wear hunter orange; put it on your dog too.

Finding the trailhead: From the intersection of Brooks and Reserve Streets go south on Highway 93 for 23.3 miles. Turn right onto North Kootenai Creek Road (Road 3020). Continue 2 miles to the trailhead at the end of the road. **GPS:** N46 43.23' / W113 34.55'

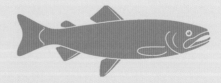

Kootenai Creek is one of the most popular hikes in the northern Bitterroot Valley. On any given day the Kootenai Creek Trail (53) can host hikers from Missoula, local horse packers, steep-creek kayakers lugging boats on their shoulders, hot-shot rock climbers laden with climbing racks, or visiting anglers who appear to have just stepped out of an Orvis advertisement.

This notch is one of the narrower canyons in the range, creating an up-close experience. Massive granitic boulders filter the crystal-clear waters of the creek as they run aggressively down the hillside forming cataracts and pools. Green shrubs frame the creek and, even in the dog days of summer, create an oasis effect.

The falls and pools in Kootenai Creek are some of the Bitterroot canyon's best.

Other Bitterroot creek bottoms are reserves for old-growth forest—wide, lush, overgrown. Kootenai Canyon is more a V shape than the classic Bitterroot "U". The result is a narrow bottom that features the creek in its constant quest to drop to the valley floor and join the Bitterroot River. The pool and drop plunges create a series of mini private retreats that trail users can sidle into. There is no architect like the chaos of nature, which has created a veritable botanical spa in these untouched Montana mountains. Steep cliff faces and solid slabs of granite punctuate the canyon walls high above the creek here on the edge of the Idaho Batholith.

Leaving the trailhead, the hike runs along the side of the canyon. Almost immediately a challenge presents itself. How that challenge is handled will vary from party to party. Hikers seeking the bosom of nature will find a private swimming hole in Kootenai Creek, complete with a terraced granite deck and a garden of broad-leafed greenery from which to view the mink and otter frolicking on rocks just to show their sheer of joy at living in such a beautiful place.

The trail traces the creek for the length of this hike. Hikers who wish to push beyond the first stunning and available pool will find an assortment of these fine water features farther upcanyon. Keep stretching your legs until the time comes to dip a toe in the water and watch an ouzel (also known as a dipper) scamper beneath the surface of the water—literally walking on the rocks below the surface of the creek, pecking at unsuspecting insects and their larvae.

Dippers are small, dark-colored birds that can be sighted on the creek's edge, nervously flicking their bodies in what could be envisioned as a handless pushup. It can be quite surprising to then see these creatures chuck themselves into strong runs of mountain current. These little birds can be accidentally consumed by salmon and large trout while carrying on beneath the water's surface. Dippers are a sign of a clean environment and require pure waters to thrive. The solitude and lack of development, along with the percolation of the water through granitic soils, makes water flowing out of the Selway-Bitterroot Wilderness some of the cleanest on Earth.

You encounter a classic pool at 0.8 mile. At 1.1 miles you reach a spectacular low-water beach with a lovely grove of ponderosa pine and cottonwood. The trail climbs up among some cliffs and gets away from the creekside. At 2.8 miles a rocky overlook marks a good turnaround spot. Retrace your steps to the trailhead.

MILES AND DIRECTIONS

0.0 Start at the side of the hill above the creek. Follow the trail up the creek and canyon.

0.8 There is easy access here to a large, deep pool and big boulders for sitting.

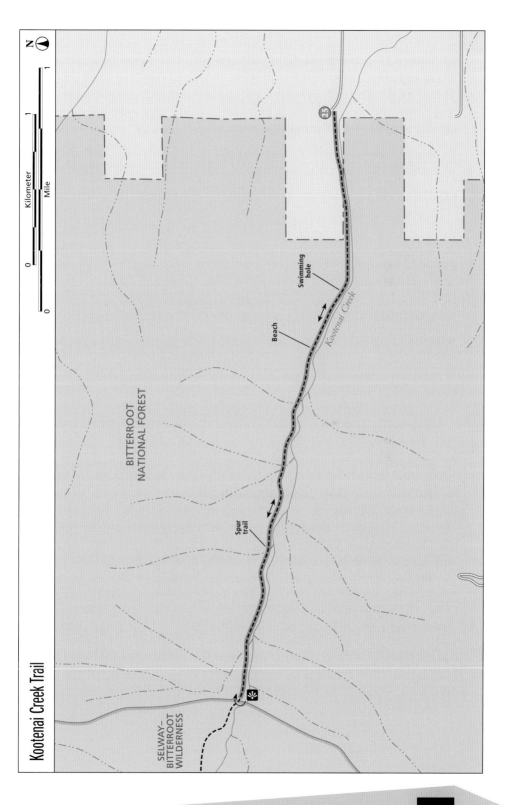

Kootenai Creek Trail

0.9 Pass a small campsite just off the trail to the left, near the creek in some ponderosa pines.

1.1 Come to a nice low-water beach and pool.

2.0 A spur trail to the left leads to the creek.

2.4 The trail skirts a series of cliffs on the right. There are big views of the creek below.

2.8 The trail leads to rocky point overlooking the creek below. This is your turnaround point.

5.6 Arrive back at the trailhead.

Options: Extend your hike by proceeding up the Kootenai Creek Trail to the turnaround point of your choice.

HIKE INFORMATION

Breweries: Two microbreweries have made a big name for themselves in the little burg of Stevensville, situated at the mouth of Kootenai Creek:

Wildwood Brewery, 4018 US 93 North, Stevensville; (406) 777-2855; wildwoodbrewing.com

Blacksmith Brewing Company, 114 Main St., Stevensville; (406) 777-0680; blacksmithbrewing.com

The Idaho Batholith

The Idaho Batholith is a collection of granite slabs reaching from western Montana into central Idaho. The mass stretches 200 miles long and 75 miles wide. It is this formation that gives the Bitterroot Mountains its solid granite base. The result, with the help of glacial activity, is a dramatic and sharp mountain range. The alpine splendor surrounded by vast reserves of big-forest habitat make this chunk of land the wildest in the United States outside of Alaska. Much of this land is protected, but much of it faces threats from mining, logging, and development interests. The Clinton Roadless Rule of 1999 has slowed development of these unprotected acres, but many area conservationists argue that full wilderness protection is still needed to preserve the character of these mountains for generations to come.

Big Creek Trail

The Big Creek Trail (11) is in the biggest drainage in the Bitterroot Range. The broad valley is blanketed in thick cedar and fir forest; its boulder-choked stream is lined with lush shrubs. This hike takes you into the Selway-Bitterroot Wilderness boundary and is home to a wide variety of wilderness species. Pileated woodpeckers, goshawks, lynx, and gray wolves roam this canyon, along with a host of other wildlife.

The hike leads you through dense canopy to the pack bridge over the creek, with options to extend the journey.

Start: Big Creek Trailhead
Distance: 3.0 miles out and back
Hiking time: About 1.5 hours
Difficulty: Easy
Trail surface: Dirt; singletrack
Best season: Spring through fall
Other trail users: Equestrians; hunters in fall
Canine compatibility: Dogs permitted
Land status: Bitterroot National Forest
Fees and permits: None required
Schedule: None
Maps: USGS Victor; USDAFS Bitterroot National Forest, available at the Stevensville Ranger Station
Trail contacts: Stevensville Ranger District, 88 Main St., Stevensville, MT 59870; (406) 777-5461; www.fs.usda.gov/main/bitterroot/home
Special considerations: High water in spring turns the creeks of the Bitterroot Mountains into raging torrents; use caution. The current can pin people underwater against rocks and logs. Hunting season, from late October through November, can be busy. Wear hunter orange; put it on your dog too.

Finding the trailhead: From the intersection of Brooks and Reserve Streets, go south on Highway 93 for 29.9 miles. Turn right onto Bell Crossing Road. Go 0.5 mile and turn right onto Meridian Road. The road bends left after 0.2 mile and becomes Curlew Orchard Road. Follow this road west 1.3 miles toward the mountains. It becomes Curlew Mine Road and then Big Creek Road. After 0.6 mile go right on Big Creek Trailhead Road at a junction with a road leading to Glen Lake. It's another 1 mile to the trailhead, at a roundabout loop. **GPS:** N46 27.89' / W114 12.78'

This broad Bitterroot Mountain canyon is well named. Big Creek is the biggest drainage in the Bitterroot Range. The lower part of the creek makes for good day hiking; the Big Creek Trail (11) winds among lush groves of cedar and fir that fill the canyon bottom. Like all Bitterroot canyons, the walls of Big Creek are carved into sheer granite faces—a sanctuary for the fleet-footed mountain goat from all predators except the golden eagle.

The creek is popular with horse packers and fly fishermen as well as hikers. The waters support a healthy population of cutthroat trout. Big Creek Lake sits at the top of the drainage, an immense stretch of water nestled amongst alpine peaks 9.0 miles up the trail. To reach it is a bit of an expedition but worth it if you have the time.

Late summer can bring low water to the Bitterroot Canyons. High water produces dangerous torrents.

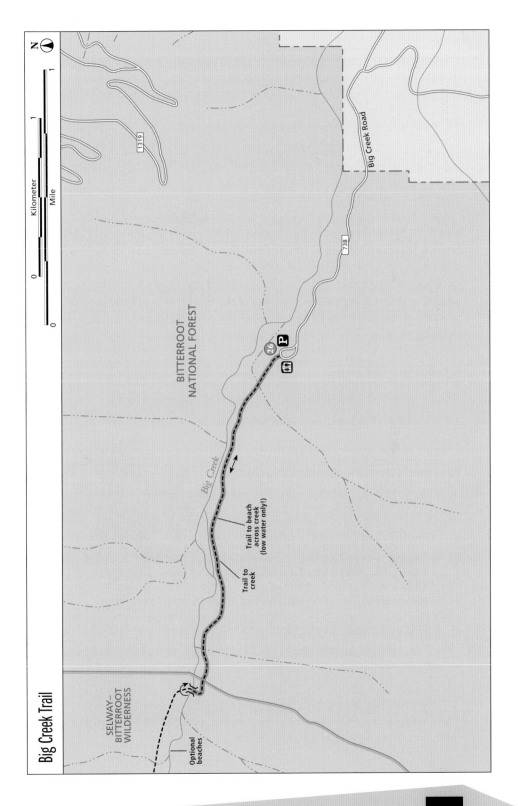

Big Creek Trail

N

Kilometer
0 1
Mile
0 1

1319

BITTERROOT
NATIONAL FOREST

Big Creek

Trail to creek

Trail to beach
across creek
(low water only!)

26

P

738

Big Creek Road

SELWAY–
BITTERROOT
WILDERNESS

Optional
beaches

The walk up Big Creek is the type where you're sure you just saw Bigfoot's shadow flashing across the base of a weathered cedar tree. Those who find joy in losing themselves in a maze of thick tree trunks should immediately lace up their boots, throw a snack in the backpack, and steer for Big Creek.

Park somewhere in the roundabout loop and head up the creek on the dirt path located on the west end of the trailhead. You will immediately be thrust into the dense forest, winding on a nice trail on the south side of the creek. Big views are limited by the canopy, but micro-views are numerous: broad thimbleberry leaves, a jagged fern, a bush heavy with huckleberries.

Several small spur trails lead to the creek's edge, branching off on the right side of the trail and leading to secret beaches, deep swimming holes, ands scenic ribbons of current. After 1.3 miles on the trail, you reach the Selway-Bitterroot Wilderness boundary, marked with a wooden forest service sign. Continue on until you hit "the bridge," as area locals call it. If you only want a short jaunt among the trees along the lower section of the creek, this is as good a place as any to turn around. Those who want to venture on should push upstream past the pack bridge 0.3 mile to a couple of beaches.

MILES AND DIRECTIONS

0.0 Start from the roundabout trailhead and head west up Big Creek.

0.7 A trail leads to a beach on the far side of the creek.

0.9 A small trail leads to the creek on the right.

1.3 The trail crosses the Selway-Bitterroot Wilderness boundary.

1.5 Reach the pack bridge, your turnaround point. Return the way you came.

3.0 Arrive back at the trailhead.

Options: Beyond the pack bridge over Big Creek, the trail continues over Pack Box Pass and into a big wilderness in the heart of central Idaho. A short continuation of this hike takes you to some nice beaches only 0.3 mile past the pack bridge.

For those up to an 11-mile day, Tipi Rock is a good destination. This house-size chunk of granite lies on a large flat 5.5 miles from the trailhead. There's good camping here.

Of course Big Creek Lake is the big enchilada in this neck of the woods. To reach its shores and return to the trailhead in one day is going to cost you 18 trail miles.

Glen Lake Trail

Glen Lake is a high-country Bitterroot Mountain gem. Craggy granite spires erupt above the lakeshore. You're not in the canyon bottoms anymore! The elevation of the trailhead is high, making this excursion less painful than it could be. The Glen Lake Trail (232) offers big views down into the Bitterroot Valley and Big Creek, thanks in part to the 2006 Gash Creek Fire that burned hot through the area. The trees are scorched for the most part, but the understory is recovering nicely. You will pass a couple of large throne-size rock outcrops on a ridge you will cross during the approach to the lake.

Start: Glen Lake Trailhead
Distance: 5.4 miles out and back
Hiking time: About 3 hours
Difficulty: Moderate
Trail surface: Dirt; singletrack
Best season: Summer and fall
Other trail users: Equestrians; hunters in fall
Canine compatibility: Dogs permitted
Land status: Bitterroot National Forest
Fees and permits: None required
Schedule: None
Maps: USGS Gash Point; USDAFS Bitterroot National Forest, available at the Stevensville Ranger Station

Trail contacts: Stevensville Ranger District, 88 Main St., Stevensville, MT 59870; (406) 777-5461; www.fs.usda.gov/main/bitterroot/home/
Special considerations: High water in spring turns the creeks of the Bitterroot Mountains into raging torrents; use caution. The currents can pin people underwater against rocks and logs. Hunting season, from late October through November, can be busy. Wear hunter orange during hunting season; put it on your dog too. The road is narrow and primitive for the last 8 miles. Make sure your vehicle can handle the trip.

Finding the trailhead: From the intersection of Brooks and Reserve Streets go south on Highway 93 for 29.9 miles. Turn right onto Bell Crossing Road. Go 0.5 mile and turn right on Meridian Road. The road bends left after 0.2 mile and becomes Curlew Orchard Road. Follow this road west toward the mountains 1.3 miles. It becomes Curlew Mine Road and then Big Creek Road. After 0.6 mile go left on FR 1321 and follow it for 7.8 miles to the trailhead. After 4 miles an unmarked road leaves the trailhead road to the right. Stay left and climb several switchbacks. The trailhead is on the left. **GPS:** N46 26.14' /W114 15.15'

Glen Lake Trailhead lies at 6,629 feet—an advantageous elevation for those who like to scamper through the high country without facing the physical punishment of hiking up the side of a hill. This is a nice treat at times. The Glen Lake Trail (232) leads you over a ridge to a big bowl you will traverse to reach the 7,542-foot-high lake after more than 900 feet of elevation gain. It's not a quad killer, though. The gradient is steady and stretched out over some distance.

Most of the hike will take you through area scorched by the Gash Creek Fire, which raged through the area in 2006, reducing the forest to a pile of skinny dead sticks. The forest here isn't what it once was, but there is a stark beauty in the blackened trees, purple fireweed, and big-peak vistas in the distance through the now-open canopy.

The hike starts out from a low-key trailhead on the left side of the road. Views of the Bitterroot Valley stretch out below. You can make out the Sapphire Mountains across the valley. The trail is a singletrack dirt path that begins to climb steadily uphill and to the north. It works its way through occasional patches of

Fireweed begins the cycle of recovery after a fire at Glen Lake.

unburned trees as it makes its way toward an obvious ridgeline crowned with two distinctive rocks. The giant thrones overlook Sweathouse Creek and Glen Creek, which flows from Glen Lake.

The trail turns to the west here, cresting through the natural saddle near the monument rocks and moving across the sidehill of the bowl on the other side. The trail descends slightly into a small saddle. As it climbs up the other side of the saddle, there are big views down into and across Big Creek. The trail moves across the side of another face of the bowl toward a band of cliffs. The lake is nestled in a cirque at the base of the cliffs at 2.7 miles.

The lake itself is a classic high-Bitterroot number surrounded by craggy granite peaks. It's small, but on sunny days it shimmers like a jewel. A few green trees that survived the fire provide some shelter. This cirque was formed when the head of a glacier scooped a pocket into the bedrock where water could collect. A pool thus formed is also called a tarn.

Considering all the trees killed by the fire, the site looks healthy, with a fresh understory making its way up among the standing survivors of the great blaze. Lush greenery typically follows a fire like this. The green grasses nourish deer and elk, which is good for hunters. After a few decades the grasses yield to huckleberries, which is good for bears and people who like pie. Eventually the forest retakes a foothold. Squirrels frolic, songbirds chirp; then, with the snap of a lightning bolt on a hot summer day in an area that hasn't seen rain in months, the whole process begins again.

Retrace your path from the lake's edge to the trailhead.

MILES AND DIRECTIONS

0.0 Start on the singletrack trail that leads north from the trailhead on the left side of the road.

1.3 Arrive at the throne rock ridge. This is the Selway-Bitterroot Wilderness boundary. The trail begins to veer left (west) and cuts across the sidehill of the bowl.

1.7 The trail descends into a saddle.

1.9 The trail climbs out of the saddle. There are views into Big Creek to the right (north). The trail then cuts across another sidehill of the bowl.

2.6 Glen Lake comes into view at a trail junction. The trail to the left leads to the lake outlet. The trail to the right climbs up to an upper lake. A spur trail leads to the water's edge. Follow this spur to the lakeshore.

2.7 Arrive at the lakeshore. Retrace your steps to the trailhead.

5.4 Arrive back at the trailhead.

Options: At the trail junction at 2.6 miles, take the right-hand trail. It leads to an hourglass-shaped upper lake and will take you up the hill to the north of (behind) the lake. The climb is 300 feet and 0.5 mile. Retrace your steps to Glen Lake and then back to the trailhead.

Other than rocks, trees are the least-flammable thing in the forest. While needles and branches may burn during a forest fire's quick inferno, even during the hottest of blazes, the tree itself very rarely catches fire. The tree that remains can stand for over a hundred years, housing insects and birds. When it falls, it will hold the soil in place and slowly turn to dirt itself, providing fertile ground for future trees.

🌿 **Green Tip:**
Keep to established trails as much as possible. If there aren't any, stay on surfaces that will be least affected, such as rock, gravel, dry grasses, or snow.

Glen Lake Trail

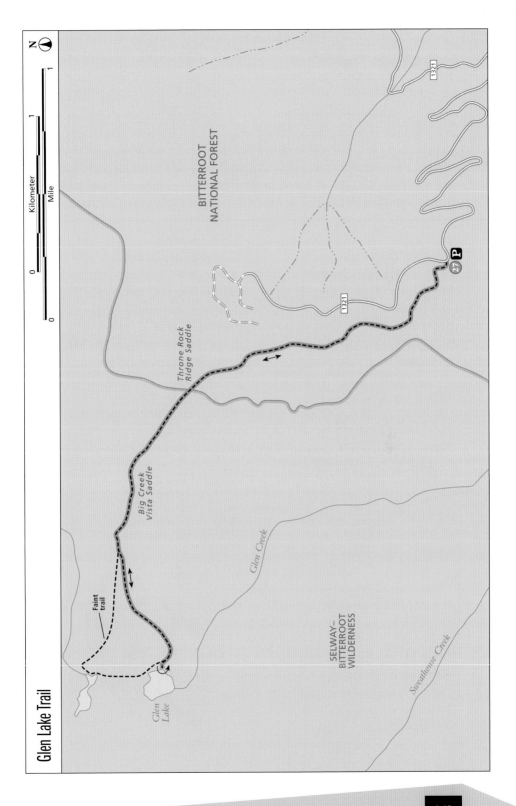

BITTERROOT NATIONAL FOREST

1321

Throne Rock Ridge Saddle

Big Creek Vista Saddle

Faint trail

Glen Creek

Glen Lake

SELWAY-BITTERROOT WILDERNESS

Sweathouse Creek

N

Kilometer

Mile

Bear Creek Trail

The Bear Creek Trail (5) is one of the most scenic hiking trails in the Bitterroot Mountains. The creek erupts into a series of waterfalls at 1.4 miles. Granite slabs serve as platforms and form a bedrock meadow next to the creek, allowing access to the cataracts. Pinnacle-topped canyon walls pop up above the creek. Big pools, good for swimming in late summer, punctuate calm spots in the whitewater chaos. Go 0.2 mile upstream from the bedrock meadow to find a more secluded falls and pool.

Start: Bear Creek Trailhead
Distance: 3.2 miles out and back
Hiking time: About 1.5 hours
Difficulty: Easy
Trail surface: Dirt; singletrack
Best season: Spring through fall
Other trail users: Equestrians; hunters in fall; kayakers in spring
Canine compatibility: Dogs permitted
Land status: Bitterroot National Forest
Fees and permits: None required
Schedule: None
Maps: USGS Gash Point; USDAFS Bitterroot National Forest, available at the Stevensville Ranger Station

Trail contacts: Stevensville Ranger District, 88 Main St., Stevensville, MT 59870; (406) 777-5461; www.fs.usda.gov/main/bitterroot/home

Special considerations: This hike terminates at a series of waterfalls on Bear Creek. Hiking near these falls is dangerous at high water. Don't scramble on any wet rocks, where you could fall into the creek. Admire the creek from a distance. Hunting season, from late October through November, can be busy. Wear hunter orange when hiking during hunting season; put it on your dog too.

Finding the trailhead: Drive 35 miles south on Highway 93 from the intersection of Brooks and Reserve Streets. Turn right onto Bear Creek Road and drive 2.3 miles. Turn right onto Red Crow Road and go 0.8 mile. The road makes a 90-degree turn to the left. Go 0.3 mile. The road turns into Bear Creek Trail. Continue 2.8 miles to trailhead for. **GPS:** N46 22.78' / W114 15.16'

THE HIKE

The Bear Creek Trail (5) is a highly scenic trek that leads to a series of scenic falls. None of the waterfalls are a classic straight-down drop. Instead the creek plunges over a number of granite drops and rockets through narrow notches in a chaotic display. The size of the cataracts varies with the season. In spring you might see steep-creek kayakers running their boats down the rowdy stretch of water.

Looking at Bear Creek Falls you might think you are witnessing an unstoppable force collide with an immovable object as water pummels granite. Each season the snowmelt pounds down on the hearty rock, not making big changes but constantly chipping away. The water always wins, and the force of the water eventually will obliterate the granite. But for now the granite deflects the frigid waters over its back in the form of rooster tails and other frothy features.

As soon as you leave the trailhead you begin to discover the pristine rocky beaches that line the pool of Bear Creek. Massive grand fir, mountain ash, and huckleberry make up the forest.

Waterfalls don't always have to be big to be beautiful, though larger falls abound in this area of Bear Creek.

Early on, the trail cuts across a section of the canyon's side where giant granite boulders have slid down throughout the years to create an open area. The trail returns to the forest and climbs up the canyon before reaching the waterfall area at 1.4 miles. Trees yield to a bedrock meadow that affords views up to pinnacles on the north side of the canyon. As the creek flows through the meadow, it gives access to a series of drops. You want to leave the main trail here.

Explore the myriad nooks and crannies up and down the creek. A trail worn from use runs directly up the creek from the bedrock meadow, probing the pools, which are perfect for a dip in late summer. Use caution walking through here at high water, and certainly don't do any swimming then. The pools give way to falls.

After meandering up the creek from the bedrock meadow, you encounter a particularly large drop into a deep pool. At the base is big granite slab. You couldn't ask for a nicer slice of paradise.

This is a good turnaround spot. Retrace your path to the bedrock meadow and then back down to the trailhead.

MILES AND DIRECTIONS

0.0 Start at the trailhead and follow Bear Creek Trail up the creek to the west.

1.3 A spur trail descends to a flat rock on the creek.

1.4 Mossy flat rocks create an overlook point for waterfalls on Bear Creek. There are more swimming holes and cataracts upstream. To reach them, leave the main trail here, veering right and following a well-worn path directly up the creekside. (**Note:** This portion of the trail may be impassable during high water.)

1.6 Reach a big flat-rock slab next to a deep pool and waterfall. Retrace your steps to the bedrock meadow.

1.8 Return to the bedrock meadow. Head back down the Bear Creek Trail to the trailhead.

3.2 Arrive back at the trailhead.

Options: You can continue up Bear Creek on the main trail from the bedrock meadow. The creek has three forks. The trail to the South Fork (304) breaks off 3.5 miles from the trailhead. The North and Middle Forks divide at mile 6.0. The North Fork doesn't have an official trail and is a real Bitterroot bushwhack adventure. If you choose to go up the North Fork you'll reach Bear Lake 8.0 mile from the trailhead. Continue on the Bear Creek Trail past the North Fork and you will enter the Middle Fork, reaching spectacular Bryan Lake 8.0 mile from the trailhead. The trail continues another 1.5 miles to Bear Creek Pass.

Bear Creek Trail

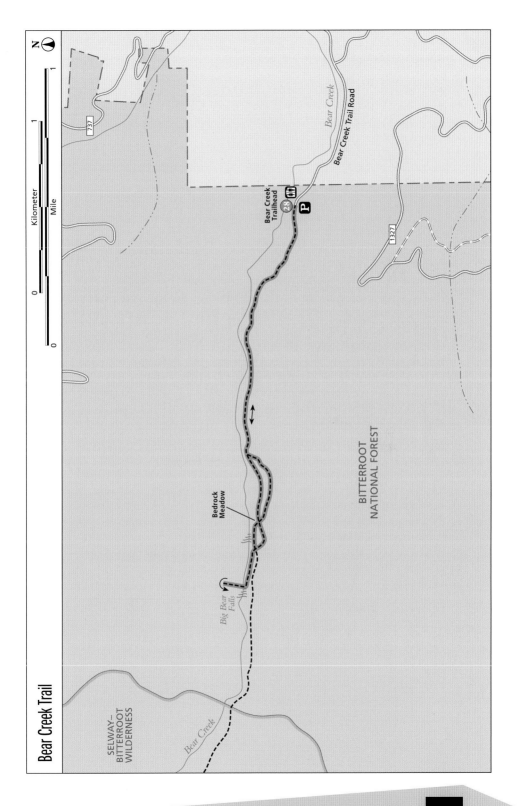

- N
- Kilometer
- Mile
- 737
- Bear Creek
- Bear Creek Trail Road
- Bear Creek Trailhead
- P
- 1327
- Bedrock Meadow
- Big Bear Falls
- Bear Creek
- SELWAY–BITTERROOT WILDERNESS
- BITTERROOT NATIONAL FOREST

Hike tours: Big Wild Adventures, 222 Tom Miner Creek Rd., Emigrant; bigwild adventures.com. For hikers who want support on a longer journey in the Bitter-root Mountains, these expeditions explore the Bitterroots' canyons, climb peaks, search out wildlife, and camp at high-country lakes.

High-Water Danger

Any roaring creek is an obstacle to be taken seriously. The Bitterroot Moun-tains have plenty of these raging ribbons of water when the snow melts during mid-May and June. When crossing creeks—whether a valley-bottom gusher or a side-canyon trickle—assess whether you think you can make it across. If you have any doubts as to whether you can make it, don't cross. Turn around, backtrack, and live to cross another day. Anything over mid-thigh deep is generally too deep to walk through.

It's tempting to cross barefoot, but it's dangerous, especially in the wil-derness, where you depend upon your ankles to get you back to the trailhead without a costly evacuation. Wear your boots, or carry special lightweight water shoes or sandals to cross the creek. A hiking stick is invaluable when dealing with a raging torrent. If you don't have one, don't fret; nature pro-vides. Find a sturdy stick that you know will hold your weight.

Once you are in the water, face upstream, leaning into your hiking stick, and side-shuffle across the current, minding any boulders and logs on the creek bottom. Move slowly and be mindful of your feet. Don't get them wedged into any debris on the creek bottom.

If your pack has a waist belt fastened, unbuckle it. This will help you get out of your pack quickly if you go in. Keep in mind that the high water is ice cold. Be sure your body can handle the temperature for the amount of time required to cross the creek. The steeper the creek, the more force it's going to exert on you. The narrower the location, the deeper. Look for an area with a flat gradient and wider creek bed to find a crossing that isn't too deep or swift.

Bear Creek Overlook Trail

A granite slab perched on a canyon rim above Bear Creek opens up the majesty of the high Bitterroot Range. A wide swath of forest in the U-shaped valley below gives way to granite basins. Along the spine of the range, Sky Pilot Peak and Gash Point command the view. To the east you can make out the Sapphire Mountains on the far side of the Bitterroot Valley. The hike gains just over 1,000 feet as it switchbacks through forest toward a giant castle rock that towers directly above the natural viewing platform. Watch for mountain goats.

Start: Bear Creek Overlook Trailhead

Distance: 4.8 miles out and back

Hiking time: About 2 hours

Difficulty: Strenuous; steep climb

Trail surface: Dirt; singletrack

Best season: Summer and fall

Other trail users: Equestrians; hunters in fall

Canine compatibility: Dogs permitted

Land status: Bitterroot National Forest

Fees and permits: None required

Schedule: 24/7

Maps: USGS Gash Point; USDAFS Bitterroot National Forest, available at the Stevensville Ranger Station

Trail contacts: Stevensville Ranger District, 88 Main St., Stevensville, MT 59870; (406) 777-5461; www.fs.usda.gov/main/bitterroot/home

Special considerations: Watch for thunderstorms building on hot summer afternoons. Lightning could be dangerous on this canyon rim. High water in spring turns the creeks of the Bitterroot Mountains into raging torrents; use caution. These currents can pin people underwater against rocks and logs. Hunting season, from late October through November, can be busy. Wear hunter orange when hiking during hunting season; put it on your dog too.

Finding the trailhead: Drive 35 miles south on Highway 93 from the intersection of Brooks and Reserve Streets. Turn right onto Bear Creek Road and drive 2.3 miles. Turn right onto Red Crow Road and go 0.8 mile. The road makes a 90-degree turn to the left. Go 0.3 mile. Turn right and stay on Red Crow Road. Go 1 mile and turn left onto Pleasant View Drive. After 1.6 miles turn right onto Gash Creek Road. Continue 2.4 miles and turn left onto Bear Creek Overlook Trail Road (Road 1325). Follow the switchbacks up the mountain for 3.6 miles to a gate. The trailhead is here, more of a turnout on the side of the mountain. **GPS:** N46 23.74' / W114 16'

THE HIKE

Elevation is everything in the Bitterroots. The slightest change in it opens up new perspectives on the range. Even though the Bear Creek Overlook is only 0.8 mile (as the chickadee flies) from Bear Creek Falls, half of that mileage is straight up a sheer granite cliff. At the overlook, slabs of granite yield to the sky. But the big sky that stretches between the canyon walls is quickly interrupted by the rippling crest of the Bitterroot Range, filling your full field of vision. Sky Pilot Peak (8,792 feet) shines a few miles in the distance. Chiseled, tall, symmetrical, it commands attention. But so do the dozens of other points peeking up from ridgetops, including local favorite Gash Point (8,866 feet). The vista extends down the mountain chain a ways but is limited to the general vicinity of Bear and Big Creeks, being only 7,022 feet high.

Hikers who have climbed to this view have dubbed the range "Montana's Alps." The moniker is fitting, as the Alps are known to be a postcard-perfect range. But a better way to understand the astonishing view might be to think of the European mountains as the "Swiss Bitterroots."

Fortunately for today's hiker, the Bear Creek Overlook Trail (126) does not require wings. Instead you can approach this marvel from a turnout on the side of FR 1325. It winds up the nose of the ridge that eventually becomes the canyon rim for Bear Creek, gaining a good amount of elevation and delivering big views of the Bitterroot Valley and Sapphire Mountains to the east. The road ends as at a gate and a trail begins, taking you the rest of the way.

The trail mostly switchbacks as it climbs the 1,088 feet to the overlook, although the last 0.5 mile is more gradual and proceeds along a ridgetop to the destination. This hike is right on the edge of the Gash Creek Fire, which burned hot in 2006, scorching virtually every tree in its path. You encounter evidence of the fire's edge at 1.7 miles. Some of the burned timber has been downed by wind and water, forming a mountain meadow.

As you push on through the trees, a granite "castle" guards the canyon rim. The trail runs right up to the monumental rock and then slides behind its left (south) side before curving back to the right (west) behind and below it. Here a terraced flat-rock slab creates a natural viewing platform up the Middle and North Forks of Bear Creek and beyond. The jagged heart of the Bitterroot Range beats before your eyes, its rugged nature surprising some visitors. The largest peaks rise several miles back from the Bitterroot Valley, at the head of the Bitterroot Mountain canyons, and are therefore concealed without your gaining some elevation.

Mountain goats and mouse-like pikas make their home up here. Retrace your path to return to the trailhead.

MILES AND DIRECTIONS

0.0 Start up the trail from the parking area on the side of the road. Take either the right or left fork to begin. The left fork switchbacks; the right fork cuts the switchback. Follow a series of switchbacks uphill.

1.7 Enter a burned area where downed timber creates a mountain meadow. The trail begins to straighten and level out on a ridgetop.

The granitic spine of the Bitterroot Range drops jaws from the Bear Creek Overlook.

2.2 A huge castle-like rock sits on the ridgeline. The trail descends to the left (south) of the rock and briefly winds around the slope to the west.

2.4 Reach a rock slab that overlooks the canyon and the rugged divide of the Bitterroot Range. Return the way you came.

4.8 Arrive back at the trailhead.

Options: Adventurous and hearty souls can extend the journey up the canyon rim. Assess your abilities realistically, and be sure you are a competent outdoors person before continuing. The route leads farther up the ridge that runs to the northwest. It is completely off-trail. Wander up the hill; the east side of the ridge is gradual and will allow you to veer around any obstacles you can't overcome on the ridgetop. The west side drops straight down into Bear Creek. Be sure to note your back trail so that you can retrace your steps back to the overlook and on down to the trailhead.

HIKE INFORMATION

Hike tours: Big Wild Adventures, 222 Tom Miner Creek Rd., Emigrant; bigwild adventures.com. For hikers who want support on a longer journey in the Bitter-root Mountains, these expeditions explore the Bitterroots' canyons, climb peaks, search out wildlife, and camp at high-country lakes.

The Pika

The pika is a bit of a redheaded stepchild when it comes to getting as much attention as the much larger mountain goat, mountain lion, or black bear. The pika looks like a large mouse with exceptionally big rounded ears but is actually a member of the rabbit family. Pikas live among talus rockslides in the high mountains. You will know one of these wily little creatures is in the area if you hear a shrill squeak that sounds like a *meep*. Pikas work hard all summer collecting grasses, drying them into hay, and then storing them down in their rock palaces for winter.

Sadly pikas are becoming endangered. They are sensitive to heat and cannot survive more than 6 hours in temperatures above 80°F. All parts of the the Rocky Mountains, including the Bitterroot Range, continue to have their hottest summers on record. As a result pikas are forced to scamper through the heat to higher elevations. Unfortunately mountain peaks only stretch so high, and eventually the animals find no shelter.

Bear Creek Overlook Trail

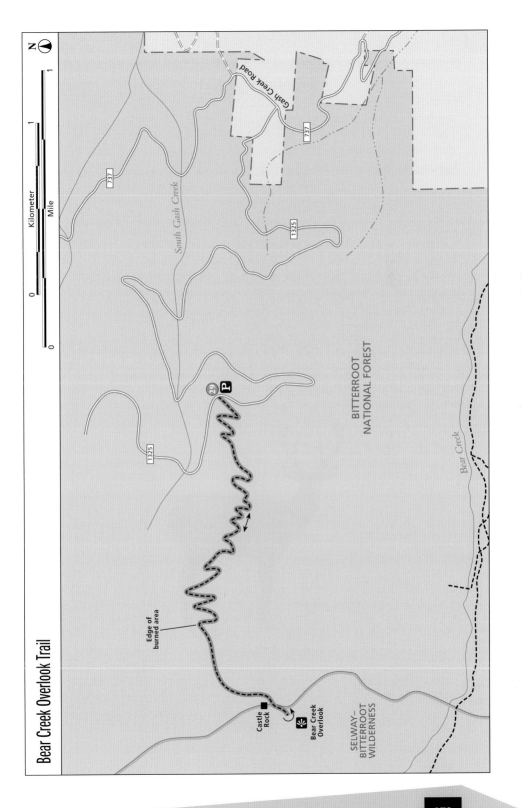

Bitterroot Glaciers

A glacier is a mass of ice that can be thousands of feet tall, even over a mile high. A glacier is formed when more snow collects during winter months than melts during summer months. When this process repeats itself over time, the giant ice masses are formed.

In the case of the Bitterroot Mountains, these alpine glaciers were formed in valleys that had already been formed by water erosion. These glaciers occasionally unfroze. This melt occurred at the base of the glacier, where it made contact with the ground. When the glacier refroze, it picked up rocks and debris, moving it down the canyon and eventually creating the U-shaped valley.

Sharp pyramidal peaks like Sky Pilot Peak are formed by the action of three glaciers. Each glacier scoops an amphitheater into a chunk of granite, sculpting the tip into a sharp point. A mountain with four such scooped sides is known as a "matterhorn."

Boulder Creek Falls Trail

Boulder Creek flows through one of the most scenic and remote canyons in the Bit-terroot Valley. Views of Trapper and Boulder Peaks stretch above the sheer granite walls in this classic, broad U-shaped canyon. Mountain goats are frequently seen on the canyon walls. The entire creek is a boulder- and trout-choked torrent, but Boulder Falls is a legendary cascade, dropping over a granite cliff. Groves of fat ponderosa pines blanket the canyon's lower elevations. The creek is a tributary to the West Fork of the Bitterroot River in the southern Bitterroot Mountains.

Start: Boulder Creek Trailhead

Distance: 10 miles out and back

Hiking time: About 5 hours

Difficulty: Strenuous due to distance and elevation gain

Trail surface: Dirt; singletrack

Best season: Summer and fall

Other trail users: Equestrians; hunters in fall

Canine compatibility: Dogs permitted

Land status: Bitterroot National Forest

Fees and permits: None required

Schedule: None

Maps: USGS Piquett Creek and Boulder Peak; USDAFS Bitterroot National Forest, available at the West Fork Ranger Station

Trail contacts: West Fork Ranger District, 6735 West Fork Rd., Darby, MT 59829; (406) 821-3269; www.fs.usda.gov/main/bitterroot/home

Special considerations: High water in spring turns the creeks of the Bitterroot Mountains into raging torrents; use caution. These currents can pin people under-water against rocks and logs. Be especially careful crossing Crow Creek, at 3.0 miles, and around the falls. Hunting season, from late October through November, can be busy. Wear hunter orange when hiking during hunting sea-son; put it on your dog too.

Finding the trailhead: Go south 65.6 miles on High-way 93 from the intersection of Brooks and Reserve Streets. Turn right onto West Fork Road and drive 13.2 miles. Turn right onto Sam Billings Road, which becomes Boulder Creek Road. Continue 1.2 miles to the trailhead. **GPS:** N45 49.78' / W114 15.16'

THE HIKE

magine an enormous canyon carved into granite bedrock at the base of some of the Bitterroot Mountains' tallest peaks. On the canyon's hillsides are groves of ponderosa pines as fat as grain silos. Above those hillsides are sheer faces of granite shooting up to pinnacled tops and dotted with mountain goats. Down the center of the canyon runs a boulder-choked creek that in many states would be considered a small river. Up this ferocious creek lies a massive falls where you can sit at the top, dangle your legs, and contemplate the life cycle of a mosquito as the sun sets in the west, casting alpenglow and shadows across the cliff faces.

View from the top of Boulder Falls looking down the canyon.

Such places do exist—for example, Boulder Creek's famous falls. Located on a tributary to the West Fork of the Bitterroot River, this waterfall sits squarely in the Selway-Bitterroot Wilderness in the southern Bitterroot Mountains.

The Selway-Bitterroot Wilderness is the third-largest wilderness area in the United States outside of Alaska. When combined with the nearby Frank Church River of No Return and Gospel Hump Wildernesses (separated by dirt roads) to the south, this complex of wildlands is the largest in the lower forty-eight states.

All of Montana's wilderness creatures can be found here, including black bear, gray wolf, mountain lion, lynx, wolverine, elk, moose, and deer. But the canyon's star is the famous mountain goat herd that dots the gray canyon walls with white. Flora includes thimbleberry, Oregon grape, huckleberry, and bearberry. Big ponderosa pines dominate the lower elevations of the canyon. Lodgepole pine and Douglas fir fill in the rest of the canopy.

Follow the trail up the canyon from the trailhead. It starts as a doubletrack but quickly whittles down to a proper singletrack wilderness trail. The path nears the creek at 0.6 mile. A massive jumble of boulders provides a clue as to how Boulder Creek received its name. These boulders provide good cover for small trout, which can be seen darting among the pools between plunges on the creek. Also at 0.6 mile, a spur trail leads a short distance to the left. It takes you up to a rock overlook of a powerful cataract. Return to the trail and turn left, continuing up the canyon.

The trail breaks into a boulder field at 1.8 miles, giving you a good chance to eyeball the highest peak in the Bitterroots—10,157-foot Trapper Peak rising roughly 5,000 feet above the trail.

At 3.0 miles the trail crosses Crow Creek, flowing down from the north wall of the canyon. This tributary is sizable any time of the year, and a log crossing usually helps alleviate the burden of crossing the tributary. During high water you may not be able to cross this torrent.

The trail continues to climb, in spots rather steeply, as it meanders among the canopy of ponderosa pines. It gets away from the creek and up on the side of the canyon. The journey continues on with stunning views of forest and canyon, not to mention the opportunity to encounter wildlife.

Just before the falls, the forest gives way to a meadow formed by the roaring avalanches that carve up the canyon during winter. The falls beckon in the distance. The trail climbs to the head of the falls via some switchbacks. At 4.9 miles you arrive at the same elevation as the top of the waterfall. Turn left off the trail on a spur that leads into a primitive camp spot at the falls.

Thick slabs of granite compose the surface around the falls. Big views stretch in every direction. There are a couple of different places to take in the waterfall. Explore and enjoy, then retrace your steps to return to the trailhead.

MILES AND DIRECTIONS

0.0 Start at the parking area and walk up Boulder Creek Trail.

0.6 Detour off-trail to an overlook of a small cataract in Boulder Creek. Return to the trailhead and turn left. Continue up the canyon.

1.8 The trail breaks out of the forest and into a boulder field with views of Trapper Peak above.

3.0 The trail crosses Crow Creek on a series of logs. Use extreme caution getting across this creek at high water.

4.9 Turn left off the trail and walk to an obvious waterfall.

5.0 Arrive at Boulder Falls. Retrace your route to the trailhead.

10.0 Arrive back at the trailhead.

Options: Families wanting a shorter hike can walk the level trail 0.6 mile to the spur trail that leads to an overlook of a roaring cataract. The pools below the falls can serve as swimming holes during low water.

HIKE INFORMATION

Food/lodging: West Fork Lodge, 5857 West Fork Rd., Darby; (406) 821-1853, westforklodge.com. This regional outpost has a restaurant, bar, and rooms; close to the Boulder Creek Trailhead.

Hike tours: Big Wild Adventures, 222 Tom Miner Creek Rd., Emigrant; bigwild adventures.com. For hikers who want support on a longer journey in the Bitterroot Mountains, these expeditions explore the Bitterroots' canyons, climb peaks, search out wildlife, and camp at high-country lakes.

🍃 **Green Tip:**
Pack out what you pack in, even food scraps, which can attract wild animals.

Boulder Creek Falls Trail

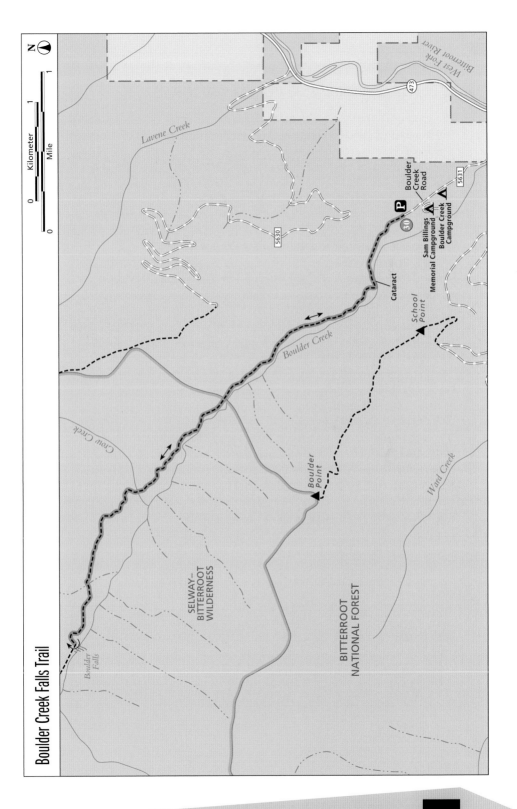

The Brandborg Legacy

The southern Bitterroots are home to a local family of wilderness champions: the Brandborgs. Guy Brandborg served as forest supervisor of the Bitterroot National Forest for twenty years, beginning in 1935. During his time at the helm, Brandborg argued that the forest should be managed sustainably, even though the post–World War II building boom was putting a great strain on forests like those in the Bitterroots. Upon his departure from the agency in 1955, Brandborg became a conservation activist, arguing for sustainable logging to become commonplace in national forests. His vision came to fruition with the National Forest Management Act of 1976.

Guy Brandborg passed on in 1977. Today his efforts to encode sustainable forestry are known in agency history as the Bitterroot Controversy.

Meanwhile, Guy's son Stewart became interested in government policies that affect the natural world and cut his teeth studying mountain goats in the Bitterroot Mountains. His work led him to Washington, D.C., where he worked with the National Wildlife Federation, eventually taking a position with the Wilderness Society in 1960 beneath the legendary Howard Zahniser. The then-controversial legislation focused on passing the National Wilderness Preservation Act, which was signed into law in 1964. Soon suitable landscapes were designated wilderness, including more than 100 million acres of wild parks, refuges, and rivers in Alaska.

Stewart Brandborg returned to his beloved Bitterroot Valley from D.C. in 1986, where he continued his work with Friends of the Bitterroot. Though he is retired these days, Brandborg still finds time to work with Missoula's Wilderness Watch, which monitors wilderness areas nationally.

Kenai Nature Trail

The Lee Metcalf Wildlife Refuge is the last tract of undeveloped land in the Bitterroot Valley's bottomland. The area serves as a slice of habitat for migrating birds and provides a beautiful backdrop for hikers. Thick marshes of cattail stretch to the river's banks, choked with thick stands of cottonwood. To the west, the Bitterroot Mountains erupt out of the valley floor, towering more than 6,000 feet above the refuge. The trail extends from the refuge's headquarters building out to a wildlife viewing shelter equipped with a spotting scope.

Start: Lee Metcalf Wildlife Refuge Headquarters Building
Distance: 2.1 miles out and back
Hiking time: About 1 hour
Difficulty: Easy
Trail surface: Paved doubletrack; dirt singletrack
Best season: Year-round
Other trail users: None
Canine compatibility: No dogs permitted
Land status: US Fish and Wildlife Service

Fees and permits: None required
Schedule: Dawn to dusk
Maps: USGS Stevensville; USDAFS Bitterroot National Forest, available at the Stevensville Ranger Station
Trail contacts: Lee Metcalf National Wildlife Refuge, 4567 Wildfowl Lane, Stevensville, MT 59870; (406) 777-5552; www.fws .gov/leemetcalf/index.html
Special considerations: Waterfowl hunting in the fall

Finding the trailhead: From the intersection of Brooks and Reserve Streets go south on Highway 93 for 16.3 miles. Turn left onto the Eastside Highway (Road 203). Drive over the Bitterroot River. The road curves to the right after 1.8 miles. After another 5.2 miles the Eastside Highway turns 90 degrees to the right in an intersection with Moiese Lane (straight) and Ambrose Creek Road (left). Go 1 mile and turn right onto Wild Fowl Lane. The road turns 90 degrees after 0.5 mile. Go 0.1 mile and turn right. Go another 0.1 mile turn left into the parking area for the headquarters building. **GPS:** N46 33.33' / W114 04.59'

THE HIKE

The Lee Metcalf Wildlife Refuge is a 2,800-acre expanse of wetlands and riparian area along the banks of the Bitterroot River in the center of the Bitterroot Valley. The refuge is one of the last undeveloped tracts of land in the Bitterroot Valley, one of Montana's fastest growing regions. The main focus of the refuge, founded in 1963 largely thanks to Metcalf, is to preserve habitat for migrating birds and other wildlife, with a special emphasis on managing the habitat to provide for threatened and endangered species. More than 200 species of birds have been documented in the refuge. A number of ponds cater to diving ducks; other areas house shorebirds. A variety of mammals make their home among the cattails and cottonwoods.

The Kenai Trail moves along the edge of two ponds. The views of the Bitterroot Mountains and the range's canyons are stunning. The mass of granite rises more than 6,000 feet from the valley floor to its highest peaks. As if a several-thousand-foot rise isn't imposing enough, the flatness of the refuge makes the mountains to the west look even more massive. Views of wetlands, dotted with lonely old snags, give way to a thick layer of forest on the braided and meandering river's edge, forming the western boundary of the refuge.

A viewing platform on the edge of the wetlands that make up the Lee Metcalf Wildlife Refuge.

The constant movement of ducks, geese, and herons among the reeds and water makes for a meditative gaze across the open space. In spots the trail serves as a demarcation line between development and the last bastion of wildlife sanctuary in the Bitterroot Valley. It's a stark contrast. The refuge side is an oasis of life. A drama, marked by squawking and flapping, plays itself out each day among a sea of green reeds. The other side of the path is a dusty farming field scraped bald of life. If one needed to conjure up what the definition of "wasteland" looks like, this view would illustrate the point. A dilapidated railroad track and rotting stacks of wood lie at the edge of the field, near where the Bass family laid down its roots in 1864.

The hike starts at the refuge headquarters; the trail begins on the left (west) side of the building. It starts out as a sidewalk and crosses an administrative road that leads from the maintenance facility near the headquarters building. Go straight here and connect with a paved roundabout, perfect for wheelchair access, after you cross over a pond on a bridge. Turn right onto the roundabout loop. At 0.3 mile turn left onto the dirt path that leads north into the wetlands of the refuge.

This trail meanders frequently, creating a series of small curves as it wanders between dusty farm fields and wetland splendor. The trail crosses the administrative road again at 0.8 mile. After this point the trail dips behind a berm, allowing you to focus solely on the refuge. The wildlife-viewing structure situated on a busy pond at 1.1 miles is equipped with a spotting scope to help you add a few birds to your life list.

This is the turnaround point for the hike. When you arrive at the paved roundabout, turn left at 1.9 miles. Turn left again at 2.0 miles on the path that will return you to the trailhead.

MILES AND DIRECTIONS

0.0 Start at the parking area walk on the left side of the headquarters building and pick up the paved path that leads into the refuge. After about 370 feet, the paved trail crosses a jeep trail. Stay on the pavement. Go straight, crossing a bridge over a pond.

0.1 Turn left onto the circular path.

0.3 The paved path begins to circle back toward the trailhead. Turn left onto a dirt path and head north into the refuge.

0.8 The trail crosses an administrative road. Continue straight on the singletrack trail.

1.1 Arrive at a covered wooden viewing shelter with a spotting scope. Turn around here.

1.9 Return to the paved trail; go left.

2.0 Turn left toward the headquarters building.

2.1 Arrive back at the trailhead.

Lee Metcalf's Legacy

The refuge is named for former Montana Senator Lee Metcalf, who served Montana in both the US House and Senate from 1952 until his death in 1978. His conduct and vision during his time in office have canonized him as a politician uncorrupted by the often shady antics within the D.C. Beltway. Named one of the most influential Montanans of the twentieth century, he was also known to be a ferocious political competitor when it came to achieving his vision.

Metcalf was born in Stevensville and raised on a nearby ranch. He went to college at Stanford after the Montana university system. He served in World War II, where he fought in Normandy and the Battle of the Bulge. Upon arrival in Washington, D.C., Metcalf became a champion of worker's rights, advocating a strong minimum wage. He was a Medicare visionary, implemented the Peace Corps, championed funding for education, and expanded the G.I. Bill.

Metcalf's other passion was preserving open spaces for both wildlife habitat and the enjoyment of generations to come. He earned the nickname "Mr. Wilderness" with the passage of the Wilderness Act in 1964. The Great Bear and Absaroka-Beartooth Wildernesses resulted from his efforts, as well as the wilderness near Big Sky that bears his name. The irony of the Lee Metcalf Wilderness, created five years after his passing, is that it is fragmented by development. Metcalf had always envisioned large wildernesses uninterrupted by ski resorts, roads, logging, or mining.

Many consider Metcalf's lasting legacy for Montanans to be his passage of the Montana Wilderness Study Act of 1977, which set aside over 1 million acres of land to be preserved for wilderness designation in the future. This was some of Metcalf's final legislative work. He died a few months later, in January 1978. Unfortunately, since his death Montana's delegation in D.C. has codified very little of that land as wilderness.

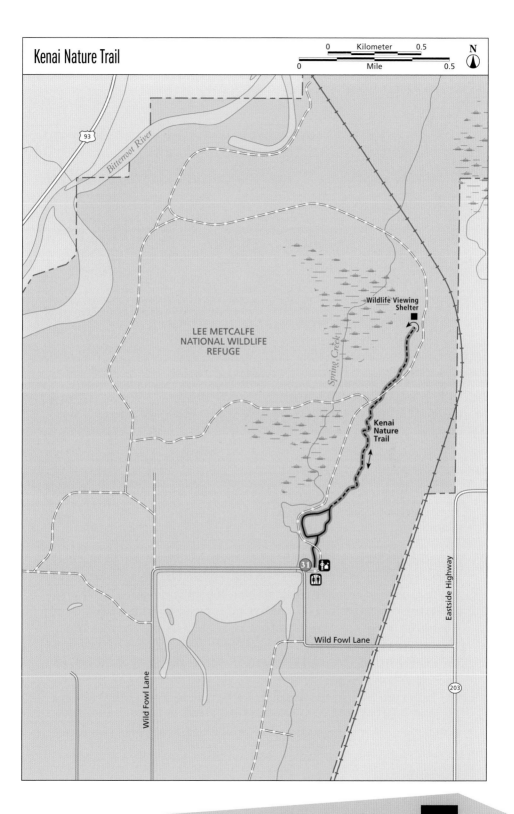

Kenai Nature Trail

0   Kilometer   0.5
0   Mile   0.5

N

93

Bitterroot River

LEE METCALFE
NATIONAL WILDLIFE
REFUGE

Spring Creek

Wildlife Viewing
Shelter

Kenai
Nature
Trail

31

Eastside Highway

Wild Fowl Lane

Wild Fowl Lane

203

West of Missoula

The view east from the summit of Cha-paa-qn.

To the west of Missoula lies a lush rain forest that is the southern tip of a tract of trees stretching up into British Columbia. This forest is unique because of its coastal qualities so far from the Pacific Ocean. The symbol of Lochsa Country has always been the mighty salmon, which wriggles its way up to the headwaters of creeks high in the mountains of Idaho, such as Warm Springs and Weir Creeks. The same western red cedars that towered when Lewis and Clark rode through the country still stand today in the wilderness over the hill in Idaho, only an hour's drive from Missoula.

Before you get into Lochsa Country, Missoula's backyard, Lolo Creek, has plenty of good hiking. Near the Lolo Hot Springs Area you can find some gems with historic value and natural beauty. Unique rock features hide within the canopy of the trees, which, while not as big as those in Lochsa Country, still make a nice forest. When the larches turn color on the hillside in October, the view is stunning.

A little to the north of the Lochsa and Lolo Creek is the Great Burn. In 1910 a firestorm that hasn't been seen since swept through the area with such vigor that it leveled entire ranger districts overnight. The result in the landscape south of Superior is wide-open grassland dotted with patches of trees. It makes for scenic country. People who wander into the Great Burn never come out the same. They see something while there that changes them. And they decide to return to this area again and again.

Hiking through the thick brush in Lochsa Country before climbing Wendover Ridge.

This section of rugged singletrack path is the original trail used by Nez Perce Indians and the Lewis and Clark expedition. You can put your foot exactly where their moccasins and boots once tread. This is a National Historic Trail designated to commemorate both parties. The trail is a rough go, steep at first; then it traverses parklike ponderosa stands and jagged rocky outcrops. You can turn around at any point, making this hike as long or as short as you wish. If you want to truly follow in the footsteps of those intrepid travelers, shuttle your vehicle or arrange for a ride and hike all the way to Lolo Hot Springs.

Start: Lolo Trail at Howard Creek Trailhead

Distance: 6.0 miles out and back, with shorter options

Hiking time: About 3 hours, depending on length

Difficulty: Strenuous; moderate for shorter hikes

Trail surface: Forested dirt path

Best season: Spring through fall; late fall for the larches

Other trail users: Horses; hunters in fall

Canine compatibility: Dogs permitted

Land status: USDA Forest Service

Fees and permits: None required

Schedule: None

Maps: USGS Garden Point; USDAFS Lolo National Forest Map, available at the district office

Trail contacts: Lolo National Forest Supervisor's Office, Fort Missoula Building 24A, Missoula, MT 59804; (406) 329-3750; www.fs.usda.gov/lolo/

Finding the trailhead: From the intersection of Reserve and Brooks Streets on the south side of Missoula, take Highway 93 south. Drive 7.5 miles to Highway 12 in Lolo. Turn right onto Highway 12. Drive 18.7 miles west to Howard Creek Road (Road 238) and turn right. Drive another 0.1 mile and park in the turnout on the right. The turnout has a pit toilet and some historical signs. The trail starts  across the road at a sign describing the different types of footwear that have traversed the historic trail. There are two trails. They both lead to the same place, but the easier climb is to the right. **GPS:** N46 46.444' / W114 26.429'

THE HIKE

There are many ambiguities about the Lolo Trail, chiefly how it got its name. Historians will agree on one thing, though: It was never an easy place to traverse for those unaccustomed to the region.

For ages the route was used by both the Nez Perce and Salish peoples. The Salish called the route "The Road to the Nez Perce." The Nez Perce called it "The Road to the Buffalo." Lewis and Clark called the narrow canyon "Traveler's Rest Creek," named for a place where they sought brief respite on a plain at the mouth of the drainage. This location is now an interesting state park just outside the town of Lolo that's well worth visiting.

The first map to bear the name Lolo Fork belonged to John Mullan, who punched his famous wagon road, now I-90, into the region in 1854, opening trade from the Missouri River to the Columbia and realizing Thomas Jefferson's vision for an intercontinental trade route. He gleaned the name from locals. Historians suspect that "Lolo" was a man named Lawrence, who hunted and trapped in the drainage until he was killed by a grizzly bear. The words "Lolo Trail" appeared in Gen. Oliver O. Howard's journals and maps during his pursuit of the non-treaty Nez Perce in 1877.

Peering through a grove of ponderosa at larch trees turning color with autumn's cooler nights.

Names aside, this section of trail is difficult to travel with as much gear as early explorers often carried. It's timbered, snowbound much of the year, holds little game, and rises and falls in elevation.

In a journal entry on September 12, 1805, William Clark wrote of the expedition's journey through the section of the trail beginning at Howard Creek ". . . passed on the sides of the steep, stony mountains, which might be avoided by keeping up the creek, which is thickly covered with undergrowth and fallen timber. Crossed a mountain 8 miles without water and encamped on a hillside on the Creek after descending a long, steep mountain." The party camped 2 miles downstream of Lolo Hot Springs.

As you hike the narrow Lolo Trail at Howard Creek today, views of the road and a channelized Lolo Creek lie below you for part of the journey. This perspective offers a tale of two worlds—the modern and the primitive. Test your mettle here, and decide which you prefer. Mullan scouted the Lolo Trail for a road to the sea but wrote, "This route I found the most difficult of all I examined." During their flight along this trail, the Nez Perce traveled the exact path now available to hikers, only with 700 people and 2,000 horses. Imagine those numbers passing by as you journey along the steep sidehill.

At 0.3 mile on the hike, you encounter a sign that says ORIGINAL LOLO TRAIL. You can turn left here and return to the parking lot for a short 0.4-mile loop. But you are here to tackle the original trail, if only for a short distance. Turn right and pass the sign that says CAUTION STEEP TRAIL. Continue following the markers for the Lewis and Clark Historic Trail.

The trail traverses through stands of ponderosa pine that have been logged, and at mile 1.2 you encounter the legendary "stony mountains" described by Clark. The views here are amazing. This is a good place to turn around, though if you continue the trail takes on a more primitive feel.

At 1.7 miles the trail crosses gated FR 2180. Pick up the path on the other side and continue following trail markers up the ridge. After crossing the road, the trail feels as though few travelers have set foot on the ancient path in decades. The forest takes on less of a managed feel; the trail gets away from highway noise, and sign of elk and moose becomes prevalent. You are now squarely in the footsteps of the parties that traversed this ridge centuries ago.

The path meanders over the shoulder of a forested point, descends through a saddle, and begins to climb another timbered point after 0.5 mile. Views of Howard and Petty Creeks stretch to the north. At 3.0 miles a ponderosa grove on the ridgetop is another good turnaround location. Here there are views of Upper Lolo Creek.

If you wish to continue, it is another 2.0 miles to where the trail descends to Lewis and Clark's former campsite, now a State of Montana maintenance building. The trail continues 2.0 miles beyond that, roadside, to Lolo Hot Springs.

Lolo Trail at Howard Creek

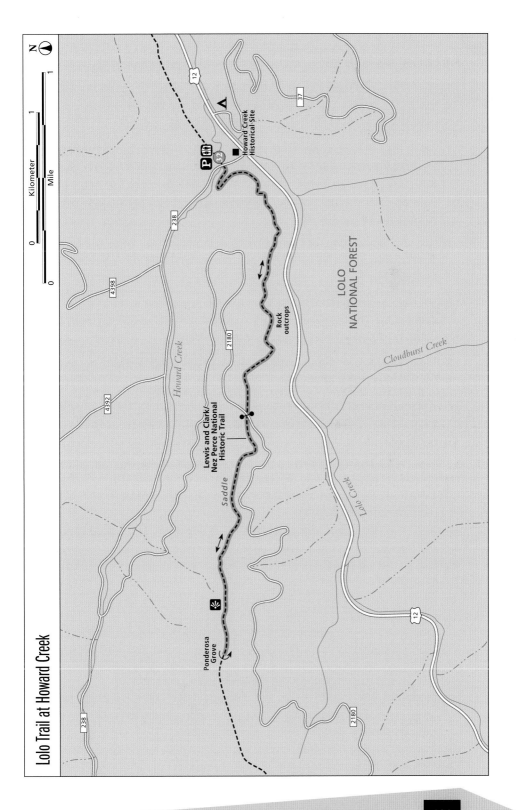

MILES AND DIRECTIONS

0.0 Start at the parking lot on Howard Creek Road (Road 238). Cross the road to a historical sign and the trailhead. There are two trail options. Go right (north) on the easier path and climb the switchbacks.

0.3 Reach the ORIGINAL LOLO TRAIL sign at a trail junction. (**Option:** Turn left/east to return to the parking lot for a 0.4-mile loop.) Turn right (west) and pass a CAUTION STEEP TRAIL sign to follow the Lolo Trail. The trail crosses the side of the hill through a stand of ponderosa pines spared by a heavy thinning operation. The area is parklike and open.

1.2 Pass the famous outcrops noted by Clark in his journal. Enjoy the rocky slopes. (**Option:** If you are feeling winded, turn around here for a 2.4-mile out-and-back hike.)

1.7 The trail crosses gated FR 2180. Continue following signs and trail markers up the ridge. The trail takes on a primitive feel and gets away from views of Highway 12 below. Animal sign becomes prevalent.

1.9 The trail crests over the shoulder of a forested point and begins to descend gently into a saddle of Douglas fir.

2.7 The trail begins to climb another forested point after following a gentle ridgetop for 0.5 mile. There are views into Howard and Petty Creeks to the north.

3.0 Reach a ponderosa grove on the ridgetop that offers views to the west of Upper Lolo Creek. Return the way you came..

6.0 Arrive back at the trailhead.

Options: Over the course of the next 2.0 miles the trail steeply descends back down to Highway 12 and then runs near the road 2.0 miles beyond that to Lolo Hot Springs. Consider parking a vehicle at either of these locations for a one-way shuttle hike.

HIKE INFORMATION

Local events/attractions: Traveler's Rest State Park 6717 Highway 12 West, Lolo; (406) 273-4253; travelersrest.org. The park is on the way to the trailhead from Missoula. Stop in to learn more about the Lewis and Clark Expedition.

Food/lodging: The nearby Lolo Hot Springs Resort (406-273-2290; lolo hotsprings.com) offers an indoor hot pool and outdoor swimming pool, as well as showers, restrooms, lodging, dining, and beverages.

Hike tours: Lewis and Clark Trail Adventures, 912 East Broadway, Missoula; (406) 728-7609; trailadventures.com. They offer hikes along sections of the Lolo Trail.

Lee Creek Interpretive Trail

This hike is perfect for families who want to explore the area near the Lewis and Clark Trail. You won't have to eat the family dog or walk barefoot through the snow to enjoy the sweeping valley views afforded by this journey. Enjoy granite rock outcroppings, ridgetop hiking, fat stands of ponderosa pines, giant lone larches, and a lush creek bottom on this loop. Follow along with the interpretive brochure offered at the trailhead as it describes twenty numbered sites you will encounter along the way. Nearby Lolo Hot Springs is a nice way to unwind after the hike; the resort offers an indoor hot pool and a cooler outdoor pool.

Start: Lee Creek Trailhead
Distance: 2.8-mile loop
Hiking time: About 1.5 hours
Difficulty: Moderate; brief uphill
Trail surface: Forested dirt path followed by dirt road
Best season: Spring through fall; in late fall the larches are beautiful.
Other trail users: Bikers, equestrians; hunters in fall
Canine compatibility: Dogs permitted
Land status: Lolo National Forest
Fees and permits: None required
Schedule: None

Maps: USGS Lolo Hot Spring, Montana; USDAFS Lolo National Forest, available at Fort Missoula
Trail contacts: Lolo National Forest Supervisor's Office, Fort Missoula Building 24A, Missoula, MT 59804; (406) 329-3814; www .fs.usda.gov/lolo/
Special considerations: Wear hunter orange when hiking during hunting season; put it on your dog too. Drinking water is available in the Lee Creek Campground during summer.

Finding the trailhead: From the intersection of Reserve and Brooks Streets on the south side of Missoula, take Highway 93 South. Drive 7.5 miles and turn right onto Highway 12 in Lolo. Go 26.6 miles west until you intersect Lee Creek Road (699); turn left. Immediately turn right into the parking area at the entrance to the campground. Park your car here and walk up Lee Creek Road 0.1 mile. The trailhead is on left side of road and is marked by a wooden sign that says Lee Creek Interpretive Trail. For reference, Lee Creek Road is 1.3 miles past Lolo Hot Springs Resort. **GPS:** N46 42.33' / W114 32.22'

Most of the Lee Creek Interpretive Trail has been worked over by human hands during its existence. While this walk is a far cry from wilderness, it is still a great way to hear the call of a mountain bluebird, smell the vanilla scent of a ponderosa pine (go ahead and stick your nose in the thick, red bark and take a sniff), or feel fertile earth squish beneath your feet.

The trail is marked by twenty numbered sites, and a corresponding brochure describes the features along the way. This relaxing hike is an education in forestry and the lasting effects of forest management and is a great way to spend part of the day.

This viewpoint over Lee Creek is accessed relatively easily. ALESHA BOWMAN

The landscape here is part of the checkerboard legacy. Checkerboard forest ownership is defined by land that alternates between federal and private control. Abraham Lincoln signed the deal putting this type of management into effect in 1864. When viewed on a map, the white and green section squares resemble a checkerboard. The private land was originally granted to railroad companies to encourage development. In the case of Lee Creek, no railroad was ever developed nearby and these lands were sold to logging companies. The modern result can be one section that is heavily logged while the next is relatively intact. This can make for a fragmented habitat. However, in 2010 the Montana Legacy Land Acquisition resulted in the USDA Forest Service taking control over most of the checkerboard lands.

The hike starts with a gradual incline. Shortly you reach a trail junction marked with a sign that points right to Lolo Hot Springs. Turn left and follow the trail as it climbs the face of a ridge through a quaint grove of Douglas fir. Markers tell tales of old logging sites, rowed terraces used for replanting trees, and the different tactics Douglas firs and lodgepole pines use to regenerate.

Farther down the trail, you come to an awe-inspiring rock outcrop with sweeping views of the valley below. Veer right onto the short spur that leads to the outcrop. This is one of the grandest moments of the entire hike, though more beauty waits down the trail. It's easy to picture yourself as an early explorer scouting a route over neighboring mountains. In fact, Lewis and Clark wandered a short distance from here. It is unknown if one of their scouts may have encountered this lookout. Surely, though, countless Nez Perce hunters scanned the forest for game from this point. In late autumn the golden stands of Western larch dominate the view. Large ponderosa pines mark this location too.

After returning to the trail from the rock outcrop, turn right and continue up the ridge, which levels out shortly, totaling roughly 400 feet of elevation gain from the trailhead. Compare the recovery of a section of forest burned by wildfire to recovery of former logging operations witnessed below. Massive 150-foot larch trees dot the landscape as you cruise across the flat ridgetop.

After you walk the ridge, the forest gets noticeably thicker and takes on an untrammeled atmosphere. Intersect the Lee Ridge Trail (295) at mile 1.4. To complete the loop, veer right and downhill into a draw housing a babbling brook. Continue your descent until you hit the road; follow it back to the parking area.

MILES AND DIRECTIONS

0.0 Start at the parking lot adjacent to the campground gate and walk up Lee Creek Road (Road 699).

0.1 Arrive at the trailhead for the Lee Creek Interpretive Trail (23), on the left (east) side of Lee Creek Road.

0.3 Reach a junction with a trail going to Lolo Hot Springs. Turn to the right (southeast).

0.6 A small spur trail veers right (south) at the site of a large rock outcrop. Carefully wander out on the rocks and enjoy the view. When you've finished taking in the scenery and enjoying the rocks, retrace your steps to the main trail and turn right (east). The main trail proceeds up the ridge.

1.4 The Lee Ridge Trail (295) intersects the path; veer right (north) and downhill.

1.7 Cross a small stream on a primitive bridge.

1.9 Return to Lee Creek Road. Turn right (north) and walk down the road.

2.8 Arrive back at the parking area.

Options: At the junction with the Lee Ridge Trail, bear left and proceed 8.0 miles to the top of Lolo Pass, or continue as far as you care to wander. This is a strenuous option, and at times the trail can be overgrown. Make sure you have sufficient food and water and proper clothing, as well as adequate wilderness navigation skills. A shuttle is possible if you go all the way to the pass.

HIKE INFORMATION

Food/lodging: The nearby Lolo Hot Springs Resort (406-273-2290; lolo hotsprings.com) offers an indoor hot pool and outdoor swimming pool, as well as showers, restrooms, lodging, dining, and beverages. The hot springs is 1.3 miles to the east on Highway 12..

Camping: Lee Creek Campground is open for picnicking and camping (fee). It offers 22 sites in two loops and is open May 28 until Labor Day. Contact the Lolo National Forest for more information: (406) 329-3750.

The western larch is a deciduous conifer. After the aspen and cottonwood have dropped their colorful leaves, the larch loses chlorophyll in its needles and entire hillsides turn yellow. Native Americans used larch sap to heal cuts and to concoct syrup. Larch bark was steeped to create a tea for coughs and colds. In the fall when the larch changes color, they are often confused for beetle kill.

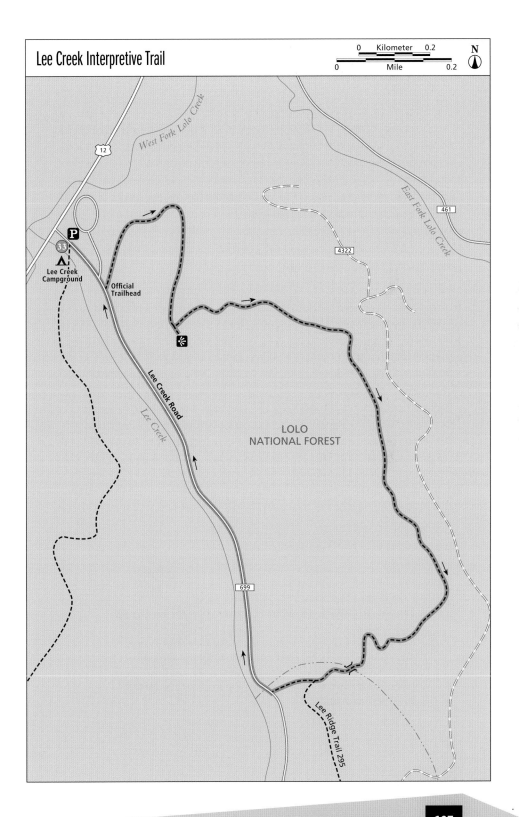

Lee Creek Interpretive Trail

0 Kilometer 0.2

0 Mile 0.2

N

West Fork Lolo Creek

East Fork Lolo Creek

12

461

4322

P

33

Lee Creek Campground

Official Trailhead

Lee Creek Road

Lee Creek

LOLO NATIONAL FOREST

699

Lee Ridge Trail 295

LOCHSA COUNTRY
Wendover Ridge

At the crossroads of historical discovery and love for nature lies the Wendover Ridge Trail (25). This arduous path climbs all the way out of the Lochsa River Canyon. Follow the footprints of Lewis and Clark on one of the most physical days the expedition endured. This section of trail is one the last sections that is completely unchanged from the time of the expedition. The trail starts among the big cedars of Wendover Creek and climbs more than 3,000 feet to a stunning vista point of the Lochsa Canyon and the east face of the Bitterroot Range. Continuing on you reach the Lolo Motorway. A short hike on the motorway delivers you to Snowbank Camp, where Lewis and Clark boiled snow to make horse soup.

Start: Wendover Ridge Trailhead
Distance: 7.7-mile shuttle
Hiking time: About 4 hours
Difficulty: Strenuous due to distance and elevation gain
Trail surface: Dirt; singletrack
Best season: Summer and fall
Other trail users: Equestrians; hunters in fall
Canine compatibility: Dogs permitted
Land status: Nez Perce-Clearwater National Forest
Fees and permits: None required
Schedule: None
Maps: USGS Cayuse Junction; USDAFS Nez Perce-Clearwater National Forest, available at the Powell Ranger Station
Trail contacts: Powell Ranger District, 192 Powell Rd., Lolo, MT 59847; (208) 942-3113; www.fs.usda.gov/nezperceclearwater

Special considerations: This is a point A to point B hike, requiring you to leave a vehicle at Snowbank Camp on the Lolo Motorway or arrange to be picked up there. Bring plenty of water; this ridge is notoriously dry, as Lewis and Clark discovered. It's also remote once you leave Highway 12—be prepared!

Finding the trailhead: Drive south from the intersection of Brooks and Reserve Streets on Highway 93 for 7.5 miles. Turn right (west) onto Highway 12 and drive 48.7 miles over Lolo Pass. Park in the Wendover Campground. Pick up the trail on the north side of Highway 12 at mile marker 158. **GPS:** N46 30.65' / W114 47.00'

  Finding Snowbank Camp: It is 14.2 miles to Snowbank Camp from the Lochsa Lodge (for the shuttle). Turn east onto Highway 12 from Lochsa Lodge and go 0.2 mile. Turn left onto Parachute Hill Road (Road 569), which becomes the Lolo Motorway (Road 500). Follow the road for 4.4 miles. Turn left at a junction to stay on the Lolo Motorway. Go 2.5 miles more until you reach Papoose Junction. Go straight, staying on the Lolo Motorway, for 6.8 more miles to Snowbank Camp, a parking area on the right. The Wendover Ridge Trail intersects the Lolo Motorway 6.2 miles past Papoose Junction, coming up the hill from the left. **GPS:** N46 34.95' / W114 49.28'

THE HIKE

The hike up Wendover Ridge is not to be taken lightly. If you do venture up this scenic and historic trail, you'll remember the rewards for a lifetime. Thick cedar forest yields to open burn as you work your way up the ridge, opening up to a big view of the Lochsa Canyon and the rugged east face of the Bitterroot Mountains.

Wendover Ridge is named for Bert Wendover, who came to the Clearwater country in 1913 after his doctor told him he was dying. He wanted to spend his final years living in the paradise and solitude of the Lochsa Country. In those days the Lochsa Valley was pure wilderness. He built a cabin, hunted, trapped—and left the area twenty years later in fine health.

Lewis and Clark made this particular ridge famous when they wandered off the Lolo Trail, the aboriginal route through this part of the Bitterroot Mountains. The Corps of Discovery accidentally followed a spur fishing trail to the cedar flat at modern-day Powell. The team realized their error and set about climbing the ridge to get back onto the Lolo Trail.

The day was brutal. Falling rain made the trail, choked with deadfall, slippery. The horses took the brunt of the beating, tumbling and rolling down the hill. One of the horses carried Lewis's desk. When the horse slid down the hill, the desk was smashed. Apparently the horse regained its footing and continued on. Other horses were not as lucky that day.

After climbing the ridge without water for either men or horses, Clark found a spring at 4.8 miles. The horses needed more than 10 gallons of water per day. The corps halted at the spring for 2 hours and watered up.

The corps found the Lolo Trail again on the ridgetop that separates the Lochsa drainage from the North Fork of the Clearwater. They pressed on until after dark looking for water. An old snowbank that had survived the summer eventually served their needs. Making a sparse camp, they melted the snow for drinking water and to make soup from a horse that had been slaughtered the previous day. Exhausted and still hungry, they fell asleep quickly that night.

To get your boots into the prints left by the corps, leave the Wendover Campground and find the trail across Highway 12. The trail is west of Whitehouse Pond and is located on the west side of Wendover Creek. It quickly begins climbing the face of Wendover Ridge. The trail is heavily forested with massive trees. Imagine crawling over, or around, a succession of these toppled beasts.

The trail crosses Wendover-Badger Road at 1.1 miles and continues up the nose of the ridge, reaching the ridgeline shortly after. Continue walking the ridgeline for the rest of the journey to the Lolo Motorway and Snowbank Camp. At times the trail meanders to one side of the ridge or another. A nice vista point opens up at 3.4 miles, exposing views of the dense forested ridges that make up the region. The trail runs just east of the historic Wendover Ridge Rest Site—the site where Clark halted the hike up the ridge to rest and water the horses.

A crew of hearty travelers retraces one of the most grueling sections of the Lewis and Clark Trail and are rewarded with big views of the Bitterroot Mountains.

Continuing up the ridge you enter a burned area and reach an impressive vantage point at 6.1 miles. A short spur trail leads to a rocky knoll where the views of the Lochsa Valley and the Bitterroot Mountains stretch for miles. From there the trail exits the burn, descends briefly to a saddle, and climbs the final pitch to intersect the Lolo Motorway at 7.1 miles. Turn left onto the motorway. The road winds and descends into Snowbank Camp, and your shuttle, at 7.7 miles.

MILES AND DIRECTIONS

0.0 Park at the Wendover Campground and pick up the trail on the north side of Highway 12. A trail sign marks the path as the Wendover Ridge Trail (25).

0.1 The trail leaves the creek bottom and begins to climb a series of switchbacks up the face of Wendover Ridge.

1.1 The trail crosses the Wendover-Badger Road (Road 5621) and picks up on the far side, climbing the ridge nose.

2.5 The trail enters one of the first open meadows.

3.4 Enjoy a vista point of forested ridges.

4.8 Reach the Wendover Ridge Rest Site, situated on a knoll on the ridgeline. The Corps of Discovery rested here after a tough morning. Maybe you should too!

5.8 The trail makes a short descent into a small saddle on the ridge. This is the beginning of a burned area with standing snags.

6.1 A small spur trail leads up to a scenic rock knoll. The views are outstanding.

6.4 Enter unburned forest again and begin descending.

6.6 Reach the bottom of the shaded saddle. The trail flattens out and begins to climb again.

7.1 Intersect the Lolo Motorway. Turn left and walk down the winding road.

7.7 Arrive at Snowbank Camp, a parking area on the right, and pick up your shuttle.

Options: If you don't want to run a shuttle, and are physically fit, consider the 15.4-mile hike up to Snowbank Camp and back to the road. If you go only to the Lolo Motorway and turn around, it is 14.1 miles. You are still facing a 3,300-foot ascent and descent, so don't get in over your head. Remember the descent can be the most grueling part. It is 9.6 miles to the Wendover Ridge Rest Site and back.

Other options include hiking from the hairpin turn where the Wendover-Badger Road crosses the trail at 1.1 miles. This will eliminate the initial switchbacks from the journey, although the trail still gains elevation as it runs along the ridge top. It is 7.4 miles round-trip to the Wendover Ridge Rest Site from here. If you want to see the upper section of the trail without climbing the lower part of the ridge, start from the Lolo Motorway at the top and hike down until you are satisfied; then retrace your steps.

HIKE INFORMATION

Local events/attractions: DeVoto Memorial Cedar Grove, mile marker 165 on Highway 12. Historian Bernard DeVoto edited the Lewis and Clark journals here. Short trails explore the massive cedars.

Travelers' Rest State Park, 6717 Highway 12 West, Lolo; (406) 273-4253, state parks.mt.gov/travelers-rest/. This is a must stop for Lewis and Clark enthusiasts. It is located just outside Lolo on the drive to Wendover Ridge.

Camping: Powell Campground, mile marker 162 on Highway 12, Powell, ID; (208) 942-3113; recreation.gov (reservations). This large campground on the banks of the Lochsa River near the Lochsa Lodge and Powell Ranger Station is 4 miles east of the Wendover Ridge Trailhead.

Food/lodging: Lochsa Lodge, 115 Powell Rd., Lolo; (208) 942-3405; lochsalodge .com. Historic and new cabins surround this welcoming lodge that has long been a popular stopover point for travelers. A restaurant, general store, and gas pump are on the premises.

Hike tours: Lewis and Clark Trail Adventures, 912 East Broadway, Missoula; (406) 728-7609; trailadventures.com. This tour company is run by history experts who specialize in getting hikers' boots in the footprints of the Corps of Discovery. A guided trip takes care of shuttle problems.

It was feast or famine for the Corps of Discovery. During plentiful times, each man ate 9 pounds of meat per day. When times were lean, they drank bear-grease soup and ate animal-fat candles.

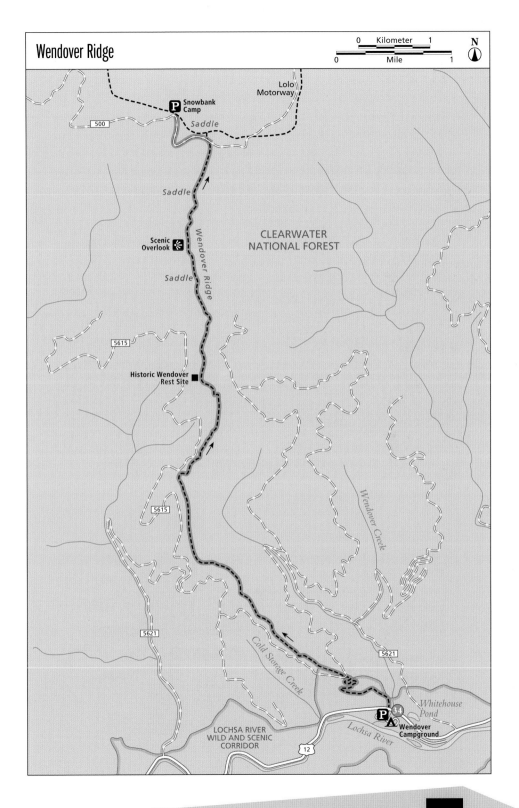

Wendover Ridge

0 Kilometer 1
0 Mile 1

N

Lolo
Motorway

P Snowbank
Camp

500

Saddle

Saddle

Scenic
Overlook

Wendover Ridge

CLEARWATER
NATIONAL FOREST

Saddle

5615

Historic Wendover
Rest Site

5615

Wendover Creek

5621

Cold Storage Creek

5621

Whitehouse
Pond

P 34
Wendover
Campground

Lochsa River

LOCHSA RIVER
WILD AND SCENIC
CORRIDOR

12

Warm Springs Creek Trail

This is one of the most popular hikes in the Nez Perce-Clearwater National Forest. The broad trail meanders through a cedar flat near where legendary trapper and miner Jerry Johnson once resided. The trail leads up the creek and past a hot spring area at the base of a cliff. The trail continues, reaching a second hot spring area in a rocky meadow next to the creek. Several pools dot the area in between granite boulders.

Start: Warm Spring Trailhead
Distance: 2.4 miles out and back
Hiking time: About 1 hour
Difficulty: Easy
Trail surface: Dirt; singletrack
Best season: Year-round
Other trail users: Equestrians; hunters in spring and fall (rarely)
Canine compatibility: Dogs permitted
Land status: Nez Perce-Clearwater National Forest
Fees and permits: None required
Schedule: Open 6 a.m. to 8 p.m.
Maps: USGS Tom Beal Park; USDAFS Nez Perce-Clearwater

National Forest, available at the Powell Ranger Station
Trail contacts: Powell Ranger District, 192 Powell Rd., Lolo, MT 59847; (208) 942-3113; www .fs.usda.gov/nezperceclearwater
Special considerations: Though many folks chance a night hike into Jerry Johnson Hot Springs, don't do it; the area is for day-use only, and the fine is $200. Help keep this heavily used area looking good by packing out your trash—other people's too.

Finding the trailhead: Drive south from the intersection of Brooks and Reserve Streets on Highway 93 for 7.5 miles. Turn right (west) onto Highway 12 and go 54.8 miles. The journey will take you over Lolo Pass. The trailhead is a big turnout on the right side of the road labeled Warm Springs Creek, near Mile Marker 152 and 10 miles west of the Lochsa Lodge. **GPS:** N46 28.47' / W114 53.12'

THE HIKE

A few steps up the Warm Springs Creek Trail (49) are all that you need to slip away from the grid of Missoula and into the old-growth cedar forest that defines the Lochsa Country. The soft, broad path is dusted with layers of cedar duff. The murmur of Warm Springs Creek flowing into the Lochsa River drifts beneath the canopy of trees.

It's easy to see why legendary trapper and miner Jerry Johnson built his cabin here in the wilderness, though his desire to explore these mountains may have been driven by motives other than fresh mountain air.

Johnson was born in Prussia, though he acquired his knowledge of minerals in New Zealand at a young age. He spent decades exploring the wildernesses of the Cascade and Rocky Mountains for precious metals. Chance brought Johnson

A happy hotspringer soaks in Jerry Johnson Hot Springs. YUVAL AVNIEL

to the Lochsa during the 1880s. Chance also brought Native American Isaac Hill into Johnson's camp one night. Legend has it that Hill was starving and Johnson nursed him back to health. In return Hill told Johnson of a creek bed littered with gold nuggets. At once, Johnson begged to be taken to the spot.

After buying supplies, Hill led Johnson to Warm Springs Creek, where Hill became sick. Still they pushed on into the high country of modern-day Tom Beal Park. Johnson carried Hill up to a high point on the side of what is now known as Grave Peak. There Hill died, but not before pointing to a peak in the distance and then pointing at the sun. Johnson buried him on a ridge near the peak.

Jerry Johnson never left the Lochsa Country, thick with grizzlies in those days. He was haunted by the "Lost Indian Prospect," and in the years to come he fruitlessly searched the area for the large placer mine. He built a cabin just downstream from the confluence of Warm Springs Creek and the Lochsa. Johnson spent his final years kicking around Missoula and is buried in the Missoula cemetery.

After Johnson scoured the land to no avail, other woodsmen continued his search, also in vain. To this day, people still talk about and look for the gold. But Isaac Hill's secret has yet to be uncovered, which speaks to the vastness of the granite folds that make up the Bitterroot Range. Today most hikers come to scour the region in search of other treasure: wild animals, bold scenery, and hot waters to soothe their bodies.

From the parking area the trail starts on the far side of Highway 12, infamous for its kamikaze truck drivers. Proceed across the footbridge over the Lochsa River. On the far side of the bridge you'll find a trail junction. Go right onto the Warm Springs Creek Trail. The trail follows the Lochsa River briefly before turning to follow Warm Springs Creek itself. At 0.3 mile the trail reaches a point overlooking the creek. It then continues on among the cedar and fir, gaining a little elevation at 0.7 mile.

The trail enters an open area above the creek at 1.0 mile. A cliff area down at the creek's edge houses a hot springs area. These springs are extremely hot, and at low water they mix with cold creek water to form pools fit for a soak. A spur trail leads down to the springs.

Continuing up the Warm Springs Trail, you pass a flat on your right that once served as an overnight camping area for the springs. At 1.2 miles you enter a rocky meadow on the creek dotted with hot springs. Enjoy the springs and turn around here, retracing your path back to the trailhead.

MILES AND DIRECTIONS

0.0 Start at the pullout and carefully cross Highway 12. Follow the trail across the wooden footbridge over the Lochsa River.

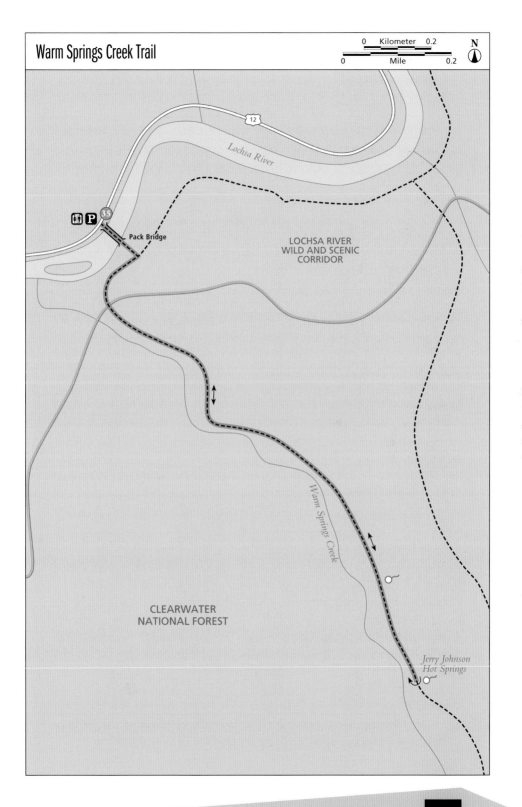

Warm Springs Creek Trail

Lochsa River

12

Pack Bridge

LOCHSA RIVER
WILD AND SCENIC
CORRIDOR

Warm Springs Creek

CLEARWATER
NATIONAL FOREST

Jerry Johnson
Hot Springs

0.1 On the far side of the bridge, turn right at the trail junction, following Warm Spring Trail (49).

0.2 The trail curves to the south.

0.3 The trail arrives at the banks of Warm Springs Creek and then cuts back into the forest.

0.7 The trail begins to climb.

1.0 A spur trail to the right leads down to a hot springs area on the creek's edge.

1.1 Another spur trail to the right leads to a flat used for camping in the past.

1.2 Enter a creekside meadow containing various hot pools. Turn around and retrace your steps to the trailhead.

2.4 Arrive back at the trailhead.

Options: Beyond the hot springs the trail extends up Warm Springs Creek for several miles into the Selway-Bitterroot Wilderness. A waterfall on the far side of a footbridge, 2.4 miles farther up the creek, is a good turnaround point. Retrace your steps to the hot springs and then back to the trailhead.

Another option is to turn left at the trail junction on the far side of the footbridge. Follow the trail upstream along the river. The stock bypass trail will cut off to the right before you cross a footbridge. The trail follows the river for about 1.0 mile and then begins climbing steeply uphill to Hot Springs Point, another 2.5 miles.

HIKE INFORMATION

Local events/attractions: DeVoto Memorial Cedar Grove, mile marker 165 on Highway 12. Historian Bernard DeVoto edited the Lewis and Clark journals here. Short trails explore the massive cedars.

Food/lodging: Lochsa Lodge, 115 Powell Rd., Lolo; (208) 942-3405; lochsalodge .com. Historic and new cabins surround this welcoming lodge that has long been a popular stopover point for travelers. A restaurant, general store, and gas pump are on the premises.

Camping: Powell Campground, mile marker 162 on Highway 12, Powell, ID; (208) 942-3113; www.recreation.gov (reservations). This large campground on the banks of the Lochsa River near the Lochsa Lodge and Powell Ranger Station is 10 miles east of the Warm Springs Trailhead.

Organizations: Friends of the Clearwater, PO Box 9241, Moscow, ID 83843; (208) 882-9755; friendsoftheclearwater.org. This local conservation group's website offers a wealth of information on the Nez Perce-Clearwater National Forest.

Weir Creek Trail

The Weir Creek Trail leads to a popular hot spring tucked alongside a creek in a cedar grove. The trail has a steady gradient and cuts across a sidehill through the forest. It can be dangerous in winter, with ice forming on the narrow trail. Steep slopes give way from the trail to the creek bottom. The hot spring, situated just above the creek on a rock outcrop, is deep and large. Weir Creek is located over Lolo Pass, along the Lochsa River in Idaho. A primitive trail continues up Weir Creek through pristine old-growth temperate rain forest.

Start: Weir Creek Trailhead
Distance: 0.8 mile out and back
Hiking time: About 45 minutes
Difficulty: Easy
Trail surface: Dirt; singletrack
Best season: Spring through fall
Other trail users: Hunters in spring and fall (rarely)
Canine compatibility: Dogs permitted
Land status: Nez Perce-Clearwater National Forest
Fees and permits: None required

Schedule: None
Maps: USGS Greystone Butte; USDAFS Nez Perce-Clearwater National Forest, available at the Powell Ranger Station
Trail contacts: Powell Ranger District, 192 Powell Rd., Lolo, MT 59847; (208) 942-3113; www .fs.usda.gov/nezperceclearwater
Special considerations: The trail is dangerous when ice covered.

Finding the trailhead: From the intersection of Brooks and Reserve Streets, drive 7.5 miles south on Highway 93. Turn right onto Highway 12 in the town of Lolo. Drive 64.9 miles to the west, over Lolo Pass into Idaho, along the Lochsa River. The trailhead is located 20.1 miles past the Lochsa Lodge. The small unmarked parking area on the right is partially blocked by a guardrail. It's easy to drive past the first time. **GPS:** N46 27.48' / W115 02.10'

THE HIKE

Although in Idaho, the Lochsa Canyon is Missoula's backyard river valley. One of the Lochsa's many tributaries is Weir Creek, famous for its fish runs, clear waters, and hot springs. A drive up Lolo Creek and over Lolo Pass will get you into the inland temperate rain forest of the Lochsa River, with its towering cedar groves, rainy days, and remote wilderness.

Weir Creek is part of the 22,000-acre Weir Creek Roadless Area. The Weir Creek drainage and the Post Office Creek drainage to the east make up the bulk of this wild land. Numerous side creeks feed into these drainages. At the head of

View from the rustic pool at Weir Creek.

the creeks runs the Lolo Motorway, the ancient travel route through the region. The roadless area is home to gray wolf, mountain lion, wolverine, and fisher. Moose, elk, deer, and mountain goat frequent the area too. Bears can wander through, though they rarely do.

The Weir Creek Trail (931) was rebuilt in 2013. The hike begins in the creek bottom. The trail is wide and obvious, leading among big western red cedars and grand firs. This is the southern tip of the inland temperate rain forest, a unique habitat that extends up into British Columbia. It is known for being especially lush, even though it's more than 400 miles to the coast in a direct line. Somehow this region has a coastal feel to it, from the big trees and dampness in the air to the chinook salmon and steelhead in the rivers.

The massive oceangoing fish migrates 900 miles, following the bends of the river. The beasts wiggle against the current for days to lay their eggs in the rocky beds of mountain creeks in central Idaho, including Weir Creek. The Lochsa River supports healthy salmon and steelhead runs each year. Spring and fall are the best times to see the 2- to 3-foot fish make their way up the shallow stream. Sitting quietly next to Weir Creek and watching is the best way to catch one of these lunkers wriggling up a small waterfall. These wily creatures have excellent eyesight, making them hard to encounter.

Native Americans traditionally built fishing weirs on the river and side creeks to corral salmon into a channel blocked by sticks or stones, as noted by Lewis and Clark when they traversed the region in the early 1800s. Bull and cutthroat trout make their home in Weir Creek as well.

The Wild and Scenic Lochsa River has a tremendous spring runoff that swells the narrow river to its banks. The annual event creates a series of powerful rapids that draw river enthusiasts from around the country. Lochsa means "rough waters" in the Nez Perce language. Weir Creek becomes a powerful tributary torrent that can easily sweep hikers away. Never attempt to ford the creek during high-water conditions.

The trail passes some creekside camping spots shortly after leaving the trailhead. The trail gets away from the creek and begins to climb up the hillside at 0.1 mile. It gains more than 200 feet, rising above the creek, before topping out at 0.3 mile. The trail descends gradually until entering a rocky clearing perched above the creek level. A series of hot springs are located here, with the largest and most popular pool for soaking just below the trail.

Though the hike is not especially arduous, this scenic treat eases troubled muscles. The hot waters top 105°F. Mixed with the smell of cedars on the breeze, it all comes together. Sit back and watch Weir Creek flow through a rain forest meadow and be happy to have hiked to such a beautiful place.

MILES AND DIRECTIONS

0.0 Start at the trailhead and follow the trail up the creek, north and away from the road.

0.1 The trail begins to climb.

0.3 The trail cuts across a slope high above the hill. It tops out and then begins to descend.

0.4 The trail enters a rocky clearing on a little bluff above the creek. There are a series of hot springs in this area. Turn around here and retrace your path to trailhead.

0.8 Arrive back at the trailhead.

Options: Continue on above the hot springs. The trail is primitive, formed by years of use. There's a nice cedar grove in the creek bed 0.5 mile above the hot springs. Continue as far as you want up into the roadless area. This area may become flooded during high water.

HIKE INFORMATION

Local events/attractions: Lochsa Historical Ranger Station, mile marker 121.5 on Highway 12, 48 miles east of Kooskia; (208) 926-4274. Open Memorial Day to Labor Day, this interpretive museum transports visitors back to the days when the Lochsa was a wilderness outpost inaccessible by road.

Food/lodging: Lochsa Lodge, 115 Powell Rd., Lolo; (208) 942-3405; lochsalodge. com. Historic and new cabins surround this welcoming lodge that has long been a popular stopover point for travelers. A restaurant, general store, and gas pump are on the premises.

Camping: Wilderness Gateway, mile marker 122 on Highway 12, 100 miles west of Missoula; (208) 926-4274; reserveamerica.com (reservations). Nestled in the heart of nature, Wilderness Gateway has something for everyone.

Organizations: Friends of the Clearwater, PO Box 9241, Moscow, ID 83843; (208) 882-9755; friendsoftheclearwater.org. This local conservation group's website offers a wealth of information on the area surrounding Weir Creek.

To be considered for Wild and Scenic designation, a river must possess outstanding scenic, geologic, and historic value to be preserved for future generations.

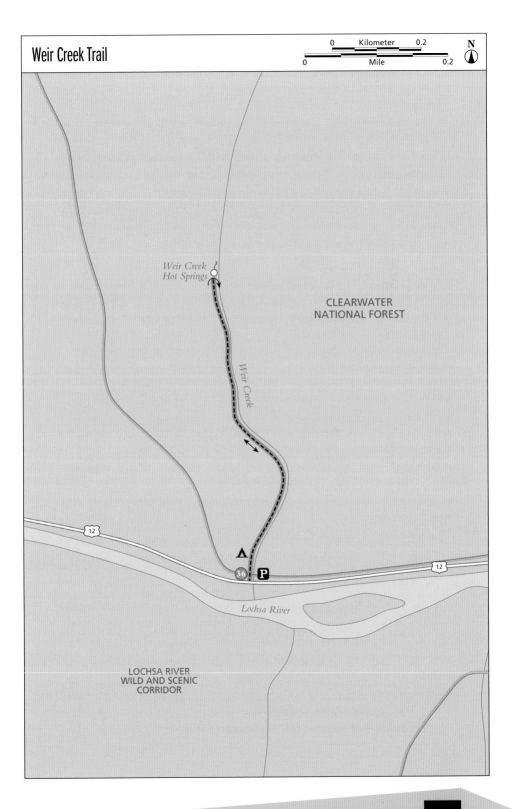

Weir Creek Trail

0 Kilometer 0.2

0 Mile 0.2

N

Weir Creek Hot Springs

CLEARWATER NATIONAL FOREST

Weir Creek

12

36

Lochsa River

LOCHSA RIVER WILD AND SCENIC CORRIDOR

SOUTH OF SUPERIOR
Lost Lake Trail

This hike west of Missoula is in an often-overlooked section of the state south of Superior. This pocket of the Bitterroot Mountains is its northern- and westernmost reaches. The broad canyons yield to stout mountains. Cirque lakes dot the landscape. The lowland forest is lush. Views stretch on when you get into the upper canyon, past the waterfall. The area is isolated and receives very little foot traffic. Any of Montana's wild creatures can be encountered here. Though the habitat screams moose, bear, and elk, wolverine, lynx, and wolf are also around. The clear green waters of the lake itself are nestled on the side of the canyon beneath the forested Mink Peak.

Start: Lost Lake Trailhead

Distance: 7.6 miles out and back

Hiking time: About 4 hours

Difficulty: Strenuous due to distance and elevation gain

Trail surface: Dirt; singletrack

Best season: Summer and fall

Other trail users: Equestrians; hunters in fall

Canine compatibility: Dogs permitted

Land status: Lolo National Forest

Fees and permits: None required

Schedule: None

Maps: USGS Illinois Peak; USDAFS Lolo National Forest Map, available at the district office

Trail contacts: Superior Ranger District, PO Box 460, 209 West Riverside, Superior, MT 59872; (406) 822-4233; www.fs.usda.gov/lolo/

Special considerations: Grizzlies have been sighted out here. Be bear aware. This area is also very remote and requires driving on a primitive access road. Make sure you have emergency supplies for yourself and your vehicle; make sure your vehicle has good tires and brakes. Be wary in this area during hunting season; it gets a lot of pressure. Wear hunter orange when hiking during hunting season; put it on your dog too. The roads and even the trails can get pretty busy after opening day of rifle season in late October.

Finding the trailhead: From Reserve Street in Missoula, drive 53.7 miles west on I-90 to exit 47 in Superior. Turn left onto 4th Avenue East and go 500 feet. Turn left onto River Street and go 300 feet across the interstate. Turn left onto Diamond Road. Go 1.7 miles and turn right onto Cedar Creek Road. Go 5.5 miles and turn right onto primitive Oregon Creek Road (Road 7865). After 12.9 miles arrive at the Lost Lake Trailhead at a switchback in the road, just before the road is gated. The trailhead is marked by a sign. **GPS:** N47 07.65' / W115 06.11'

THE HIKE

The Bitterroots take on a different feel here than in their southern reaches. Instead of steep, narrow canyons cut into craggy granite masses, the valleys here are broad and open, with pockets of trees. This area is near the proposed Great Burn Wilderness, named for the great forest fire of 1910 that swept through this part of the state and consumed 3 million acres of forest in three days. Thus the wide open spaces today.

Missoula is the closest urban center, and most of the immediate locals tend to stick to motor and horse travel, so hiking enthusiasts have these valleys to themselves. Idaho is a mile to the southwest of the lake, along with millions of acres of frontier. Sandwiched between two larger wildernesses—the Cabinets to the north and the Selway to the south—the proposed wilderness area (roadless land along the state line between Lolo Pass and Lookout Pass) begins just beyond the lake and serves as a unique landscape and wildlife corridor.

The Great Burn isn't one of the big sexy wildernesses near Missoula, but its pull is magnetic. People who play here become transfixed and have to return to explore more of the area. There's something about it; it feels untouched and pure.

The Great Burn is noted for its wide open spaces.

The region is as famous for its more than forty lakes as it is for its meadows and exposed mountainsides. One of those lakes is Lost Lake. The hike up the valley, through the forest, past the waterfall, and into the bowl of the upper canyon is unrivaled. It's an experience of serenity and solitude that can be hard to find on other Missoula-area trails. Hiking crowds tend to ignore this region, leaving the area south of Superior quiet—a good thing for the roaming grizzly, wolverine, and lynx that cherish this habitat.

The hike begins at the Lost Lake Trailhead, in the Lost Meadows at the drivable end of Oregon Creek Road (Road 7865). A small sign marks the obvious trail at a turn in a lonely switchback just below a gated fence.

Immediately after you begin the hike, a spur trail kicks out to the left and leads down into the Lost Meadows (a decent place for a primitive walk-in camp). Stay on the side of the hill and continue hiking up the creek through the trees. The vegetation is thick in the creek bottom, watered by 70 inches of precipitation annually. Spruce and cedar trees are complemented by a lush understory of thimbleberry and alder. Wildflowers are abundant: paintbrush, aster, fireweed. Several side creeks feed across the trail.

At 1.0 mile you cross a notable side creek, which comes down in the form of a small cascade. Just beyond the crossing is a major trail junction. The left fork leads 0.2 miles down to the creek and to Lost Creek Falls. Take the right fork and climb two long switchbacks, the second of which is quite a bit steeper than the first. The trail traverses below a cliff face around into a subalpine meadow and runs directly alongside the creek at 2.3 miles. While this is a beautiful spot, it gets better 0.5 mile down the trail when you get into the head of the upper canyon. The trail slides across a large sidehill meadow in a bowl filled with shrubs and pockets of forest. There are views of rocky cliff faces above. This is one of the high points of the hike.

The trail continues to climb, and just before you crest the ridge that hides Lost Lake, there are views of the bowl and valley below. At 3.5 miles you begin a short descent into Lost Lake, reaching it at 3.6 miles.

The lakeshore is forested. The water is a brilliant, clear green. Mink Peak rises rounded and timbered above the far side of the lake. Watch for mink, otter, beaver, and other water lovers.

The return hike is along the same route. Enjoy!

MILES AND DIRECTIONS

0.0 Start at the trailhead, marked by a sign at the end of Oregon Creek Road, on a switchback just before the gate. After 200 feet a spur trail goes left into Lost Meadows. Stay on the main trail. Go straight, continuing up the creek through the trees.

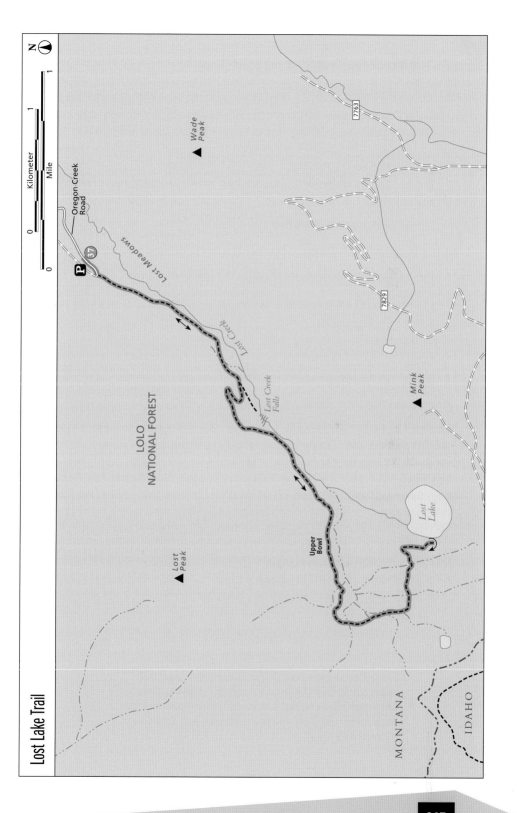

Lost Lake Trail

0.5 Cross a small, clear creek. The trail is fairly level.

1.0 Cross a small cascading creek.

1.1 Reach a trail junction. Left leads 0.2 mile to Lost Creek Falls. Go right and climb the switchbacks.

1.3 The forest opens with views during a steeper uphill.

1.7 The trail travels creekside through a lush meadow after passing below a large cliff face.

2.3 A small creek flows over the trail.

2.6 Cross a small creek. Continue through the forest, gaining more elevation.

2.8 The trail traverses through meadow on the side of the canyon.

3.1 The trail crosses a steep, small cascade.

3.4 A small window in the trees opens up for a view of the bowl below.

3.5 The trail descends to the lake.

3.8 Reach the lake. Retrace your steps to the trailhead.

7.6 Arrive back at the trailhead.

Options: The trail is fairly level to Lost Creek Falls for those who want a more gradual hike. Turn around here instead of hiking into the upper canyon for a 2.6-mile out-and-back hike.

HIKE INFORMATION

Organizations: The Great Burn Study Group, 1434 Jackson St., Missoula, MT, 59802; (406) 240-9901; Greatburnstudygroup.org; thegreatburn@yahoo.com. This Missoula-based group works in the field with volunteers, hiking and monitoring the backcountry of the proposed Great Burn Wilderness. They also host an annual event where hundreds of pounds of trash are pulled out of the woods.

Edge effect is a concept that says wildlife habitat gets better the farther it is from a road. Nonnative species can wreak havoc on habitat, as can more frequent fires, development of food sources, pollution, and erosion—all caused by roads.

Cha-paa-qn holds a special place in the heart of Missoulians. Its iconic pointy tip dominates the western skyline. It's also a fairly attainable peak to stand upon, as a road gets you close to the top, though the walk is no slouch. The trail rises 2,269 feet on its journey to the summit. The last 0.3 mile is a legitimate rock scramble, though the views are rewarding if you want to turn around here. The view from the top is exceptional. The 360-degreee panorama includes several mountain ranges and valleys, including great views of the Mission Mountains.

Start: Sleeping Woman Trailhead
Distance: 5.8 miles out and back
Hiking time: About 3 hours
Difficulty: Strenuous due to elevation gain
Trail surface: Dirt; singletrack
Best season: Summer and fall
Other trail users: Equestrians; hunters in fall
Canine compatibility: Dogs permitted
Land status: Lolo National Forest
Fees and permits: None required
Schedule: None
Maps: USGS McCormick Peak and Hewolf Mountain; USDAFS Lolo National Forest, available at the district office
Trail contacts: Ninemile Ranger District, 20325 Remount Rd., Huson, MT 59846; (406) 626-5201; www.fs.usda.gov/lolo/
Special considerations: The last 6.4 miles of road is narrow, primitive, and slow going. It can take more than 30 minutes to drive. The trail only goes to 2.6 miles. You will have to rock-hop up a steep slope to reach the summit. Or you can turn around at 2.6 miles, which affords a nice view of the Ninemile Valley.

Finding the trailhead: From Reserve Street go 18.8 miles west on I-90 to the Ninemile exit. Turn right (north) onto the Frontage Road for 1.4 miles. Turn right (north) onto Remount Road and continue 2.6 miles to the Ninemile Ranger Station. The road becomes Edith Peak Road (Road 476). Go 1.8 miles to a fork in the road; veer left onto Butler Creek Road (Road 456). The road goes north and then turns west. FR 2178 turns off Road 456 after 2.7 miles. Follow FR 2178 for 6.4 miles to the primitive trailhead at a roundabout at the end of the road. There is no sign. **GPS:** N47 07.93' / W114 23.30'

THE HIKE

Cha-paa-qn Peak, or "Shining Peak" in Salish, is an iconic symbol for the city of Missoula. The pointy peak, snow covered half the year, dominates the western view and rises more than 4,000 feet from the valley floor. Peering over several mountain ranges, this talus island in the sky serves as a perfect observation point for the region. Cha-paa-qn is also one of the most accessible of the peaks that surround Missoula. Road access gets you more than halfway up the slope. The mountain rises above the Ninemile Valley and is part of the Reservation Divide, a chain of high points that define the reservation boundary.

The Sleeping Woman Trail (707) is the most direct approach to the mountain. Even though it has a little more uphill than the Reservation Divide Trail (98), it's fewer miles. The hike up to the peak leads through a healthy forest of lodgepole pine and Douglas fir. Huckleberry bushes blanket the forest floor, making this a popular spot with huckleberry pickers. Grizzly bears frequent the area as well. The region serves as a crossroads between the Mission and Cabinet Mountains and the Great Burn roadless area to the south, making it a popular travel route for bears. Bear grass stalks adorned with tiny white flowers emerge from clumps of long, drooping grass that dot the forest floor.

Why do they call it Big Sky Country?

The trail from the parking area leads north-northeast. Aside from a couple of switchbacks, the trail maintains this bearing for the 2.9 miles to the top. The first 0.6 mile is a pleasant meander through the forest at a moderate gradient. Then the trail begins to steepen for more than 1.0 mile as it climbs up the side of a ridge above Stony Creek. The trail eventually levels out on the ridgeline at 1.9 miles, just before intersecting the Reservation Divide Trail (98) at 2.2 miles. This trail runs from Edith Peak Road to Kennedy Creek. You want to continue straight on a path marked by a pile of rocks. You continue to climb and come face to face with the big bald peak at 2.6 miles, where a big rock cairn marks the end of the official trail.

The back face of Cha-paa-qn doesn't look like the classic alpine pyramid you see from Missoula. It's more rounded. Snags dot the talus face that leads the last 0.3 mile to the summit.

The trail through here is primitive, created by foot traffic polishing the boulders over decades of use. There are several trails, all of which get you to the top. Make sure you stay within the limits of your ability. Talus slopes can be dangerous; the rocks can shift, and even the smallest readjustments can cause great harm. When a rock becomes dislodged and really gets rolling down the hill, you must get out of the way or face being crushed. Try to avoid this situation by not being in the "fall line" of any rocks that a hiker above you can dislodge. If you're hiking in a group, this may mean spacing out along the route at times.

For the most direct and easiest route, continue straight up the hill from the big rock cairn but veer a little to the right to pick up the path created by use. This will take you on a trajectory just to the left of the row of snags on the hillside. Pick your way through the boulders to the summit.

From the top you can see half of western Montana. At a distance, the Swan, Mission, Rattlesnake, Sapphire, Anaconda-Pintler, and Bitterroot Mountains are in view, broken up by the Missoula, Clark Fork, Jocko, Mission, and Ninemile Valleys. Old forests and lakes dot the closer ridges and peaks that form the Reservation and Ninemile Divide. The view is an array of alpine peaks, lush high country, and drier valley bottoms. With a slight breeze blowing and the sun shining brightly, who could think of a better place to get away from it all?

Retrace your steps to return to the trailhead.

MILES AND DIRECTIONS

0.0 Start at the unsigned trailhead. The trail begins to the northeast and makes a moderate ascent through the forest.

0.6 The trail begins to steepen as it climbs the side of a ridge.

1.4 Enter two big switchbacks.

1.9 The trail levels out on a ridgeline.

2.2 Arrive at a junction with the Reservation Divide Trail (98), which runs across the trail. Continue straight to Cha-paa-qn; the trail is marked with a pile of rocks.

2.6 Reach the base of Cha-paa-qn's rounded, rocky summit. A large rock cairn marks this spot. From here there are a number of primitive trails to get you to the summit. All require significant rock hopping. The best route to the summit from the rock cairn is to veer a little right but proceed essentially straight up; you will find a path worn from use. Stay just to the left of the line of snags that dot the hillside. Pick your way through the boulder garden that marks the final approach.

2.9 Arrive at the summit of Cha-paa-qn for 360-degree views. Retrace your steps to the trailhead.

5.8 Arrive back at the trailhead.

Options: You can hike either direction on the Reservation Divide Trail, encountered at 2.2 miles. The left-hand option eventually heads north and toward Kennedy Creek. The right-hand option heads east toward Edith Peak Road. Both trails tend to be on ridgetops through the forest.

HIKE INFORMATION

Local events/attractions: Ninemile Remount Depot, 20325 Remount Rd., Huson, MT 59846; (406) 626-5201. Located at the Ninemile Ranger Station, this livery stable was once the headquarters of the entire region's firefighting efforts. It's listed on the National Registry of Historic Places.

Food/lodging: Nine Mile House, 28030 Hwy 10 West, Huson; (406) 626-2546. Call this old-school establishment to see if they will be open for dinner and drinks when you finish your hike.

Sleeping Woman Trail to Cha-Paa-qn Peak

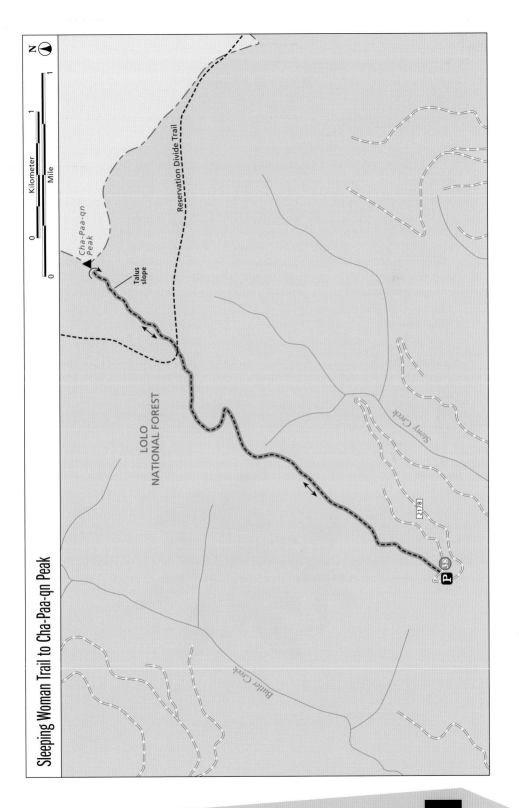

Cha-Paa-qn Peak

Talus slope

Reservation Divide Trail

LOLO NATIONAL FOREST

Stony Creek

Butler Creek

2178

N

Kilometer

Mile

What's in a Name?

During aboriginal times the Salish Indians called the distinct peak on the Missoula Valley's western horizon *Cpaaqn,* which translates as "Shining Peak." Captain John Mullan, who blazed the first European road through the area, called it Skiotah Peak in 1863. At some point the local name became Squaw Peak, which was officially adopted by the Montana Board of Geographic Names in 1918.

During the 1970s a new understanding of the word emerged. "Squaw" was traced back to an Iroquois word, *otsiskwa,* which literally translated to a word for female genitalia. Whether or not that European use of the word emerged on the East Coast and spread west, Montana tribes find it offensive. And as a place-name, it was a considered a reminder of conquest.

In 1999 the Montana Legislature passed House Bill 412, which created an advisory committee to rename seventy-six geographic locations in Montana bearing the word "squaw." In 2004 Missoula's epic landmark was officially changed to Cha-paa-qn Peak, an anglicized corruption of the Salish word *Cpaaqn.* Since the word *Cha-paa-qn* alone means Shining Peak, it was redundant to add an extra "peak" to the name. With this name change Cha-paa-qn has come to symbolize a new day for Native American communities.

Vista Point Loop

The Vista Point Loop is a relatively wild experience in a Recreation Area that caters to several uses in addition to hiking. The heavily used trail offers a moderate incline and a rewarding view. The journey begins by traversing the big meadow from the trailhead. The trail eventually works into a hillside covered in ponderosa pines and after a few switchbacks summits an unassuming knoll with incredible views of the Missoula Valley and surrounding mountains. The region is a restoration success story after decades of mismanagement.

Start: Blue Mountain Recreation Area Trailhead
Distance: 4.1-mile lollipop
Hiking time: About 2 hours
Difficulty: Moderate
Trail surface: Dirt; single- and doubletrack
Best season: Year-round
Other trail users: Bikers, equestrians
Canine compatibility: Dogs permitted
Land status: Lolo National Forest
Fees and permits: None required
Schedule: Closed 10 p.m. to 6 a.m.
Maps: USGS Southwest Missoula; USDAFS Lolo National Forest Map, available at the district office; City of Missoula Parks, Open Space & Trails
Trail contacts: Lolo National Forest Supervisor's Office, Fort Missoula Building 24A, Missoula, MT 59804; (406) 329-3814; www .fs.usda.gov/lolo/
Special considerations: This is a heavily used hiking trail. Watch for horses and bikes on the trail. During hunting season there is no rifle hunting permitted on this loop, but archery hunting is allowed.

Finding the trailhead: From the intersection of Brooks and Reserve Streets go south on Highway 93 for 2 miles. Turn right onto Blue Mountain Road and continue 0.6 mile. The Blue Mountain Recreation Area trailhead is on your left. **GPS:** N46 49.607' / W114 05.28'

Just south of Missoula, across the Bitterroot River, Blue Mountain rises up as a series of forested ridges. The Blue Mountain Recreation Area is a good example of multiple-use forestry—and a Cinderella restoration story. The 4,900-acre complex was once part of Fort Missoula and a military training ground. Live ammunition training tore up the region for years. It was turned over to the USDA Forest Service in the early 1950s and opened to the public, but was still the site of military training.

The Bittterroot River winds across the south side of the Missoula Valley. This unique view of the valley is often overlooked.

By the 1970s Blue Mountain was considered a top priority in the state for restoration. Years of unregulated off-road motorized use had resulted in eroded hillsides and trails. Garbage dumps pocked the landscape. Cattle grazed in the creeks. Native plants suffered; weeds prevailed. Unexploded ordnance and munitions dumps littered the site.

The cleanup effort during the following decades was rigorous. Restrictions were made on where and what trail users can do. Today several different uses coexist with little conflict. Today hikers, bikers, motorcyclists, equestrians, hunters, recreational shooters, and folfers all ramble around on Blue Mountain in relative harmony.

Rifle hunting is permitted west of Road 365 only. Archery hunting is allowed throughout the recreation area. Motorcycles are confined to a certain network of trails. Some trails are hiking and equestrian only; others are shared with mountain bikers. At the top of Road 365 there is a fire lookout tower and a night sky observatory. Both attractions are open to the public—the lookout during summer, the observatory on certain Friday nights during summer.

On the Vista Point Loop, hikers share the trail with bikers and equestrians. The hike starts out in a gentle meadow with a slight incline and produces views by the time you enter the trees. There are a number of trails in the meadow, though Trail 3.04 is the most direct route. You can pick it up as a straight path right out of the parking area, where Trail 3.15 goes to the left and Trail 3.01 goes to the right. The first intersection with other meadow trails is at 0.4 mile, where six trails come together. Continue straight.

At 0.7 mile there is another trail junction with Trail 3.15. After intersecting Trail 3.04, the trail veers to the right. Continue straight through this junction.

At 1.3 miles turn left onto Trail 3.06. (Trail 3.08 goes to the right.) Continue through ponderosa pine forest. The trail climbs through a series of switchbacks and reaches the well-named Vista Point—an unassuming knoll with an unmatched view of the Missoula Valley—at 2.1 miles. Talk about a classic picnic opportunity!

The views of the Bitterroot River are especially scenic from Vista Point, as is the view of Lolo Peak. Mount Sentinel and Mount Jumbo frame the city well in the distance. The peaks of the Rattlesnake Wilderness rise above.

The trail continues past Vista Point. At 2.4 miles there is a junction with Trail 3.06. Go right and follow the trail until the next junction, with Trail 3.03, at 2.5 miles. This trail takes you down a series of switchbacks and at 2.8 miles rejoins Trail 3.04. Turn right at this junction. At 2.9 miles you return to the junction of Trails 3.06 and 3.08. Continue straight and retrace the path back to the parking area.

MILES AND DIRECTIONS

0.0 Start at the trailhead and take Trail 3.04, the obvious doubletrack, straight (west).

0.4 Reach a trail junction where six trails come together. Go straight, staying on Trail 3.04.

0.7 At the trail junction, continue straight on Trail 3.04.

1.3 Turn left onto Trail 3.06. Trail 3.08 goes to the right.

1.4 Trail 3.13 intersects on the right and left; go straight.

2.1 Reach the top of Vista Point. Enjoy the big views.

2.4 Trail 3.06 merges with Trail 3.05; turn right.

2.5 At the junction with Trail 3.03, turn right and go down switchbacks.

2.8 Rejoin Trail 3.04; turn right.

2.9 Arrive at the junction of Trails 3.08 and 3.06 again. Continue straight and retrace your steps back to the trailhead.

4.1 Arrive back at the trailhead.

Options: There are several options on this route. For a big loop, take a left at the trailhead on Trail 3.15. It merges with the Vista Point Loop. After the overlook, instead of turning on Trail 3.03, go straight. Turn right onto Trail 3.04 briefly and then left onto Trail 3.14. This will take you to an alternative trailhead. At that trailhead turn left onto Trail 3.16, then right onto Trail 3.01, to get back to the main trailhead.

HIKE INFORMATION

Local events/attractions: Blue Mountain Observatory, top of Blue Mountain Road (Road 365); (406) 243-5179; cas.umt.edu/physics/Blue_Mountain _Observatory/. On a few Friday nights per month during summer, the university hosts stargazing events with their telescope at the observatory atop Blue Mountain.

Other resources: For a good overview of Blue Mountain's many recreational opportunities, visit allmissoula.com/parks/blue_mountain_recreation_area.php.

Encountering horses on the trail can be dangerous. Always yield to horse traffic and give them the right-of-way. If possible, position yourself on the downhill side of the trail. Don't make any sudden movements, and talk to the rider to show the horse you are not a threat.

Vista Loop Trail

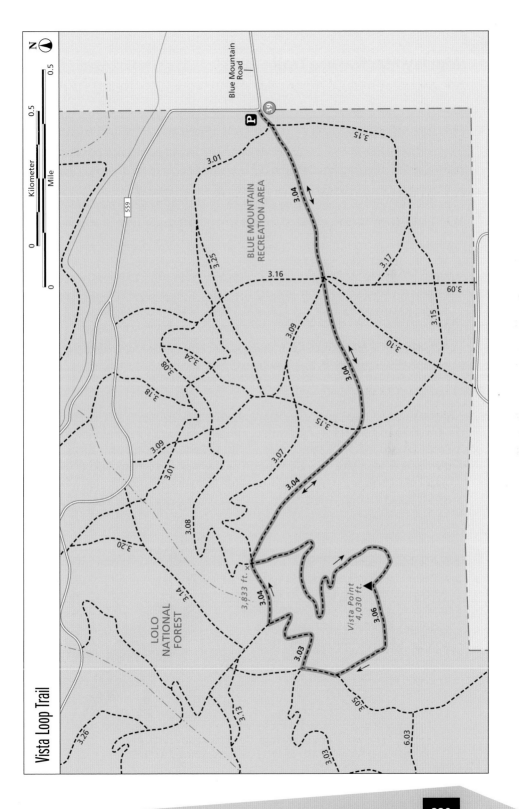

The Bitterroot River winds along the base of picturesque McCauley Butte on the edge of the Blue Mountain Recreation Area. The Maclay Flat Nature Trail leads out to the river and traces its bank. Big cottonwoods lay down shade at swimming holes. Scattered benches offer a respite where you can enjoy the murmur of the river away from the hum of the road. Large meadows offer a view of the surrounding hills. Birders can see golden eagles, hawks, and falcons in the open grasslands. A marshy area shelters a variety of songbirds. Bald eagles, ospreys, and kingfishers patrol the river bottom.

Start: Maclay Flat Trailhead

Distance: 1.9-mile loop

Hiking time: About 1 hour

Difficulty: Easy

Trail surface: Gravel; doubletrack

Best season: Year-round

Other trail users: None

Canine compatibility: Leashed dogs permitted

Land status: Lolo National Forest

Fees and permits: None required

Schedule: Closed 10 p.m. to 6 a.m.

Maps: USGS Southwest Missoula; USDAFS Lolo National Forest, available at Fort Missoula; City of Missoula Parks, Open Space & Trails

Trail contacts: : Lolo National Forest Supervisor's Office, Fort Missoula Building 24A, Missoula, MT 59804; (406) 329-3814; www .fs.usda.gov/lolo/

Special considerations: The trailhead is shared by rafters and anglers. Beware of trailers backing up and erratic traffic; watch your pets and kids. In spring the river can flood through this section, submerging parts of the trail.

Finding the trailhead: From the intersection of Reserve and Brooks Streets, go south on Highway 93 for 2 miles. Turn right onto Blue Mountain Road and follow it through some bends and turns for 1.9 miles. Turn right into the loop parking area for Maclay Flat Trailhead, marked by a large sign. **GPS:** N46 50.13' / W114 06.21'

THE HIKE

Big cottonwoods, direct access to the Bitterroot River, and big meadows mark this hike on the edge of the Blue Mountain Recreation Area. The Maclay Flat Nature Trail (14.01) is for hikers only and is accessible by wheelchair. This broad, flat path meanders through the floodplain of what was once a Salish camp where bitterroots were collected. Today interpretive signs and benches by the river make this refuge just out of town incredibly user-friendly.

Groves of ponderosa pine and native bunchgrasses attract white-tailed deer, flammulated owls, and pygmy nuthatches. Serviceberry hangs heavy with fruit in season. Black hawthorn provides forage and security for songbirds. Purple flowers of knapweed, an invasive species, dot the fields.

The river is the central attraction here. This stretch of the Bitterroot is away from the road and takes on a wild feel as it meanders along the base of McCauley Butte. Benches for picnicking are scattered along the waterfront. Anglers wet their lines for the trout that tango in the current. Swimmers dart like frogs through clear waters. The water here is clean and refreshing on a hot day. Upstream, the Bitterroot Valley lacks the industrial pollution that has marred the Clark Fork over the years (although dramatic steps have been taken to clean up its waters).

Large meadows punctuate Maclay Flat when you get away from the river.

From the trailhead follow the path straight toward the river. The hike begins through open country bordered by a thick band of tall cottonwoods. The trail dips and rises gently, curving just before reaching the river at 0.4 mile. A couple of benches perfect for picnicking are scattered about pockets of shade along the banks of the Bitterroot. River rock and steep banks don't make for the perfect beach, but access to the water's edge is possible.

At 0.6 mile Trail 14.02 intersects from the right and leads away from the river. This trail leads back to the parking area for a shorter trip. Keep going straight to complete the full loop. Just beyond, at 0.7 mile, a large aspen grove gives way to a big meadow. Another nice bench with a great view of McCauley Butte sits at 0.8 mile.

At 1.1 miles the trail takes a dramatic bend to the right and begins to run alongside the Big Flat Irrigation Ditch. Wildflowers line the trail. Continue straight past the junction with Trail 14.02, from the right, and arrive at an inland marsh at 1.5 miles. Frogs, toads, salamanders, and snakes thrive in this microhabitat. Flickers, sapsuckers, and woodpeckers call the forest around the marsh home. Foxes, raccoons, and beavers also utilize the sanctuary and resources of the tall grasses.

MILES AND DIRECTIONS

0.0 Start at the trailhead and follow the broad, gravel path straight (east) out of the parking area.

0.4 Reach a lazy stretch of the Bitterroot River, a good place for strong swimmers in late summer. The trail curves.

0.5 Intersect Trail 14.02. Go straight for the longer loop

0.7 The trail goes through a big meadow. A large aspen grove stands nearby.

0.8 Reach a bench and view of bluffs.

1.1 The trail creates a bend and encounters the Big Flat Irrigation Ditch, then runs along beside it.

1.4 Intersect Trail 14.02 again.

1.5 Inland marsh grass stretches along the trail.

1.9 Arrive back at the trailhead.

Options: Turn right onto Trail 14.02 at 0.6 mile to shave distance off the trip. Turn left when you rejoin the main trail. Total mileage for this shorter loop is 1.2 miles.

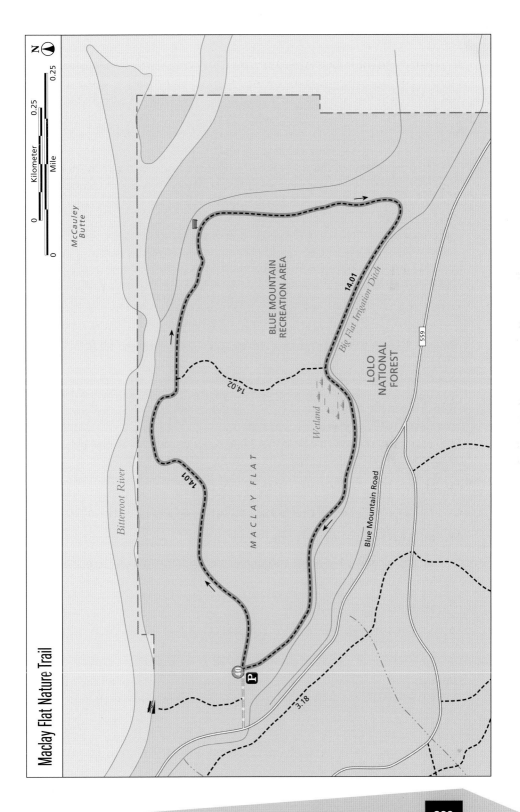

Maclay Flat Nature Trail

McCauley
Butte

Bitterroot River

MACLAY FLAT

14.01

BLUE MOUNTAIN
RECREATION AREA

14.02

Wetland

Big Flat Irrigation Ditch

LOLO
NATIONAL
FOREST

Blue Mountain Road

559

3.18

Kilometer

0   0.25

0   0.25

Mile

N

Local events/attractions: Five Valleys Audubon Society, PO Box 8425, Missoula, MT 59807; fvaudubon.org. The Missoula chapter of the Audubon Society frequently hosts bird walks in Maclay Flat and other popular hiking and birding destinations around town.

Amazing Aspens

Aspen groves are often the oldest and largest organisms in the forest. The roots of every tree are connected underground in a massive, shared root system. Each trunk that appears aboveground is just a small appendage of a beast that lies beneath the ground. The oldest known aspen grove is in Utah. It's 800,000 years old and weighs 13 million pounds, stretching over 100 acres, with 40,000 trees protruding from the ground.

Aspens have been used for years as a pain reliever. Its inner bark, which provides sugar to the body, contains chemicals similar to synthetic pain relievers, as do the leaves, which can be made into a medicinal tea. Its soft wood is pliable and can be easily molded with fire and sandstone to make a bowl, or you can take the easy route and use a knife. The white powder on the bark of the aspen can be used as a makeshift sunscreen. It also contains yeast and can be used as a starter in a bread recipe.

Aspens can be used for shelter too. In thick stands, several thin, straight poles can be harvested. The thick bark on mature trees can be used as an effective roofing material. Finally, piles of aspen leaves make feasible bedding material.

Appendix A: Honorable Mentions

I wasn't able to fit all the hikes I wanted into this book in detail, but here's some information to point you toward some other great hikes in the Missoula area.

A   *Heart Lake Trail*

This subalpine lake lies near the divide in the Great Burn section of the Bitterroot Mountains. It is a 4.0-mile round-trip to the lake.

Go west on I-90 from Reserve Street for 53.7 miles to exit 47 in Superior. Turn left onto 4th Avenue, then River Street, then Diamond Road. Go east on Diamond Road for 6.5 miles, where it becomes Trout Creek Road. Continue another 14.7 miles to a switchback and parking on your left for the Heart Lake Trail.

Lolo National Forest, Superior Ranger Station; (406) 822-4233; www.fs.usda .gov/recarea/lolo

B   *Morrell Falls National Recreation Trail*

A favorite among locals and visitors alike, this is a gentle hike at the foot of the Swan Mountains to the base of a substantial waterfall. It is 5.0 miles round-trip to the falls.

Follow MT 200 East out of Bonner for 32 miles. Turn left onto MT 83 for 15 miles. Turn right onto Morrell Creek Road. After 1.2 miles, turn slightly left to stay on Morrell Creek Road. It's another 7 miles to the Morrell Falls Trailhead.

Lolo National Forest, Seeley Lake Ranger District; (406) 677-2233; www .fs.usda.gov/recarea/lolo

C   *Lolo Peak*

Lolo Peak Trail is a demanding climb up Carlton Ridge to Carlton Lake, then up to the summit of Lolo Peak. It is a 13.0-mile round-trip to the peak.

To reach the trailhead, go 7.5 miles south on Highway 93 from the intersection of Brooks and Reserve Streets. Turn right onto Highway 12 in the town of Lolo. Go 3.7 miles and turn left on Forest Road 612. Go 8.4 miles to the trailhead located on a hairpin turn.

Lolo National Forest, Missoula Ranger District; (406) 329-3814; www.fs.usda .gov/recarea/lolo

D   Mission Falls Trail

This is a classic Montana waterfall hike at the base of the steep and sharp Mission Mountains. It is a 7.0-mile round-trip. You need a tribal conservation license to hike here, available at Bob Ward and Sons or the Missoula Fish, Wildlife & Parks.

Go west on I-90 for 5.2 miles from Missoula. Turn right onto Highway 93 and go 30.7 miles. Turn right onto Old Highway 93. After 1.1 miles turn right onto St. Mary's Lake Road. Turn left on Mission Dam Road after 0.7 mile and continue 5.3 miles to the trailhead.

Confederated Salish & Kootenai Tribes; (406) 883-2888; cskt.org/tr/fwrc_wildland.htm

E   Grizzly Creek Trail

This trail moves up Grizzly Creek, a quiet drainage near the Welcome Creek Wilderness in the Sapphire Mountains. It is a 7.0-mile round-trip.

Go 20.7 miles east on I-90 from Missoula to the Rock Creek Road exit. Turn right and follow Rock Creek Road for 11.5 miles. Turn left onto Ranch Creek Road. The trailhead for Grizzly Creek is 0.8 mile up the road on the left.

Lolo National Forest, Missoula Ranger District; (406) 329-3814; www.fs.usda.gov/recarea/lolo

F   Canyon Lake Trail

This steep Bitterroot Mountain Canyon just behind Hamilton is a granite wonderland, culminating in a beautiful cirque lake. It is 8.0 miles round-trip to the lake.

Go 45 miles south of Missoula on Highway 93 to Hamilton and turn right onto Main Street. Go west on Main Street in Hamilton for 1 mile. Turn right onto Ricketts Road and go 0.5 mile. Turn left onto Blodgett Camp Road (736) for 2.4 miles. Turn left onto Canyon Creek Road (735) and continue 3 miles to the trailhead.

(406) 363-7100; www.fs.usda.gov/recarea/bitterroot

G   Sweeney Ridge Trail

This trail climbs the ridge on the north side of Sweeney Creek with nice Bitterroot views before dropping down to Peterson Lake. It is 10 miles round-trip to the lake.

Drive 19 miles south of Missoula on Highway 93. Turn right onto Sweeney Creek Loop for 0.9 mile; it becomes Sweeney Creek Trail. Continue another 5 miles to the trailhead, at the end of some switchbacks.

Bitterroot National Forest, Stevensville Ranger District; (406) 777-5461; www.fs.usda.gov/recarea/bitterroot

H Cliff Lake Trail

This short but sweet hike starts at Diamond Lake and takes you up to one of the most scenic lakes in the western Bitterroots. It is a 2.0-mile round-trip to the lake.

Go 60 miles west of Missoula on I-90 to the Dry Creek Road exit. Turn left onto Southside Road for 0.8 mile. Turn right onto Dry Creek Road and go 9.5 miles to the junction with Diamond Lake Road. Turn left onto Diamond Creek Road; the trailhead is west of the bridge.

Lolo National Forest, Superior Ranger Station; (406) 822-4233; www.fs.usda .gov/recarea/lolo

I Boulder Lake Trail

This hike starts in Gold Creek Meadows and leads through the Rattlesnake Wilderness to Boulder Point, with a panoramic view. Below is Boulder Lake, a high-mountain lake with fish.

Go east from Missoula on I-90 for 4 miles. Exit onto MT 200 East and go 10 miles, through Bonner, to Gold Creek Road. Turn left and go 6 miles. Turn left onto FR 2103 for 5miles, then left on FR 4323 at a fork for 7 more miles to the West Fork of Gold Creek Trailhead.

Lolo National Forest, Missoula Ranger District; (406) 329-3814; www.fs.usda .gov/recarea/lolo

J Burdette Creek Trail

For a mountain trail, this remains flat as it runs up Burdette Creek past some beaver ponds. Lolo Hot Springs is nearby. It's a 10-mile round-trip to the beaver ponds.

Go south on Highway 93 from Missoula for 8 miles. Turn right onto Highway 12. Continue 26 miles to Fish Creek Road and turn right. It is 9 miles to the Burdette Creek Trailhead.

Lolo National Forest, Missoula Ranger District; (406) 329-3814; www.fs.usda .gov/recarea/lolo

K Wagon Mountain Trail

This Lewis and Clark and Nez Perce National Historic Trail leads up to Packer Meadows near Lolo Pass. Go all the way—5.0 miles—with a vehicle shuttle or partway and back to the trailhead.

Go south on Highway 93 from Missoula 8 miles to Highway 12 and turn right. Go 26.5 miles and turn left into the Lee Creek Campground. Make a quick right into the parking lot. You have to cross Lee Creek and the trail crosses a couple of logging roads before it climbs Wagon Mountain.

Lolo National Forest, Missoula Ranger District; (406) 329-3814; www.fs.usda .gov/recarea/lolo

Appendix B: Hiking Clubs and Trail Groups

Montana Dirt Girls: mtdirtgirls.tripod.com/index.html; MontanaDirtGirl@gmail .com. The Dirt Girls hike seasonally and bike the rest of the year. The group focuses on fun and skill building.

Rocky Mountaineers, PO Box 4262, Missoula, MT 59806; rockymountaineers.com. The Mountaineers have been active around Missoula for years. They have monthly meetings at The Trailhead and frequent outings.

Campus Recreation Outdoor Program, University of Montana, Missoula; (406) 243-5172; umt.edu/outdoor. For students only, UM has one of the best outdoor programs in the country. The program offers rentals and outings.

Five Valleys Audubon Society, PO Box 8425, Missoula, MT 59807; fvaudubon.org; info@fvaudubon.org. The local chapter of the Audubon Society takes frequent field trips around the region. E-mail for a current schedule of events.

The Great Burn Study Group, 1434 Jackson St., Missoula, MT 59802; (406) 240-9901; greatburnstudygroup.org. This group makes frequent outings into the Great Burn west of Missoula to monitor and clean up the area. They are also interested in your trip reports at thegreatburn@yahoo.com.

Montana Chapter of the Sierra Club, 222 North Higgins Ave., Missoula, MT 59802; (406) 549-1142; montana.sierraclub.org. The Sierra Club holds regular outings. Contact them for a current schedule of events.

Appendix C: Further Reading

Alt, David D. *Roadside Geology of Montana*. Mountain Press Publishing, 1986.

Ambrose, Stephen E. *Undaunted Courage: Meriwether Lewis, Thomas Jefferson, and the Opening of the American West*. Simon & Schuster, 1997.

Haines, Aubrey L., and Calvin L. Haines. *The Battle of the Big Hole: The Story of the Landmark Battle of the 1877 Nez Perce War*. TwoDot, 2006.

Kershaw, Linda J., Jim Pojar, and Paul Alaback. *Plants of the Rocky Mountains*. Lone Pine Publishing, 1998.

Koelbel, Lenora, and Stan Cohen. *Missoula, The Way It Was: A Portrait of an Early Western Town*. Pictorial Histories Publishing Co., 1983.

Locatelli, Mario. *The Mountain Goat Chronicles*. Stoneydale Press Publishing Co., 2008.

Moore, Bud. *The Lochsa Story: Land Ethics in the Bitterroot Mountains*. Mountain Press Publishing, 1996.

Hike Index

About the Author

Josh Mahan is a Missoula journalist and author who grew up hiking in the Bitterroot Mountains while attending junior high and high school in Darby. He received a degree in Journalism with a minor in Environmental Studies from the University of Montana. He has written for newspapers, magazines, online, (written for) an anthology; and coauthored a book for St. Martin's Press.

Josh has also worked several years in the tourism industry, taking him from the Brooks Range in Alaska to the Futaleufu River in Chile, as well as into the depths of the wildernesses around Missoula. He works each year with his family's business, Big Wild Adventures, leading trekking trips throughout the West and Alaska. In 2007 he was a member of the 1,400-mile Down the River expedition that retraced John Wesley Powell's historic first descent of the Colorado River.

Your next adventure begins here.

falcon.com

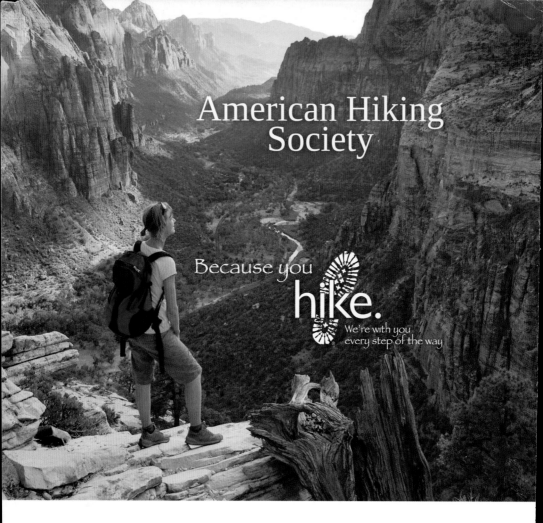

American Hiking Society

Because you
hike.
We're with you
every step of the way

As a national voice for hikers, **American Hiking Society** works every day:

- Building and maintaining hiking trails
- Educating and supporting hikers by providing information and resources
- Supporting hiking and trail organizations nationwide
- Speaking for hikers in the halls of Congress and with federal land managers

Whether you're a casual hiker or a seasoned backpacker, become a member of American Hiking Society and join the national hiking community! You'll enjoy great member benefits and help preserve the nation's hiking trails, so tomorrow's hike is even better than today's. We invite you to join us now!

American Hiking Society